CHARLES I's LORD TREASURER

Sir Richard Weston, Earl of Portland (by Van Dyck)
Courtesy of the Earl of Clarendon

CHARLES I's LORD TREASURER

Sir Richard Weston, Earl of Portland (1577–1635)

MICHAEL VAN CLEAVE ALEXANDER

Foreword by A. L. ROWSE

THE UNIVERSITY OF NORTH CAROLINA PRESS
Chapel Hill

First published in the United Kingdom 1975 by
THE MACMILLAN PRESS LTD.

ISBN 0–8078–1248–X

Library of Congress Catalog Card Number 74–34370

Printed in Great Britain

Library of Congress Cataloging in Publication Data

Alexander, Michael Van Cleave, 1937–
Charles I's Lord Treasurer, Sir Richard Weston, Earl of Portland (1577–1635).

Includes bibliograpical references and index.
1. Weston, Sir Richard, Earl of Portland, 1577–1635.
2. Great Britain—Politics and government—1603–1649. I. Title.
DA396.W47A63 941.06'2'0924 [B] 74–34370
ISBN 0–8078–1248–X

Contents

Foreword

A. L. ROWSE

As with Martin Havran's study of Cottington, we are indebted to yet another young American scholar for this further venture into the tangled undergrowth of early Stuart administrative history. We have plenty of studies of medieval administration, often *pour faute de mieux*, but few for the Tudor and Stuart periods. Impossible as it is to make the subject of administration lively, it can at least be made human, and this Professor Alexander has done for us in this careful and exhaustive study of Charles I's able Lord Treasurer.

The biographical is the best way to approach, and make clear to the intending reader, the functions and differences between these offices and officials, between Treasury and Exchequer, Upper and Lower Exchequer, between Clerk of the Nichills and Clerk of the Pells – endearing names, the latter more familiar to us as a fat sinecure for eighteenth-century politicians. Professor Alexander points out that the conception of government of these administrators under James I and Charles I, as of the Kings themselves, was 'basically Elizabethan'. Of course the creaking old system, with its inefficiency and endless disputes and delays, gave plenty of opportunity for corruption and politicians on the make.

As if they are not always with us! But at least the country was not over-governed, weighed down by bureaucracy at every level, weakened by the insupportable burdens of social parasitism. There remained plenty of room for individual initiative and enterprise, of which able people like Weston took full advantage. Of course they made money – but they created a distinguished Caroline culture, built gracious houses, the relics of which still illuminate a devastated countryside. They patronised the arts; Weston himself was a patron of Ben Jonson, and we owe to him the commissioning of Le Sueur's equestrian statue of

Charles I at Charing Cross, celebrated by the poets and familiar to us all.

Weston was a man of sense and good judgement, maligned as he has been in the history books. But they have mostly been written under the influence of the Victorian cult of Parliament and the Whig interpretation of history, with Puritan and Parliamentarian sympathies about which we need have no illusions today. The great historian of the early seventeenth century, Samuel Rawson Gardiner, not content with being descended from Oliver Cromwell, was also one of the odd sect of Plymouth Brethren.

We can do better justice today to those who carried on, and those who opposed, the King's government. Professor Tawney, who embarked on the study of Weston's predecessor and mentor, Cranfield, with the idea of catching him out, in the end found that he was one of the ablest ministers of the time with more sense of the country's best interest than most politicians. Professor Alexander gives us the evidence for a comparable view of Weston. On the other hand, he makes clear that an opponent of the King like the sainted Sir John Eliot was by no means the unselfseeking martyr depicted by the parliamentary tradition.

It is not sufficiently grasped – or not at all imaginatively – that the appalling mistakes of Buckingham and Charles I were the mistakes of youth, rash irresponsibility and wilful inexperience, as so often in history. The consequences were with Charles right up to the Civil War and to the end of his life. It is indeed hard to understand the infatuation of Charles and his father for that *homme fatal*, Buckingham. The later mishaps and misunderstandings of the 1630s, the period of the so much abused personal rule, by no means merited the explosion, and the disaster, of the Civil War. Professor Alexander makes the interesting point that Weston probably conceived of the abstention from the amenities of parliament as a temporary phase of cooling-off, meant neither to be permanent nor to introduce absolutism. Unfortunately the generation that went through the bitter experiences of the 1620s stored up their bitterness and preserved their heat. It was parliament that drove forward the revolution in the 1640s, even if their motives were not revolutionary but those of fear and self-preservation, the igniter of most wars.

By then Weston was well out of it: originally a good parliament man, popular enough in that querulous assembly, he had no real responsibility for the wrath to come, though greatly blamed. The consequences fell upon his family, as with so many others in that generation – there was no end to the tale of suffering and loss in the storm which Clarendon saw as a cloud no bigger than a man's hand approaching from the North.

Preface

Few English statesmen have been as poorly served by history as Sir Richard Weston, first Earl of Portland (1577–1635). Although an important official of James I and Charles I and for more than six years the chief minister of the crown, he has never been the subject of a biography or scholarly monograph, owing mainly to the absence of collected papers on which to base such a work. Furthermore the authors of most general histories have been unduly hostile towards him. The great Victorian scholar of the early Stuart period, S. R. Gardiner, was unsympathetic for two reasons: Weston's Catholic leanings offended the Protestantism of most Englishmen and his consistent support of royal power incensed a generation that rejoiced in the triumph of parliamentary government. Since Gardiner's day little has been written to alter his view, which was upheld so vigorously by A. F. Pollard in the *Dictionary of National Biography*. In his admirable account of the parliament of 1624, Professor Ruigh dismisses him simply as 'a timeserving courtier'; and in their studies of economic and financial developments during the seventeenth century, Barry Supple and Charles Wilson fail to give him any mention at all. In his brilliant but controversial essays on the early Stuart period, Professor Trevor-Roper likewise ignores his contributions. The only historian to challenge the traditional view is Professor Dietz, who has given such a flattering appraisal of Weston's work as Chancellor of the Exchequer and Lord Treasurer that his conclusions have been all but ignored.

Among his own contemporaries Weston enjoyed far more respect than later generations have seen fit to accord him. John Hacket, David Lloyd, and Sir Philip Warwick held him in high regard; and Lord Clarendon gave a sympathetic, if not complimentary, account of his career before 1628. Once Weston received the white staff, Clarendon's attitude begun to harden, for he was convinced that Sir Richard's access to 'unbridled power' revealed the grasping and self-serving side of his personality. Clarendon was nevertheless in sympathy with his efforts to stabilise the financial and political position of the crown, which had been so greatly weakened by the mismanagement of the preceding decades..

A more serious cause of misgovernment than even the sustained inflation of the early Stuart period, so emphasised by recent historians, was the easy and permissive attitude of the King. James I had been brought up in near-poverty in Scotland, where he had lived on a hand-to-mouth basis and never enjoyed sufficient revenues for the maintenance of his household and government. During the 1590s he realised less than £50,000 a year from all sources, which was only a fraction of the ordinary revenues of the English crown. It was thus inevitable that he came to feel that England was a richer country than it actually was and that all his problems would disappear when he ascended the English throne. Unfortunately James was slow in realising that the national obligations of England were proportionately greater than those of Scotland and that the English crown found it almost as difficult to live of its own as the Scottish crown. As a result he lost all interest in living within his yearly revenues and, after his accession in 1603, allowed the expenditures of the English government to mount at a truly alarming rate.

The lax and diffident attitude of the King would not have had such disastrous consequences had it not been for the outbreak of the Thirty Years War. Once fighting began in earnest on the continent, James was pressed from all sides to send military support to his son-in-law, the Elector Palatine of the Rhine. During the summer of 1621 a volunteer force under Sir Horace Vere landed in the Low Countries, and within three years almost £170,000 had been issued for its maintenance. Equally sizeable sums were required for the navy; and funds nearly as great were dispensed on the numerous embassies dispatched to the continent. Once the parliament of 1624 convened, an insistent clamour for war encouraged by Prince Charles and the Duke of Buckingham, the leading favourite of the time, compelled James to sever all ties with the Spanish government and intervene directly in the conflict. Both the Lords and the Commons gave pledges of financial support, which prompted the King to search for allies on the continent. Within a year he had signed subsidy treaties with the German mercenary Count Mansfeld, the States-General of the United

Provinces, and Christian IV of Denmark. There were of course no statutory limitations on the King's power over foreign policy during the seventeenth century; but when James and his ministers negotiated the subsidy treaties of 1624–5, which involved an outlay of almost £59,000 a month, they committed themselves to a policy that had no chance of success without parliamentary support. Furthermore they indirectly raised the question of whether the Lords and Commons were bound by such promises to other European rulers, promises to which they were neither asked nor allowed to accede.

As long as Buckingham remained at the helm, the crown erroneously assumed that the main economic burden for the war could be transferred to parliament and thus to the ordinary taxpayer. Yet public opinion was highly critical of the way the King had managed his revenues for the past twenty years and showed little interest in voting additional funds for him to squander. Not only did successive parliaments refuse to grant as many subsidies as his ministers demanded, but the ordinary taxpayer found ways to avoid payment of the funds required of him. Because of the crisis of confidence now developing, the receipts of the subsidies actually voted between 1624 and 1628 fell to almost one-half of what they would have been during the reign of Queen Elizabeth. Unhappily this served not to restrain the King in the realm of foreign policy but to deepen his irritability with his subjects and to increase the chances of dangerous altercations in parliament. And the accumulated bitterness that developed between crown and parliament during the 1620s was to be a major factor in bringing on the civil wars of the 1640s.

It was with this difficult and confused situation that Weston and his two predecessors as Lord Treasurer, the Earls of Middlesex and Marlborough, had to contend. As the most important financial officers of the kingdom, they had to find funds for policies they knew to be wasteful and ill-advised. Middlesex displayed rare courage and voiced strenuous objections, thereby preparing the way for his own impeachment in 1624. With his example before their eyes, Marlborough and Weston were more inclined to run with the times and do whatever they could to meet the demands of Buckingham and the King. By means of an unhealthy reliance on land sales, forced loans, and the customs duties, they managed to raise enough money to keep the government's head above water.

But when Buckingham was assassinated in August 1628 and a change of policy at last became possible, Sir Richard, who had just been entrusted with the white staff, was able to seize the initiative and lead the crown out of the tempest into less troubled waters.

In order to avoid total bankruptcy the King's new chief minister opened peace negotiations with both Louis XIII and Philip IV, and within eighteen months the treaties of Susa and Madrid had been signed, despite the protests of those concerned for the fate of European Protestantism. Weston's policy in regard to parliament was, if anything, even less popular, since he encouraged his master to rule by means of the prerogative for the next few years. The abortive session of 1629 had convinced him that there was no hope of the members' co-operation for the immediate future and that the King must avoid another parliament until tempers subsided from their currently inflamed levels. Although Weston himself had once been a respected member of the Commons, he was now identified in the public mind as a thoroughgoing royalist; and by the time he died in 1635, he had lost almost all the popularity he had enjoyed a decade earlier. Yet he had temporarily halted the decline of royal power; and had his policies been continued by his successors it is conceivable that the holocaust of the 1640s might have been avoided. With the possible exception of the proposals advanced by the Earl of Bedford in 1640, his programme offered the only chance of England's remaining on the path of gradual, evolutionary change.

From these few paragraphs it is apparent that Weston was both an important and a controversial figure. A study of his career has long been needed, not only to provide a fuller picture of the man and the place of his family in English society but also to throw some light on the operations of the central government. In recent years historians have produced a host of works on the economic, social, cultural, and religious history of early Stuart England. But aside from Professor Aylmer's analysis of the civil service of Charles I, little has been done to explain the most important administrative developments of the period. Furthermore no studies have been made of individual Privy Councillors and their role in the parliaments of the early seventeenth century. Since Weston was a high government official for nearly two decades and served in all the parliaments of the 1620s, a study of his career should give some understanding of the methods of Stuart administration and the main developments taking place in the House of Commons.

I have been engaged in this study of Weston's political career for some years. My interest in early Stuart England was kindled by Professor Stephen Baxter of the University of North Carolina at Chapel Hill, without whose counsel and encouragement this book could hardly have been written. Although he read the entire manuscript and made valuable suggestions for improvement, I naturally assume responsibility for any errors of fact or interpretation that remain. I should also like to extend my thanks to Miss Louise Hall and Mrs Kenneth McIntyre of the Reference Department of the Louis Round Wilson Library of the University of North Carolina for their cheerful and expert assistance. My gratitude is also due to Professor Burke Johnston, Emeritus Professor of English at Virginia Polytechnic Institute and State University, who called my attention to the poems by Ben Jonson in honour of Weston and his son Jerome, the second Earl of Portland.

Two research trips to England were made possible by grants from the American government, one under the terms of the Fulbright-Hays Act and the other through the auspices of the National Endowment for the Humanities, for which I would like to express my deepest appreciation. To Earl Fitzwilliam and the Trustees of the Wentworth Woodhouse Settled Estates, I am grateful for permission to quote from the papers of Thomas Wentworth, Earl of Strafford, now on deposit in the Sheffield Central Library. I am also indebted to the Marquess of Salisbury, who graciously allowed me to see whatever papers I considered important at Hatfield House. The archivist and librarian to the Duke of Norfolk, Francis W. Steer, kindly transcribed and forwarded several letters addressed by Weston to the second Earl of Arundel and Surrey; and Professor Aylmer made valuable suggestions concerning the records to be examined in the Public Record Office.

Wherever I travelled in England I was assisted with unfailing courtesy. This was true not only at York, Sheffield, and Hatfield House but also at the Essex Record Office in Chelmsford, where the administrative staff was extraordinarily helpful. In London the same circumstances prevailed at the British Museum, the National Register of Archives, and the Public Record Office. My especial thanks are due to the staff of the Round Room of the latter institution, who did so much to make my research productive. I should also like to express my appreciation to the officers of the British Museum and of the Public Record Office, for allowing me to make extracts from documents in their safekeeping, and to the Trustees of Trinity College Dublin who permitted me to use a microfilm of the diary of Sir Richard Grosvenor for the parliament of 1626.

I would be particularly remiss if I did not express my deepest gratitude to A. L. Rowse of All Souls College, Oxford, who edited the manuscript, showed me how to reduce it to a more practical length, and, in general, transformed it into a livelier book than it would have been otherwise.

In closing I wish to acknowledge the excellent work of my typists, Mrs Muriel Dyer and Mrs Diane Williams, whose copy is noted for both its accuracy and its attractiveness. To my wife Ann I owe far more than I can possibly express. Although completing her own dissertation at the time, she offered constant encouragement, read and criticised each chapter as it was finished, and helped with the re-writing of my most awkward sentences. This book is dedicated jointly to her and my mother, Mrs M. L. Alexander, whose faith sustained me not only during much of the research and writing of this work but during my graduate school days as well.

Blacksburg, Virginia
June 1974

Note on Dating and Spelling

During the seventeenth century the Julian calendar, which was still in use in England, was ten days behind the Gregorian calendar, which had been adopted by a majority of the continental states. With few exceptions the dates given in this book correspond to the Julian calendar, although the year is considered to begin on 1 January rather than 25 March. The abbreviations 'o.s.' (for old style, *i.e.* Julian) and 'n.s.' (for new style, *i.e.* Gregorian) are used whenever dates might otherwise be unclear.

For the ease and convenience of the reader I have modernised the spelling used in quotations from contemporary letters and documents. I have also made a few changes in punctuation, in order to render passages more clearly.

The history of Stuart England is stained with the trail of public finance. R. H. Tawney

An unbridled legislature, combined with an empty exchequer, is half-way to political anarchy. J. H. Plumb

1 A Journey to Prague

In June 1620 a middle-aged squire from Essex, Sir Richard Weston, lord of the manors of Skreens and Tye Hall, was selected by James I for an important embassy to the continent. Exactly why he was chosen for this diplomatic mission, which was intended to prevent the spread of the conflict known to history as the Thirty Years War, is an impossible question to answer categorically, since at least three factors contributed to the King's decision. First, Weston had been in the crown's employ for almost four years, since 1 July 1616, when he and his heir-apparent Richard were named to serve as joint collectors of the petty customs in the port of London. From that time forward the elder Weston had become increasingly active in the management of government business, particularly of a naval and commercial nature; and although he had not yet received an important bureaucratic post, he was beginning to make a name for himself as a capable man of affairs. Second, Sir Richard is likely to have had the support of the Spanish Ambassador in London, Count Gondomar, a skilful and persuasive diplomat who enjoyed the special confidence of James I. For more than a century most historians of the early Stuart period have been in agreement that Weston profited from the Spaniard's backing, and no evidence has yet been adduced to challenge this view.[1] Third, and most important of all, Sir Richard was a member of the gentry, that increasingly powerful class from which the King drew so many members of his diplomatic corps.

Born in 1577, the eldest son of Jerome and Mary Weston of Roxwell parish in Chelmsford hundred, Essex, the future ambassador and Lord Treasurer, who was knighted in the summer of 1603, was descended from a prosperous gentry family whose origins can be traced with confidence no farther than the first quarter of the sixteenth century. William Weston, the great-great-grandfather of the first Earl of Portland, was a prominent mercer in London, but the real founder of the family fortunes was his grandson Richard, who was 'bred to the law' at the Middle Temple and served as a Justice of the Common Pleas from October 1559 until his death in July 1572. This Richard Weston married three times, fathered a large family, and built up an estate consisting of several manors and numerous smaller properties worth approximately £1500 a year. His son and chief heir Jerome, a good example of Professor Tawney's 'rising gentry', more than doubled the value of the lands bequeathed to him and, in 1603, left a yearly income of more than £3500 to his own son, the future Lord Portland.[2]

Like many such families of the Tudor period, the Westons were deeply affected by the educational movements of their age. Indeed the young Richard Weston, who was eventually to bring such distinction to the family, was one of the foremost beneficiaries of the 'educational revolution' of the mid-sixteenth century, when the two universities and many of the public schools were invaded by the sons of England's ruling families. Lord Clarendon, whose views still serve as the basis of all appreciations of Sir Richard's personality, was so impressed by the extent of his learning that he characterised his education as 'very good among books and men.' Regarded as a cultivated individual by almost all his contemporaries, Weston was described by another writer as 'a great scholar . . . of various erudition, and as large observation.'[3]

From the Chelmsford grammar school, an institution founded during the reign of Edward VI, which he is likely to have attended, Weston proceeded to Trinity College, Cambridge, where he doubtless continued his study of Latin and acquired more than a rudimentary knowledge of Greek, since his parliamentary speeches during the 1620s were sprinkled with allusions to Epictetus and other Hellenistic philosophers. A careful grounding in the principles of logic and rhetoric also contributed to that urbane style which was to make him one of the most respected, if not one of the most forceful, orators in the House of Commons. After graduation from Trinity College in the spring of 1594, Weston established himself in London, where he was admitted to the Middle Temple on 18th June.[4] Both his father and his grandfather had studied at the Middle Temple, so he was merely following a now-established family tradition. During the latter part of the sixteenth century many boys from upper-class families completed their education by enrolling at one of the Inns of Court, which were capable of providing expert instruction in the principles of the common law. Yet the Inns were not just legal academies, since they doubled as finishing schools where students could learn how to dance, fence, and play tennis. Many members of the Inns also studied music and history and sought to acquire the social graces of the near-by court. At several of the Inns there was a real interest in the drama of the age: Shakespeare's 'Twelfth Night' was first presented at the Middle Temple in 1601.

Very little is known about Richard Weston's activities while he was enrolled at the Middle Temple. On 4 July 1595 he was assigned to a chamber shared with John Williams, an Essex man who had married his older sister Anne in December 1590. For these accommodations he was charged a fee of 53s. 4d. At a parliament of the benchers on 6 February 1596, he was one of fifty vacationers fined 20s. each for being absent during Christmas, and later in the same year he was one of four students appointed to provide the feast for Mr Phillipes, the Reader for the coming autumn term. Although there is no clear proof, Weston had probably left the Temple by 20 October 1600, when his place in the chamber shared with Williams was assigned to another student.[5]

Once his father died in December 1603 and he inherited a substantial yearly income, Weston decided to use a portion of his wealth to make a brief tour of western Europe. During the Elizabethan and Jacobean periods scores of ambitious young Englishmen sought advancement at Whitehall by means of Paris, the Loire valley, and northern Italy, since the broadening experiences of foreign travel usually helped courtiers to advance. Again there is no direct proof, so we must rely on the words of Lord Clarendon, who observed that 'after some years' study in the Middle Temple, and at an age fit to make observations and reflections, out of that which is commonly called experience is constituted, he travelled into foreign parts and was acquainted in foreign parts.' Another seventeenth-century writer, David Lloyd, maintained that Weston used a portion of his inheritance 'to improve himself with public accomplishment, but came off a saver and a gainer at the last, when made Chancellor of the Exchequer.' Certainly Sir Richard believed in the educational value of foreign travel, for in the period after 1629 he sent two of his own sons on an extensive European tour.[6]

On 23 February 1604 Weston received a royal licence to travel, which he made no attempt to utilise because of his unexpected return to parliament for Midhurst, Sussex on 29 March. Consequently he did not go abroad until some time after receiving a new licence on 17 October 1604.[7] How long he remained away is far from clear. Doubtless he was back in England by the following March, for his second wife, Frances Waldegrave, whom he had married shortly after the death of his first wife, Elizabeth Pincheon, early in 1603, gave birth to their first son in December 1605.

Even after his return from the continent Weston continued to be more concerned with local and family affairs than with national ones. In October 1606 he was reprimanded by the quarter sessions of Ongar, Harlow, and Waltham hundreds for allowing a bridge near his manor of Netteswell to fall into a dangerous state of repair. Within two years of this incident Sir Richard himself was serving as a justice of the peace, in which capacity he was especially active between 1608 and 1615. During the years after 1615 he continued to serve as a justice and frequently attended the general sessions at Chelmsford, but he naturally played a declining role in local and county affairs as his interest in national questions grew.[8]

Exactly when he began to think seriously about the prospect of employment at court is far from clear, although it seems likely that he was on the London scene for some years before doors began to be opened to him. Neither a pushing nor an aggressive man, despite his aspirations for the future, he lived in the environs of the capital 'some years, at that distance, and with that awe, as was agreeable to the modesty of that age, when men were seen before they were known, and well known before they were preferred, or durst pretend to be preferred.'[9] Although he was probably not the Sir Richard Weston who became embroiled in a bitter quarrel with the Earl of Salisbury in 1609, his rise to position and place was nevertheless delayed until after the Treasurer's death three years later.[10] Early in 1614 he was elected to the Addled Parliament as a knight of the shire for his home county. During that brief and ill-fated assembly, he was appointed to eight different committees, several of which were of more than routine importance.[11] Clearly he had begun to make a name for himself in the Commons and to play a more prominent role than the average member. Yet because of his steadfast refusal to join in the growing criticism of royal policy, he did not emerge as an acknowledged power in the House until 1621, after he became Chancellor of the Exchequer.

Early in 1615 Sir Richard was active in raising a loan of £3000 for the Lord Treasurer, the Earl of Suffolk, a leading member of the Howard family.[12] In this he came into contact with Sir Arthur Ingram, one of the best-known financiers of the period, who introduced him to the commercial life of London. Ingram's encouragement caused him to develop an interest in mercantile affairs, which was an obvious boon to his future career. Although never a prominent financier himself, he became acquainted with almost all the London magnates and acquired a detailed knowledge of their business methods. Probably because of Sir Arthur's support, Weston and his eldest son, Richard, were appointed joint collectors of the petty customs in the port of London on 1 July 1616, with the handsome yearly fee of £277 6s. 8d. Originally granted to the two Westons during pleasure, this position was regranted to them for life in February 1618.[13]

Through his customs work the elder Weston came into contact with Sir Lionel Cranfield, an associate of Ingram's since 1604 and Surveyor-General of the Customs since 1613. One of the most successful textile exporters of the period, Cranfield had entered politics as a supporter of the Howards but was virtually compelled to turn against them owing to the arrogance of the Earl of Suffolk, Lord Treasurer from 1614 until 1618, who insisted that he was not prepared to be 'yoked by a London apprentice.' Because Suffolk threatened to resign rather than accept Cranfield as his Chancellor of the Exchequer,[14] the latter had no choice but to look elsewhere for a patron. By 1615 he had recommended himself to Sir George Villiers, the future Duke of Buckingham and chief favourite of James I. Between 1616 and 1619 Cranfield was appointed to the Masterships of the Great Wardrobe, Court of Wards and Liveries, and Court of Requests. Because of his growing influence he was able to keep his old associate Ingram from being ruined when the Earl of Suffolk was toppled from power in 1618. Furthermore he was in a position to do favours for Ingram's friend and protégé, Sir Richard Weston.

With Cranfield's support Sir Richard was named in November 1617 to a royal commission that was charged with finding ways to reduce Household expenditure. The commission's work was largely directed by Cranfield, who had a long-time interest in administrative reform and was almost singlehandedly responsible for the new book of orders that James I signed on 1 June 1618. Reforms were thereby adopted that led to savings of £18,000 a year and enabled Household expenditure to be stabilised at some £59,000 annually.[15] Through their work on the commission of 1617–18 the two men laid the foundations of a friendship that was to continue until Weston's death in 1635. They were genuinely fond of one another, and Weston often visited Cranfield's home at Chelsea. Consequently they were able to work effectively together on the commission appointed in 1618 to make an investigation of the navy and advance proposals for its reform.

Fifteen years after the accession of James I the navy was riddled with corruption, owing to the mismanagement of the Earl of Nottingham, Lord Admiral for more than thirty years, and Sir Robert Mansell, Treasurer of the Navy since 1604. Neither Nottingham nor Mansell was a competent administrator, and neither had attempted to keep the fleet in a state of preparedness. The fighting strength of the navy had ebbed away during the first two decades of the seventeenth century, and by 1618 there were hardly 25 ships that could be considered seaworthy.[16] The first step towards naval reform was taken in May 1618, when Mansell was discharged from his post and replaced by Sir William Russell. Several months later a more significant change occurred when Nottingham was induced to surrender the admiralty to Buckingham in return for a cash payment of £3000 and an annuity of £1000 from the crown. Under the new leadership provided by Buckingham and Russell, a measure of honesty was brought back into the administration of the navy. But they wisely made no attempt to direct the work of the commission appointed on 18 June.[17]

During the summer of 1618 the ten naval commissioners found that many of the King's ships had rotted away and were now suitable only for firewood. In recent years large sums had been squandered, £10,000 on unusable cordage alone. Late in September a report of the commission's findings was presented to the King at Hampton Court. It called attention to the practice of 'buying at rates double to the market' and the multitude of new and unnecessary officials. It also outlined ways of reducing naval expenditure by £22,000 a year while improving the fleet's fighting capacity and proposed a five-year programme for the construction of ten new ships and the repair of all vessels judged to be salvageable. Such a programme would cost slightly more than £30,000, but once it had been completed the annual expenses of the navy would decline to less than £20,000.[18]

After being studied by a select group of councillors, the commissioners' recommendations were adopted, and Cranfield was soon reporting to the Lord Admiral that 'for the business of the navy we follow it daily, wherein we find all things to succeed better than we could hope.'[19] Several new ships were constructed in record time, and many older ones were overhauled and restored to effective fighting condition. Minor improvements were made in naval design and construction, but rigging and armament remained unchanged. Considerably less reliable than they were expected to be, the ships performed rather poorly in the campaigns of 1625–8. Although the commissioners succeeded in halting the navy's continued decline, they were unable to re-establish its former greatness.[20]

While helping to regulate the affairs of the navy, in which he now had a deep interest, Weston was becoming involved in a variety of public duties. Late in September 1618 he was one of four men directed to consider the establishment of a tapestry industry in England. He was also engaged in discussions between the English and Dutch East India Companies, which led to the conclusion of an important commercial agreement on 7 July 1619. Six months later he and Sir John Wolstenholme were appointed to report on English trade with the Far East during the preceding four years, their specific task being to learn whether the country was enjoying a favourable balance of trade. On 17 April 1620 he was one of eight men named to a commission to inquire into the 'corrupt dyeing of black and coloured silks.'[21]

As he became increasingly active in public affairs, rumours began to circulate that Weston was destined for an important government post. Early in 1618 John Chamberlain informed a friend that he was one of 43 suitors for the Chancellorship of the Duchy of Lancaster. A year later he was mentioned for a seat on the Court of Requests, and in January 1620 it was declared that he was about to be nominated Under-treasurer of the Exchequer to assist the ageing Chancellor, Sir Fulke Greville.[22] Although all these rumours proved false, an important reward did come his way in February 1620, when he and three other men were authorised to supervise the collection of the pretermitted customs, duties charged since the 1550s on woollen goods exported to the continent. Weston himself assumed responsibility for the duties levied on all broadcloths and kersies exported via the Thames by native-born merchants. In this capacity he distinguished himself by collecting 'the largest sums accounted for by all the collectors of the pretermitted customs.' For his outstanding work in this regard, he was granted at 21-year annuity of £500 out of his own collections on 1 June 1620.[23]

Only a few days after receiving this valuable grant, Weston was appointed co-leader of an important embassy to the Spanish Netherlands, several of the German principalities, and Bohemia. This embassy, which gave him the chance to move from the periphery to the inner circles of government, was part of the diplomatic offensive by James I to prevent the spread of hostilities from central into western Europe, the beginning of what became known as the Thirty Years War. In June 1620 James decided to send two embassies to the continent in a last desperate attempt to localise the rebellion that had begun two years earlier in Bohemia. The first was to be conducted by Sir Henry Wotton, a career diplomat who had been Ambassador to Venice and the United Provinces. Wotton left England on 28 June, visited the courts of the Duke of Lorraine and the Holy Roman Emperor, but accomplished nothing of value.[24]

The second embassy dispatched in 1620 was under the joint command of Weston and a professional military man, Sir Edward Conway, whose father had once served as Governor of the Dutch cautionary town of Brill. The two men were to travel first to Brussels, where they would confer with the Spanish Regent, the Archduchess Isabella, and her husband, the Archduke Albert, an uncle of the Emperor. While in Brussels the two ambassadors were to make a strong protest against an attack on the Palatinate, which would be supported by a remonstrance delivered in Madrid by Lord Digby, the English envoy there. From the Spanish Netherlands Weston and Conway were to travel into Germany, where they would visit Nuremberg and several of the imperial electors, including the Archbishops of Cologne and Mainz and the Lutheran Elector of Saxony, John George. After their consultations in Germany they would continue on to Prague, where they were to confer with the Elector Palatine, now in shaky possession of the

Bohemian throne, which the Habsburgs were determined to recover.[25]

Unable to commit their government to any specific course of action, Weston and Conway had virtually no hope of forestalling an invasion of the Palatinate. They were authorised only to explain their master's concern for the fate of his son-in-law's ancestral lands, to solicit support for a negotiated settlement of the conflict, and to predict what England might or might not do under certain circumstances. Extremely critical of James's refusal to take a decisive stand, S. R. Gardiner characterised the embassy as a 'bootless errand' and a 'purposeless mission.'[26] It should be added, however, that the engines of war were so well primed by 1620 that a firmer stand by the English government is unlikely to have made much difference.

Shortly before setting out the two ambassadors paid a call on Count Gondomar, to whom they described the nature of their mission and whose assistance they requested in the quest for peace. Gondomar replied that his master was equally concerned for the peace of Europe and regretted the steps he had already been compelled to take.[27] Weston and Conway began their journey during the first week of July. They were accompanied by a number of attendants, including John Dickinson, a clerk of the Council who was especially knowledgeable about German affairs and had been appointed their secretary, and a Dr Winston, who went along at Weston's invitation and personal expense.[28] A few days before their departure the ambassadors received advances of £400 each from the Exchequer, while their secretary was allotted £200. The total cost of the embassy, which lasted almost eight months, was £9087, which was rather less proportionately than the expenses of Wotton's mission, which came to £5965.[29]

Weston and his associates disembarked on the continent at Calais, whence, because of a thunderstorm, their journey to Brussels was both slow and difficult. The archduchess and her husband had left two weeks earlier for their summer palace at Marimont, some thirty miles away, to which the Englishmen were accompanied by the Count of Noyel and the Lieutenant of the Guard of Archers. At Marimont James's representatives were received first by the archduchess and then by her husband, who proved to be in perilous health. Isabella listened attentively as they explained their master's concern for the security of the Palatinate and, in response, declared that she too desired to see the maintenance of peace, 'both as a woman, and because the war tended to the prejudice of a Lady whom she does so much love and esteem.' (This was James's only daughter, the Princess Elizabeth.) Yet the Archduke Albert would not promise to withhold assistance from his nephew the Emperor in the recovery 'of that inheritance of the House of Austria, which had been taken away by force.' Nor would he deny the rumours of an impending Spanish attack on Frederick's ancestral lands, which prompted the ambassadors to object that 'unless we might be cleared and assured touching the Palatinate, we knew not in what terms we stood, nor how we should proceed.'[30]

After a long and unproductive interview with Albert, Weston and Conway were escorted into the garden of the palace, where they were entertained at a banquet held alongside an arbor 'in the middle of a very long and goodly close walk.' The following day they returned to Brussels and secured accommodations with William Trumbull, the resident English agent. At his house they conferred with such dignitaries as Don Carlos Coloma, the Spanish Ambassador in Brussels; Ambrogio Spinola, the renowned general from Genoa; and Peter Peckius, the Chancellor of Brabant, who had been summoned from Ghent to preside over the talks with them. These three officials stoutly maintained that their master, Philip III, saw no need for an attack on the Palatinate. Weston was sceptical of their assurances, however, and in a letter to Buckingham he declared 'they are unwilling to draw his Majesty to the necessity of this war, but hitherto they give us little satisfaction to the contrary.'[31]

After two weeks in Brussels the ambassadors set out for Lorraine and the Rhineland. There they were welcomed by the Archbishop of Cologne, who, after declaring his friendship for James I, maintained that England should be encouraged to participate in an alliance with the Catholic bishops of Germany and their friends. The two Englishmen showed only the most guarded interest in this remarkable proposal, although they gave a detailed account of it in a dispatch to London. During a conference on 4 August the archbishop confessed that he had just received reports of possible military action against the Palatinate and had sent letters advising against such a course to the authorities in Brussels, but he was in no position to predict what the future might bring.[32]

The ambassadors travelled on to Mainz and Trier, where they engaged in similar conversations with the ecclesiastical electors. The journey to Trier was especially difficult, for it cost them 'in going and coming, eight days, in a very troublesome way, and want of conveniences.' In the Rhineland the Englishmen passed through several towns already occupied by the imperialists, which gave them a good indication of the movements of Spinola's troops. The general and his men had already crossed the Rhine at Coblenz and were heading for Mainz.[33]

On 21 August Weston and his associates arrived at Oppenheim, where the Protestant Princes of the Union were encamped. Led by the Margrave of Anspach, the army of the Union consisted of some 20,000 men, or several thousand less than in Spinola's force. The princes clamoured to know not only whether James planned to send any assistance to them but also the exact nature of Spinola's campaign plan. When disappointed in this regard, they demanded of the Englishmen whether they would be justified in taking the offensive and landing the first blow. Weston and Conway responded that their master was opposed to such a course because he wanted the enemy to strike first and thereby brand himself the aggressor.[34] Ultimately the Protestant princes elected to remain on the defensive and await Spinola's attack, which was not long in coming. On 30 August the Spanish troops laid siege to Kreuznach, which opened its gates the next day. Spinola then turned against Alzei, which led the princes to evacuate Oppenheim for the greater safety of Worms. On 4 September the Spanish troops entered Oppenheim in triumph, unopposed and unresisted. Once this happened the Protestant princes sought to blame their cowardly behaviour on Weston and Conway, whom they denounced for forbidding offensive measures while there was still a chance of success. In Gardiner's opinion, 'It would have been well for James if all the charges brought against him and his ministers could have been met as easily as this.'[35]

Meanwhile the ambassadors had departed for Nuremberg, where they urged the municipal officials to join with England 'in counsel and all other means whereby the present troubles may be happily composed.' But the city fathers were unwilling to commit themselves and made a long and evasive reply to the English proposals. From Nuremberg Weston and his associates travelled on to Dresden, only to find the Elector of Saxony away on a military campaign. An unaccommodating man, John George refused to return from the front and insisted that any negotiations with him be by means of written memorandums. Nothing was to be accomplished by such a tedious procedure, and by 26 September the Englishmen had decided to resume their journey to Prague. This was soon reported to the Elector, who sent instructions for his ministers to place obstacles in the way of their departure. He also directed that their trunks be searched, for it had been reported to him that they were transporting a 'great store of money' from James I to his son-in-law in Prague. Weston and Conway naturally protested this latest annoyance as a violation of their diplomatic immunity and a serious affront to the honour of their King, which did not deter John George's henchmen, however.[36]

Shortly after the beginning of October the Englishmen succeeded in crossing the frontier into Bohemia. A slow and tortuous journey of almost a week brought them to a village four miles from Prague, where they were met and welcomed by Sir Francis Nethersole, the English agent with Frederick V. Although the ambassadors' arrival was long overdue, Frederick was away from his capital, having established himself at Rakovitz, a fortified camp some thirty miles to the west. As a consequence the visitors were received by Elizabeth alone, as Queen of Bohemia, whom they found to be 'in good health and full of courage.'[37] On 14 October Frederick made a hurried return to the city to confer with them. Weston and Conway made special efforts to refute the accusation, now widely reported, that their counsel had paved the way for Spinola's uncontested victories in north-western Germany. Indeed they spoke so heatedly on the subject that they left Frederick 'well satisfied . . . [and] much marvelling at the courses held by the Princes of the Union.'[38]

Yet on the main point of a peaceful accommodation with the Emperor, the Englishmen were considerably less successful. Frederick protested that he had never sought the Bohemian throne, which he could not now surrender without great loss of honour. Although his reputation and integrity were dearer to him than any of his territorial possessions, there were even more compelling reasons why he should not withdraw to his ancestral lands in the west. It was his firm belief that a renunciation of the Bohemian throne by him 'would not end the war, nor secure Religion, because these States will never receive the Emperor.' Frederick also insisted that there was no possibility of a diplomatic resolution of the problem without a suspension of arms, to which he was convinced Ferdinand II would never agree.[39] Weston and Conway must have sensed the hopelessness of their mission after the interview with Frederick. Despite the logic of some of his arguments, his inflexible attitudes were making a European conflict inevitable. Although the ambassadors remained in Prague for almost a month, they must have concluded by mid-October that all their efforts were doomed to fail.

During their stay in the Bohemian capital, the Englishmen periodically dined with Frederick and Elizabeth, since an acute shortage of funds made it impossible for them to be entertained in a grander way. On Sunday the 8th of November they were present at a dinner during which plans were made for them to accompany Elizabeth on an inspection of the troops at nearby Star Park. Before that tour could be made, the Bohemian army was attacked and overrun at the White Mountain, several miles outside the city. In this celebrated battle, the first real encounter of the Thirty Years War, Frederick's commanders were overwhelmed by an imperial army captained by Maximilian of Bavaria and Count Tilly. Once the Bohemian army was crushed, Prague was at the mercy of Frederick's enemies and a general exodus from the city began. Scores of wagons and carriages were soon to be seen on the roads leading to the north and west. A determined woman, Elizabeth refused to flee without her husband, who was frantically trying to rally support for a defence of the city. Weston and Conway were sceptical of the wisdom of making a stand and warned that all possibilities should be carefully weighed. They also sought to mediate between Frederick and his enemies by sending trumpeters to the imperialist camp to inquire about possible peace terms.[40]

During the sleepless night following the battle, Frederick and Elizabeth concluded that there was no chance of holding Prague and hastily planned their departure. Accompanied the next morning by the English emissaries, they left the city at the head of a slowly moving convoy of more than 300 wagons, carts, and carriages. After crossing the mountains to the north they arrived at Breslau, where Frederick sought vainly to enlist the services of the Silesians and Moravians in his cause. From Breslau on the 13th of November Frederick and his wife addressed urgent appeals to London for military support. Until this juncture the royal couple had refused to concede their folly in accepting the Bohemian throne. Now they could no longer ignore the gravity of their situation, which they had brought squarely upon themselves.[41]

Weston and Conway remained with Frederick and Elizabeth only a few days after the flight from Prague. Shortly after the city surrendered to the imperialists on 10 November, they secured a safe-conduct from Maximilian of Bavaria and retraced their steps in order to confer with representatives of the Emperor. As they themselves probably anticipated, these consultations achieved nothing of importance, and they soon received instructions from the Secretary of State to begin their homeward trip.[42] They returned to England by way of Dresden, Magdeburg, Hamburg, The Hague, and Antwerp. Most of their journey took place during deepest winter, when overland travel was made more difficult than usual by heavy snow and ice. Long stretches of the river Elbe were completely impassable, so of necessity they travelled by sledge and passed through villages that 'could hardly afford . . . any mean conveniences for carriages and other accommodatings.'[43] Their progress was painfully slow, and it was not until January that they arrived in Hamburg, where they were obliged to beg financial assistance of the English merchant colony. Even more laborious was their journey across northwestern Germany to The Hague and thence to Antwerp, which, because of 'the strangeness of the season,' was 'a compound of trouble, danger, and expense.' They managed to reach the Scheldt by 20 February but were unable to cross the Channel until 4 March. Once back in England they secured issues of more than £3850 from the Exchequer towards the relief of their financial difficulties.[44]

Public opinion was convinced that Weston and Conway had failed lamentably in their mission. Yet Clarendon later averred that Sir Richard conducted himself throughout the embassy 'with great prudence,' thereby winning the reputation 'of a wise man from all those with whom he treated, princes and ambassadors.'[45] This was the view held by the King, who shortly rewarded both men with high positions in the government. In November 1621 Weston succeeded Sir Fulke Greville as Chancellor and Under-treasurer of the Exchequer; and a year later Conway took over Sir Robert Naunton's responsibilities as principal Secretary of State.

2 Parliament and a Second Embassy

By the time Weston returned from the continent, the third parliament of James I had been in session for more than a month. Thus he was still abroad when the elections were held, and for the first time in almost twenty years he was absent from the House of Commons, which he was unable to enter until returned in a by-election for Arundel, Sussex on 22 November. Despite his temporary absence from the House, he remained keenly interested in parliamentary affairs and kept himself well informed of the proceedings.

The parliament of 1621 met in two sessions, with the first lasting from 30 January until early in June. During the opening weeks there was a real spirit of co-operation between James and the members, and in mid-March the government was voted two subsidies for a war in defence of the Palatinate. Although this grant would produce much less than was needed for such a war, the King was delighted by its passage, since it was the first to come his way in more than ten years. His elation was of brief duration, however, for the opposition was busily preparing an attack on various aspects of royal policy. Legal abuses were bitterly assailed, and monopolies were criticised so severely that Sir Giles Mompesson, one of the greatest monopolists of the period, was committed to the Tower, despite his close friendship with Buckingham. Of greater political significance was the campaign mounted against the Lord Chancellor, Sir Francis Bacon, who was charged with numerous malpractices in office. Reviving the process of impeachment for the first time since the mid-fifteenth century, the opposition demanded Bacon's removal from office and sentenced him to pay a fine of £40,000. As a result of the Commons' unexpected boldness, the harmonious relationship between crown and parliament disappeared, and on 4 June James announced a sudden adjournment, a move that caused surprise and dismay in many quarters. Weston was among those distressed by this turn of events, and in a letter to Sir Walter Aston he complained of 'the sudden, and much wondered at, and much lamented adjournment.'[1]

Early in June the government took disciplinary action against several of the parliamentary opposition. Sir Edwin Sandys was imprisoned, while the Earl of Southampton, who had flirted too openly with the opposition leaders in the lower House,[2] was placed in the custody of John Williams, Dean of Westminster and Bishop-elect of Lincoln. Weston was named to serve as Southampton's actual keeper; but because he did not relish the prospect of acting as a jailer, he petitioned to be relieved of his charge, which was reassigned to Sir William Parkehurst, a former aide to Sir Henry Wotton.[3]

During the summer of 1621 Weston continued to be active in the management of naval affairs, in which he now had a sincere interest. He was becoming known as an expert in matters pertaining to naval finance and was acquiring some knowledge of nautical design and equipment. This would prove invaluable when he later served as head of the first two naval boards of Charles I. He also continued to play a part in the collection of the pretermitted customs, a task first assigned him sixteen months earlier. In June 1621 the office of collector of the pretermitted customs in the port of London was granted him and his eldest son at an annual salary of £100. A large cash reward was required to make sure of the appointment: in 1621 or 1622 he released £2000 to Cranfield in return for the collectorship.[4] Because of his growing involvement in government affairs, public opinion was convinced that he was being groomed for an important post, although it was not known what office he might receive. On 28 July John Chamberlain informed a friend that

> All this last week Sir Richard Weston was [principal] Secretary (as far as common fame could make him) insomuch that it was said not to be in doing, but done, but now the report cools again and he is where he was, as likewise Sir John Suckling, who was in ill haste to be Chancellor of the Exchequer.[5]

On 23 September Weston was at last sworn of the Privy Council. Within a brief period he became one of its more regular members, missing only five of the sixteen meetings held during the remaining weeks of the year.[6] In 1621 the Council was still a small body with an average attendance of between nine and ten members. It was not too large to be an effective governing body, but the main decisions were made and implemented elsewhere by the King and his favourites. Thus the Council had limited policy-making functions and handled little more than routine administrative matters. During the autumn of 1621 the most active members were Secretary Calvert, Lord Mandeville, and Sir Julius Caesar, all politicians of the second rank.

Between September and November a major administrative shuffle occurred when both the Treasury and the Exchequer changed hands. On 28 September Lord Mandeville surrendered the white staff, the symbol of his great office, to the King, who two days later entrusted it to Cranfield. Shortly afterwards Sir Fulke Greville resigned as Chancellor and Under-treasurer of the Exchequer, both positions being granted to Weston on 13 November.[7]

Less than two weeks after obtaining this important dual post, Sir Richard was returned to parliament in a by-election for Arundel, Sussex. He was selected to fill the seat vacated by his mentor, who had recently been elevated to the peerage as Baron Cranfield.[8] Yet Sir Richard's election for the borough was made possible by its chief patron, Thomas Howard, Earl of Arundel, a nephew of the disgraced Earl of Suffolk, who had been ousted from the Treasury in 1618. Eight years younger than Weston, Lord Arundel had been educated at Trinity College, Cambridge, the same foundation once attended by Sir Richard. By the early 1620s the two men had become firm friends, bound not only by common attitudes towards government and religion but also by a mutual interest in the painting and sculpture of their age. Clearly the earl considered Weston a man of great ability, for in a letter to Cranfield he described him 'as without equal in the King's service.'[9]

During the second session of the parliament of 1621, which began on 20 November, Sir Richard emerged as one of the leading Privy Councillors in the lower House. He took an active part in the debates and gave unswerving support to the crown. As an important government official he acted as a liaison between James and the Commons, delivering frequent messages and petitions between the two. He also sent reports to Buckingham and kept him informed of the views being expressed by the members.[10]

Because the opposition was demanding a voice in the formulation of foreign policy, a major confrontation between King and parliament was virtually inevitable. For the past fifty years the crown had insisted that diplomatic matters should be determined by the prerogative alone, and James was unwilling for them to be discussed without his explicit permission. Yet he refused to do anything to restrain his favourite, who, for his own personal reasons, was giving strong encouragement to the leaders of the Commons. Despite this grave tactical error, James hoped to obtain additional financial support so that he could render assistance to the Elector Palatine. Aside from a report given by Lord Digby, however, he did very little to win support for his foreign policy. By the autumn of 1621 the upper Palatinate had been occupied by an imperial army under Maximilian of Bavaria and Count Tilly, while the lower Palatinate was on the verge of being overrun by Spinola's troops. Parliament as of old regarded Spain as the principal enemy and was clamouring for a declaration of war against Philip IV.[11] Although the Commons had only a vague idea of the King's diplomatic plans, they were hostile to another grant unless they had a voice in the projects for which the funds were to be appropriated.

On 26 and 27 November there was a long debate on foreign policy in the lower House. Sir Dudley Digges, a prominent opposition leader, called for England to join forces with other Protestant states for the defence of the Palatinate. After a lengthy discussion of Digges's proposal, Weston took the floor and delivered a persuasive speech on behalf of the crown. For two days, he declared, the House had heard numerous propositions to the same end. A series of speakers had called for the 'encouraging of old friends, raising new [ones], finding the true enemy.' The King had worked diligently to preserve the peace of Europe, even at the cost of neglecting his son-in-law's interests. The Protestant faith was being battered abroad, and the King's children and grandchildren were enduring great hardships. During the past summer James had permitted several regiments to cross over and take part in the defence of the Palatinate. 'This new army in the Palatinate hath given relief to the Palatinate, given time to the Princes [of the Union] to reunite, and behooves us [to act]. Now the King hath met us half way, done what rests in him, and leaves us to do our parts.' At present there were but three purposes for which money was needed: to provide support for the English troops in the Palatinate, to make possible a war of diversion, and to revive old friendships and develop new ones.[12]

Sir Richard's speech convinced the House that it should concentrate on the question of supply. The members were favourable to the idea of another grant, but only if steps could be taken to ensure that they had a voice in the way the funds were to be spent. While James was thinking in terms of a long war that might cost millions of pounds, a majority of the House was calculating on a brief conflict involving considerably less expenditure. On 28 November Sir Edward Coke reported for the grand committee to which the matter had been referred that it recommended a grant of 'one entire subsidy,' payable by February 1622. To increase the yield of the subsidy, the Commons decided that all aliens, recusants, and convicted Papists should be taxed at double the normal rates.[13]

Although a single subsidy was an absurdly small grant, the members had done nothing as yet to encroach on the prerogative and provoke the King's anger. On 29 November, however, they began to tread a perilous course by discussing the desirability of a war with Spain. Several members urged the King to make a formal declaration of support for the Elector Palatine. Others insisted that the government take repressive action against the English Catholics, who were felt to be in secret sympathy with their coreligionists on the continent. Almost all agreed that James should be asked to terminate the negotiations, underway since 1614, for an Anglo-Spanish marriage alliance and to select a Protestant bride for Prince Charles.[14] Of the Privy Councillors in the House, Sir Richard was clearly the most distressed by the direction the debates were now taking. After prolonged discussion of the Prince's marriage, he rose on 3 December and admonished the members not to meddle with such affairs. He continued by asserting that

> . . . as princes do best when they take counsel of this House, so we ought not to speak of that which will not be heard. No more will I meddle with the war, yet I am not against the war; but whether war did ever first begin from this House I much doubt. It's good when the King adviseth with his parliament of war, but for the parliament to advise the King of war is presumptuous. It's not enough to know what we ought to speak, but we must also know what is fit for him to hear.[15]

Although he knew this speech would be displeasing to Buckingham, Weston did not shrink from giving a clear statement of his constitutional views. He was no enemy of parliament; but he had too good an understanding of his country's history to be able to support the members' claims to complete freedom of speech. In accordance with the practices of a rapidly disappearing age, he believed that such questions as religion, foreign policy, and the succession were best settled by the prerogative.

Sir Richard's speech provoked a sharp rejoinder from the more liberally-inclined members. Sir George More, Sir Robert Phelips, and several others protested that they had done nothing to merit such reproofs from him. But many of the members were unconvinced, and Sir Henry Vane suggested an inquiry. Precedents should be studied and an effort made to determine whether earlier parliaments had ever advised the crown in regard to marriage negotiations. This investigation should be completed before the House began work on a petition to the King, 'lest we grasp more than we can hold fast.'[16] Shortly after agreement had been reached on this matter, the members received a kingly reprimand by way of the principal Secretary, Sir George Calvert, who had been directed to inform the House

> That none therein shall presume henceforth to meddle with anything concerning our Government, or deep matters of State, and namely not to deal with our dearest Son's Match with the Daughter of Spain, nor to touch the Honour of that King, or any other our Friends and Confederates.

In a note to the Speaker, James also warned that '. . . we think our self very free and able to punish any man's misdemeanors in Parliament, as well during their sitting as after: Which we mean not to spare hereafter upon any occasion of any man's insolent behavior there.'[17]

The King's two warnings caused a mood of deepest gloom to descend upon the House, which was for several days uncertain how to proceed. Eventually the members decided that a declaration should be framed to explain their position and assure the King that they had not encroached upon the prerogative. Although this declaration acknowledged that James alone was able to 'resolve of Peace and War, and of the Marriage of the most noble Prince your Son,' it also asserted that:

> . . . whereas your Majesty doth seem to abridge us of the ancient liberty of Parliament for freedom of speech . . . without which we cannot freely debate, nor freely discern of things in question before us: In which we have been confirmed by your Majesty's most gracious former speeches and messages. We are therefore again enforced in all humbleness to pray your Majesty to allow the same, and thereby to take away the doubts and scruples your Majesty's late letter to our Speaker hath wrought upon us.[18]

The House decided to entrust the presentation of its declaration to a committee of twelve members; and Weston, as leader of the delegation, was directed to 'report, or bring to the House, such answer as his Majesty shall be pleased to give or send.' On 9 December Sir Richard and his associates travelled to Newmarket to deliver the declaration, the contents of which James had already been informed. He responded by angrily maintaining that the Commons had no authority to consider the Prince's marriage without his permission. Rather than press for a long and costly war against Spain, the members would do better to thank their sovereign for keeping the realm so long at peace.[19]

On 14 December, after the Speaker had announced James's answer to the House, Sir Richard gave a lengthy account of the audience at Newmarket. James had insisted that 'he was an old and experienced King and need not [take] such lessons from you.' He had denied that he was obliged to accept the advice of persons who lent him money for military purposes, an irrelevancy that must have perplexed the average member; and he had ended by stating that 'your privileges are rather tolerations from our predecessors and us than inheritances as you term them.'[20] Once Sir Richard completed his report, the House turned to a discussion of its privileges, which several members contended had been violated. The feeling of the Commons was that their liberties were in no way dependent on the King's indulgence and toleration. Sir Francis Seymour criticised James's refusal to allow freedom of debate on matters relating to foreign policy and the Prince's marriage, and he urged the passage of a protestation 'that it is our right notwithstanding' to discuss such issues.[21]

Seymour's remarks prompted a rejoinder from Weston, who insisted that the House had no reason to be dissatisfied with the King's answer. It was Sir Richard's conviction that

The King hath granted us all our privileges only bounding his prerogative from being encroached upon. Let us make this day a happy day by accepting this favour from him. It will be nearer a discontent than a sorrow if we petition any more, or abstain from proceeding [with business].

Weston urged the members to conclude their discussion of grievances so that 'all the world might conceive well that his Majesty and his subjects agree.'[22] This was to be a recurrent theme in his parliamentary speeches during the 1620s. He repeatedly maintained that the members should adapt their views to fit the needs of royal policy. Otherwise England's enemies might conclude that the country was weak and divided, which would doubtless increase the likelihood of war.[23]

The House refused to be swayed by Weston's arguments, which Sir Thomas Crew conceded to be of great importance although fundamentally mistaken. Crew, rather than the Chancellor, reflected the true feeling of the Commons when he declared that their privileges must be safeguarded for future generations. The members must not be lulled into accepting the King's position, and Crew suggested the passage of a formal protestation, a matter the House debated furiously for three days. ' "Such heat within," wrote an old courtier to Weston, "and the Thames impassable without for frost and snow." ' Meanwhile the King had become alarmed and was directing the Speaker to permit debate only on the subject of a new subsidy bill.[24]

By 18 December the members had agreed on the wording of their protestation, which asserted

That the liberties, franchises, privileges, and jurisdictions of Parliament are the ancient and undoubted birthright of the subjects of England; and that the arduous and urgent affairs concerning the King, state, and defence of the realm, and of the Church of England, and the maintenance and making of laws, and redress of mischiefs and grievances which daily happen within this realm, are proper subjects and matter of counsel and debate in Parliament; and that in the handling and proceeding of those businesses, every member of the House of Parliament hath, and of right ought to have, freedom of speech to propound, treat, reason, and bring to conclusion the same . . . And that every member of the said House hath like

> freedom from all impeachment, imprisonment and molestation (other than by censure of the House itself) for or concerning any speaking, reasoning, or declaring of any matter or matters touching the Parliament, or Parliament-business.[25]

Knowing what the King's reaction would probably be, the members voted against presenting the document to him and merely entered it in their official journal.

When James learned of the action taken by the Commons, he acted with surprising resolution. After declaring an immediate adjournment until 8 February 1622, he ordered the arrest of several leading opposition spokesmen, including Sir Robert Phelips, Sir Edward Coke, and John Pym. Within a few more days he had grown so angry that he ordered the clerk of the House to bring the *Commons' Journal* to him at Whitehall. With his chief advisers and several of the judges looking on, he tore out the pages on which the offending protestation had been inscribed. Then he dissolved parliament.

Although the parliament of 1621 ended on an acrimonious note, it marked the opening of a new phase in Sir Richard's career. During the second session he emerged as a leading figure in the lower House, where a statement of his views was always welcomed, if not always accepted. His primary allegiance was to the King, but this did not prevent him from considering himself a loyal member of the Commons, which he was prepared to serve in any way not conflicting with his constitutional philosophy. A genial and engaging man, he had scores of friends in the lower House, which caused him to rise swiftly among the inner circle of royal Councillors. Indeed David Lloyd maintained that 'his activity in Parliament made him considerable at court, none fitter to serve a Prince than he who commands the humour of the people.'[26]

Since parliament had failed to grant him sufficient funds for an active war policy, the King had no choice but to resort again to diplomacy. Although the prospects were far from good, he could only hope for a negotiated settlement of the war over the Palatinate. As early as November 1621 he had appealed to the Emperor for a cessation of hostilities and urged that the Elector Palatine be restored to his ancestral lands in northwestern Germany. On his part Frederick V would renounce all claim to the Bohemian throne and would, on bended knee, crave humble pardon of the

Emperor. In the future he would render 'all constant due devotion' to Ferdinand II and would 'upon reasonable conditions reconcile himself with other his neighbour Princes and States of the Empire, and hold good friendship with them.'[27]

James did not receive an answer until 13 January 1622. Ferdinand readily conceded that the English government had made sincere efforts to preserve the peace of Europe, but Frederick himself had shown few signs of repentance and almost no desire to end the conflict. On the contrary his actions seemed to bespeak an intention to continue the war indefinitely. Yet the Emperor was willing to participate in a peace conference at Brussels and would grant authority to negotiate in his name to the Archduchess Isabella.[28] Despite this commitment Ferdinand had no desire to see Frederick restored to his ancestral lands. In May 1622 he confessed this in a letter to his Spanish cousin, Philip IV, to whom he revealed that he had promised the Palatinate to his Catholic supporter, Maximilian of Bavaria. All the preliminary matters had been settled, and only the 'solemn investiture' of Maximilian was left to be arranged.[29]

James suspected that the Emperor was not altogether sincere in his desire for a negotiated settlement, but he was willing to gamble that something might be achieved by a peace conference at Brussels. If only the two sides would agree to a truce, negotiations for a formal peace treaty could be opened at a later date. To conduct the preliminary talks for a truce, Sir Richard was selected. He had acquitted himself well on his previous embassy, and he had the continued backing of Count Gondomar.[30] During the conference he was to be assisted by John Dickinson, the Council clerk who had accompanied him to Prague and was again appointed his secretary. To defray the initial charges of their trip, Weston received an advance of £1500 from the Exchequer, while Dickinson was issued £240. These sums were to be applied towards their payment for the embassy, which was to be calculated at the rate of £6 per day for the ambassador and £2 a day for his secretary.[31]

On his arrival in Brussels on 6 May, Weston's reception by the archduchess was 'very honourable . . . since two days were spent in ceremony.' Once serious discussions began, he announced that he had full authority to conclude a suspension of arms and that he understood Isabella had been entrusted with similar powers.

Her deputies replied that they had received no such formal authorisation and possessed only a general letter concerning a possible cessation of hostilities. During one of the opening sessions Weston proposed the immediate declaration of a truce, which should last for the duration of the conference. Isabella's commissioners professed to like the general intent of his suggestion but maintained that a suspension of arms could only be for a predetermined period of time, such as eight, ten, or twelve weeks. If no time limit were established, either side might be tempted to prolong the talks indefinitely for its own advantage. A more fundamental question raised during one of the initial sessions was whether either side could really negotiate on behalf of the auxiliaries in Germany. The archduchess's deputies declared that they had no power to make commitments for Count Tilly, the leading general of Maximilian of Bavaria, while Sir Richard conceded that he was not authorised to make agreements binding on Christian of Brunswick, the chief auxiliary of the Elector Palatine.[32]

For two months the negotiations in Brussels proceeded harmoniously but at little more than a snail's pace. Because key decisions were always deferred, Weston came to feel that the imperialists had a deliberate plan to spin out the talks until the military situation turned more clearly in their favour. If James could be hoodwinked into abstaining from direct intervention in the conflict for the duration of the conference, the power of England would be effectively neutralised. Spain and her allies would have a free hand and might well accomplish their objectives in regard to the Rhineland and the United Provinces.

During his stay in Brussels Sir Richard received letters from friends in London and various other places. Undoubtedly the most important of these were from Sir Dudley Carleton, England's Ambassador at The Hague. Carleton was a skilful observer of the European scene, and his letters helped to keep Weston informed of military developments in Germany and the Low Countries. They also argued that the imperialists had no desire for a truce and were merely seeking to gain time 'till they be in better readiness and the King's [*i.e.* Frederick's] armies weakened by lying still.'[33] Carleton's assessment of the situation was thus in accord with Weston's, and the two men seem to have struck up a lively friendship through their correspondence. Six years later, after Weston had been named Lord Treasurer and was emerging as chief minister of Charles I, Carleton found himself appointed, with Weston's backing, principal Secretary of State.

It was probably from Carleton that Weston learned in July that Heidelberg, the capital of the Palatinate, was being besieged by an imperial army under Tilly and a Spanish force captained by Gonzales. Once he had verified this intelligence, he requested an audience with Isabella and demanded that the siege be ended immediately. The archduchess averred that she could not meet this demand, since she had no control over Tilly, who took his orders directly from the Emperor. Weston countered that she had been authorised by Ferdinand to conclude a truce and must therefore be able 'to direct his ministers to that end.' Even if she had no influence over Tilly, she had unquestioned power over Gonzales, who should be ordered to withdraw from the siege at once. Isabella conceded that Gonzales normally received his orders from Spain but insisted that he considered himself a subordinate of Tilly. Upon hearing this Sir Richard declared bitterly that James should never have sent him to Brussels. It was now apparent that the Spanish generals could accept orders from whomsoever they pleased, 'according to the variety of advantages' at the time. If James had only known this beforehand, he would never have sent an ambassador to participate in the negotiations and 'might [thereby] have prevented the receiving of such an affront.'[34]

During the next few weeks Sir Richard made no attempt to conceal his growing dissatisfaction with the Brussels talks. His letters alluded chiefly to the hypocritical arguments of the archduchess's commissioners and their wiles in preventing the conclusion of a truce. In a dispatch to Secretary Calvert he noted 'what good words, what professions we have here, but what cold effects.' He hastened to add, however, that 'the mystery of this' could be discovered only in Madrid, since the archduchess and her deputies had no independent authority and were unable to give real satisfaction.[35]

By the beginning of September Sir Richard had concluded that there was no reason for him to remain any longer in Brussels. In a letter to Buckingham, who had already begun to press for his recall, he stated that 'my chief comfort was, that whatsoever the success were, the clearness of his Majesty's intentions would appear to the whole world . . . [and] the failing is not of his side, which I think is manifest enough.' Weston was unable to report that he had secured any promises concerning the siege of Heidelberg. The archduchess had requested Tilly and Gonzales to withdraw from the siege but had as yet received no response. Sir Richard concluded with the assurance:

> I have said, and done, and used all diligences within my power to bring forth better effects, and can go no further; and therefore, I humbly beseech your Lordship, that I may have leave to return, when I shall hear that they will not remove the siege at Heidelberg. For their pretending to restore all, when all is taken, is poor comfort to me, and as little honour to his Majesty.[36]

Sir Richard's final interview with the archduchess was a rather stormy one. He announced that his master had laid down specific conditions that must be met if the talks were to continue. Tilly and Gonzales were to be ordered to withdraw from the siege of Heidelberg within six days, and a cessation of hostilities was to be proclaimed within two additional days. Should Isabella fail to meet these terms, the negotiations were to be broken off and he himself would return to England at once. To this ultimatum the archduchess could give only the weakest of answers. She declared that she had repeatedly requested Coloma, the Spanish Ambassador in Brussels, to secure additional powers from Madrid, 'whereby the business may be well accommodated.' She also implored Weston not to lose all patience and to postpone his departure until a reply had been received from Philip IV. This time Sir Richard was not to be put off. After explaining why he could not comply with such a request, he stalked angrily out of the room.[37]

On 16 September Sir Richard learned, probably from Sir Francis Nethersole, that Heidelberg had just surrendered to Tilly's army. He then made the final preparations for his departure and arrived in London shortly before the end of the month. On 29 September he was received by the King, and several days later he submitted an account of his embassy to the Council.[38] Although he had accomplished little of value, he was not held responsible for the outcome. On the contrary public opinion was favourably impressed by his conduct of the talks, and he was warmly commended for uncovering the true designs of Philip IV and the Emperor. His actions were applauded in the parliament of 1624;

and because of his repeated denunciations of Spanish 'trickery,' he was hailed as a courageous man who was not afraid to give honest counsel to the King.[39]

Weston's second embassy to the continent prompted rumours that he was about to be named principal Secretary of State. While still in Brussels he was mentioned as a candidate for the post from which Sir Robert Naunton had been suspended several months earlier.[40] Despite his proven diplomatic talents Sir Richard did not secure the office, which would have amounted to a significant promotion for him. In January 1623 the seals of the vacant Secretaryship were entrusted to Sir Edward Conway, his associate on the embassy to Prague, who had been performing the duties of the position since the previous autumn. Conway was a brusque man with little talent for the niceties of diplomacy, and Weston would doubtless have made a more effective Secretary. It is possible in fact that he would have made greater contributions in that capacity than he did as Chancellor of the Exchequer and later as Lord Treasurer. But Conway had extensive military experience, and Buckingham and the King wanted someone of his background to advise them in such matters. There was another reason why Weston was deliberately passed over. A man of greater independence and more important political connections than Conway, he would have been much more difficult for the favourite to control.[41]

3 The Man and His Family

By the time he returned from the continent in September 1622, Sir Richard had passed his forty-fifth birthday. Still in good health and at the height of his powers he was a man of relaxed and polished manners who excelled in the arts of the courtier and had a skilful way of 'removing prejudice and reconciling himself to wavering and doubtful affections.' Lord Clarendon admired his talents and noted how he

> . . . did swim in those troubled and boisterous waters in which . . . Buckingham rode as admiral with a good grace, when very many about him were drowned, or forced on shore with shrewd hurts and bruises: which showed he knew well how and when to use his limbs and strength to the best advantage, sometimes only to avoid sinking, and sometimes to advance and get aground. And by this dexterity he kept his credit with those who could do him good, and lost it not with others who desired the destruction of those upon whom he most depended.[1]

Those 'upon whom he most depended,' and whose destruction was desired by the general public, was never clarified by the noble historian. Perhaps they were Buckingham and his creatures, whose prestige showed a marked decline between 1625 and 1628; but more probably Clarendon had in mind the Roman Catholic friends in whose company Weston was often seen. When in April 1622 he set out on his second embassy to the continent, a shrewd observer noted how he was accompanied by 'Sir Anthony Magnie, a great papist, and more of the [same] stamp.'[2] Sir Richard's sympathy for Catholicism, and his penchant for choosing Catholic friends, was no doubt a result of his second marriage to Frances Waldegrave of Borley, Essex, with whom he had now lived for almost twenty years. Although he himself had been reared in the Anglican faith, his second wife was a staunch Catholic who insisted on keeping her own private chaplain. Only rarely did the second

Lady Weston attend the services of the established church, and in the parliaments of 1624–6 questions were raised as to whether the whole family should be made subject to the recusancy laws. In 1628 Sir Richard's name was included on a list of government officials having 'wives, children, or servants who were recusants or non-communicants.'[3] A perceptive analysis of the religious practices of Sir Richard and his dependents was given by Lord Clarendon, who knew so much about the private lives of Jacobean and Caroline officials.

> His wife and all his daughters were declared of the Roman religion; and though himself and his sons sometimes went to church, he was never thought to have zeal for it; and his domestic conversation and dependents, with whom only he used entire freedom, were all known Catholics, and were believed to be agents for the rest.[4]

When he died in 1635 it was widely believed that he had become a convert to Catholicism. According to one letter-writer, it was 'whispered and believed that he died a Roman Catholic, and had all the ceremonies of that church performed at his death. And none but such [as were Catholics] were present with him when he died.'[5] Like his paternal grandfather the judge, who served under both Mary and Elizabeth, Sir Richard was a man whose conscience was somewhat elastic or, at the very least, adaptable. While he probably preferred Catholicism he was willing to forgo it for the political advantages offered by Anglicanism, although his policy as Treasurer was rarely influenced by religious considerations of any kind. In 1628 he made a public pledge of £400, which he apparently never paid, for the rebuilding of Old St Paul's, which had fallen into a state of advanced decay. He clearly understood the importance of attending the established church and occasionally prevailed upon his wife to go, although she never agreed to take communion by Anglican rites. As Treasurer he made strenuous efforts to win his wife over to occasional conformity. In November 1628 a resident of the capital observed to a friend how 'my Lord Treasurer's lady, that all her life hath been a Papist, doth now come to church.'[6]

While troubled by the possible consequences of his wife's religious views, Sir Richard was obliged to give increasing attention to the well-being of his many offspring. As the father of five sons and six daughters, he had heavy responsibilities, especially during the 1620s, when his children began to come of age. The two daughters by his first wife, Elizabeth Pincheon of Writtle, Essex, who had died in 1603, were raised at home and given the limited educational training the age deemed necessary for girls. Yet he arranged fashionable marriages for both daughters and probably gave them substantial dowries, if the requirement of his father's will that he furnish £800 each to his sisters Winifred and Margaret can be trusted as an indication. Sir Richard's eldest daughter, Elizabeth, was married in 1623 to Viscount Netterville in the peerage of Ireland, a known Roman Catholic.[7] Sir Richard's second daughter, Mary, born in 1602, was married in September 1629 to Walter, son and heir of Lord Aston of Forfar, in the peerage of Scotland. According to the painter Rubens, who was in England at the time, Mary's wedding ceremony was 'conducted by priests, according to Catholic rites.'[8]

By his first wife Sir Richard had only one son, Richard, born in 1600 or 1601, who matriculated as a Fellow Commoner at Trinity College, Cambridge in Easter term 1615. He did not complete the requirements for a degree but continued in the family tradition by enrolling at the Middle Temple, London on 16 May 1617. He was charged an entry fee of £4 and was bound with Andrew Jenour and Benjamin Tichborne, a cousin of the Westons from Hampshire.[9] Sir Richard had high hopes for his eldest son, who seems to have been an intelligent and enterprising young man. Beginning in July 1616 the two Westons were engaged together in collecting the petty customs in the port of London, and five years later they were named joint collectors of the pretermitted customs, also in the port of London. In May 1621 Sir Richard agreed to a generous financial settlement for the benefit of his son, who was granted the manor of Tye Hall, worth almost £325 a year, and various smaller properties in Chelmsford hundred, Essex. In April 1622, when Sir Richard set out on his second embassy to the continent, he was accompanied by his namesake, who fell ill at St Omer and was forced to return home.[10] Because of his chronically poor health the younger Weston took almost no part in public affairs during the remainder of the 1620s. Not until August 1631, when he was appointed one of the five receivers of composition money for knighthood fines in Staffordshire, did he become active on the political scene once again.

Because Richard died childless and unmarried in the spring of 1634, approximately a year before his father, the latter's principal heir was his second son, Jerome, who was born in December 1605 and was the first of eight children born to Sir Richard and his second wife. Like both his father and his half-brother, Jerome attended Trinity College, Cambridge, where he matriculated as a Fellow Commoner in Easter term 1623. He received his degree in the spring of 1626 and then enrolled at the Middle Temple.[11] During the parliament of 1628–9 he sat for Gatton, Surrey, a borough controlled by the Copleys, a Catholic family of Lincolnshire; and in 1630 he and his brother Thomas were sent on a lengthy European tour. After the death of Lord Dorchester in February 1632, his father attempted to secure his appointment as principal Secretary of State; and somewhat later Jerome's nomination as Master of the Court of Wards and Liveries was proposed. Although unsuccessful in these endeavours, the elder Weston did arrange for his son to marry Lady Frances Stuart, a sister of the fourth Duke of Lennox and a distant cousin of the King himself.

By his second wife Sir Richard had three other sons, Thomas, Nicholas, and Benjamin, who were born in 1609, 1611, and 1614 respectively. As younger sons they were not given the same expensive education that Sir Richard provided for his two first born. None was admitted to the Middle Temple, although Thomas was allowed to enrol at Wadham College, Oxford. He matriculated in the spring of 1626 and took his degree three years later.[12]

By his second wife Sir Richard had four daughters, Catherine, Frances, Anne, and Mary. Frances became the wife of Philip Draycote of Paynesley, Staffordshire, while Anne was the first of the four wives of Basil, Earl of Denbigh. Anne had no children and died in Venice on 10 March 1635, a few days before her father. Two of Sir Richard's daughters, Catherine and Mary, were staunch Catholics and died in exile after the outbreak of the Civil War. Catherine fled to the continent in 1642 with her husband, Richard White of Hutton, Essex. She died after residing for several years in Rome and is said to have been buried in the church of Santa Maria Maggiore. Sir Richard's youngest daughter, Mary, to whom he left £4000, took up residence in 1653 at the Augustinian convent of St Monica's in Louvain. Although she never became a nun, she lived in a special apartment that was constructed for her beyond the chapel until her death some years later.

In view of the many children he had to support, it was fortunate for Sir Richard that he enjoyed a sizeable income during the 1620s. From July 1616 he and his eldest son received a yearly fee of £277 6s. 8d. for collecting the petty customs in the port of London; and from July 1621 until the summer of 1624 they drew a joint salary of £100 from their post as collectors of the pretermitted customs. In addition the elder Weston had been awarded a 21-year annuity of £500 out of the receipts of the latter in June 1620. As Chancellor and Under-treasurer of the Exchequer, he had a salary of £287 6s. 8d. a year, plus a small allowance for robes. From these sources alone he received approximately £1000, which does not include the miscellaneous fees and gratuities paid by clients and suitors. These increased his income considerably, and he probably received more than £2000 a year in all.[13] Sir Richard could also expect to receive additional rewards from the crown from time to time. In December 1621 he and Lord Middlesex shared in a seven-year grant of all fines charged on alienations of crown lands, which were normally reserved for the Treasurer and the Chancellor of the Exchequer. In October 1624 the King authorised him to hold a weekly market and two fairs each year on his manor of Neyland in Suffolk.[14]

Considerably greater than these rewards were the revenues he derived from the estate bequeathed to him late in 1603. This estate, which had been skilfully built up by his father and grandfather, consisted of lands scattered across the counties of Bedford, Suffolk, and Essex. In Bedfordshire the chief Weston property was the manor of Rudlonds (or Rudlandesfelde), a tract of 1000 acres or more that had been purchased from Sir William Paulet in 1575.[15] In Suffolk Sir Richard had inherited the large and valuable manor of Neyland, the most important single property owned by the Westons before the accession of Charles I, when Sir Richard began the development of an extensive estate near Roehampton, Surrey. Neyland had an annual value somewhat greater even than that of Skreens, the family estate near Chelmsford, which was worth approximately £600 a year during the first decade of Charles I. When Sir Richard was raised to the peerage in April 1628, he elected to take the title of his barony from Neyland rather than from any of his other lands.[16] Located within a short distance of Neyland were the two Essex manors of Horseley Park and Barwick Hall, which were situated only a few miles north of Colchester, in Lexden hundred. Probably administered as a unit and thus by a single steward, the three adjacent manors of Neyland, Horseley Park, and Barwick Hall had a collective value of at least £1200, and more likely £1400 or £1500, annually.[17]

The bulk of Sir Richard's inheritance was located in the hundreds of central Essex. Here was the family estate of Skreens, which consisted of 400 acres of arable land, 200 acres of pasture, 100 acres of meadows and woods, ten messuages, eight gardens and four cottages. Although the manor house was a simple wooden structure, it had served as the principal family seat since its purchase in 1554. Just to the east of Skreens was the smaller manor of Tye Hall, which nevertheless had its own private park and produced in conjunction with Skreens yearly revenues of almost £925. Acquired by the Westons in 1594, Tye Hall itself was moated and stood several hundred yards from the southern side of the road leading towards Roxwell. Also situated in central Essex were the manor of Netteswell in Harlow hundred and several other manors originally purchased by Richard Weston the judge, such as Markes in Dunmow hundred and Frayes and Long Barnes in Ongar hundred. If the average value of these four properties was as great as that of Tye Hall, which was not one of the Westons' larger manors, they should have produced approximately £1300 a year between them. Rounding off the properties inherited by Sir Richard were the manor of St Lawrence Hall and scores of smaller tracts in various sections of the county. Altogether these lands amounted to a sizeable estate that must have produced revenues of £3500 a year at the very least.[18]

Like most other gentlemen of the age Sir Richard hoped to raise his family to the ranks of the titled aristocracy: Lord Clarendon believed that no man had greater social aspirations or sought to achieve more for his family. To this purpose he engaged in speculative transactions throughout the course of his career, particularly in conjunction with his Hampshire cousins, Sir Walter and Sir Richard Tichborne, but he acquired no additional properties for himself until after the accession of Charles I.[19] Despite his periodic dabblings in the land market Sir Richard found it difficult to increase the wealth of his family. In an age when rents tended to lag behind the general price level, gentlemen who gave little thought to problems of estate management were bound to encounter economic hardship. Weston was no exception to this rule, and there is no reason to believe that he ever took steps to improve his estates or wring higher rents from his tenantry. Indeed the surviving evidence suggests just the opposite: that he was a complacent landlord who was content to accept token payments from those who lived and worked on his lands. On 6 March 1606, for example, he leased at a yearly rental of a single penny a large tract lying between Roxwell and Chelmsford, which included a water mill and 'a parcel of pasture with a tenement.'[20] Thus he cannot be regarded as one of those grasping landlords, described in Chapter VI of Professor Stone's *Crisis of the Aristocracy*, who surmounted their financial difficulties after 1600 by steeply increasing their rents at the cost of alienating their tenantry.

It is clear that Weston did not manage to increase the size of his estate during the first quarter of the seventeenth century. Because of heavy family obligations, including the dowries of £800 each he was required to provide for his two youngest sisters, he was actually forced to sell land. In 1605 he temporarily lost possession of Long Barnes in Ongar hundred, Essex to Philip Courtman and several of his associates. Exactly when he regained possession of this manor is far from clear, but the *Victoria History of Essex* affirms that he did in fact do so and that he sold it sometime after 1623.[21] Perhaps it was the temporary loss of Long Barnes that prompted him to sell his other properties in Ongar hundred. In 1611 he sold the manor of Frayes to Thomas Yonge, and two years later he disposed of the advowson of Beauchamp Roding church, which had been a family perquisite since 1560. In 1617 he parted with Netteswell, a tract of more than 500 acres, which was purchased by Sir William Martin.[22] Despite these land sales, which must have reduced his annual revenues by more than £800, Sir Richard still owned the greater part of the estate inherited from his father at the accession of Charles I. Certainly he had not spent 'the best part of his fortune,' as Lord Clarendon charged.[23]

Unlike the 'mere gentry' of the period, Weston developed a sincere interest in mercantile affairs; and in November 1617 he was admitted a free brother of the East India Company, probably through the influence of Sir Arthur Ingram. In later years he never became especially active in company ventures, although he did on occasion advance moderate amounts. Sometime before 1623 he invested £500 in company stock; and not long before he received the white staff in 1628, he purchased an additional block of shares worth £800. By the standards of the time he made only a small profit on these investments. The second joint-stock, in which he was a participant, produced a net return of 12% on invested capital, whereas the first joint-stock had produced a net return of 87%.[24] Undoubtedly he was disappointed by this, one of his few direct ventures into the world of commerce.

Sir Richard was also briefly concerned with the management of the great farm of the customs, which had been established shortly after James's accession and accounted for almost a third of the royal revenues. The great farm was responsible for the collection of all customs duties on imported products except for those few specially exempted items which were, for the most part, assigned to the petty farms. Until 1621 the great farm was dominated by a syndicate led by William Garway, but it then fell under the control of a rival group organised by Sir Paul Pindar. Sometime in 1620 or 1621 Sir Richard acquired two shares of stock in the great farm, which he retained only until the summer of 1623, when he disposed of them both for £500.[25]

Although an account of Weston's estate and financial interests can be given easily enough, it is more difficult to provide a description of the man himself. He was clearly a cautious person who seldom confided in others, and only a few of his personal papers have survived. While still in his prime he was pleasant and agreeable and made a uniformly favourable impression. Lord Clarendon, who was eventually to become one of his bitterest critics, acknowledged that he was a man of commanding appearance and that he was able 'to please some very much and to displease none.' Although he made scores of enemies as Lord Treasurer, he was commonly regarded to be a 'bold, stout, and magnanimous man' before being entrusted with responsibility for the royal finances.[26] The best surviving likeness of Weston is the full-length portrait of him with the white staff that has been attributed to Van Dyck. This study reveals that he was probably of above-average height and that he became much too heavy as he grew older. As a young man he had participated in such outdoor sports as hunting and hawking,[27] but as he entered middle age the pressures of work took a greater share of his time and precluded regular exercise. Consequently he gained a great deal of weight, although his corpulent body was supported by rather spindly legs. He remained an imposing man, however, with a kindly face that was dominated by a long straight nose, the effect of which was softened by the beard and moustaches that he wore. Although neither shy nor retiring, he was never loud or flamboyant; and the cut of his expensive clothes was inevitably conservative and restrained.

The overriding impression that a study of his career leaves is that he was a man of placid and unruffled disposition. Sure of himself and his place in the world, he had no reason to show the impatient and aggressive behaviour of a Strafford, whose thirst for power was much greater. This does not mean that he was never petulant, for he clearly had a temper. But it generally took a real provocation to arouse his anger, and his normal mood was so genial and contented that it bordered on complacency. Endowed with a sound but altogether conventional intelligence, he retained a lifelong interest in scholarship and learning. Once he became Treasurer he received occasional presents of expensive foreign books from lesser officials who wished to benefit from his favour. Deeply interested in the arts, he entrusted commissions to Van Dyck and the sculptor Le Sueur and had a number of poems dedicated to him by Ben Jonson. One of these, 'An Epigram,' reveals Jonson's clear understanding of his liking for the arts.

If to my mind, great Lord, I had a state,
  I would present you now with curious plate
Of *Noremberg*, or *Turkie*; hang your roomes
  Not with the Arras, but the Persian *loomes*.
I would, if price, or price could them get,
  Send in, what or *Romano*, *Tintaret*,
Titian, or *Raphael*, *Michael Angelo*
  Have left in fame to equall, or out-goe
The old Greek-hands in picture, or in stone.
  This I would doe, could I know *Weston*, one
Catch'd with these Arts, wherein the Judge is wise
  As farre as sense, and onely by the eyes.
But you, I know, my Lord; and know you can
  Discerne between a Statue and a Man;
Can doe the things that Statues doe deserve,
  And act the businesse, which they paint, or carve.
What you have studied are the arts of life;
  To compose men, and manners; stint the strife

Of murmuring Subjects; make the Nations know
What worlds of blessings to good Kings they owe;
And mightiest Monarchs feel what large increase
Of sweets, and safeties, they possesse by Peace.[28]

So refined, apparently, were Weston's tastes that an especially persistent suitor compared him in 1633 to the great Lord Burghley, Queen Elizabeth's chief minister for forty years, and maintained that 'none hath brought to the place [of Treasurer] a judgment so cultivated and illuminated with various erudition as your Lordship.'[29] In short, Sir Richard was a man of 'wisdom and breeding,' which helps to explain why he was able to win the confidence and friendship of both James I and Charles I.

That Weston rose rapidly in the royal favour during the 1620s is also to be explained by his abilities as a parliamentarian. A member of every parliament between 1601 and 1629, he had a thorough knowledge of the procedures employed by the lower House. A smooth and easy debating style ensured that his views would always receive a hearing. A man of conservative but not reactionary temperament, he retained his basically Elizabethan outlook throughout the course of his career and was rarely inclined to speak out against misuses of the prerogative. Indeed he stood loyally by the crown throughout the Buckingham era, despite the chronic mismanagement of those years. Yet his attitude was a moderate and conciliatory one, and this, in conjunction with the respect felt for him, enabled him to play a prominent part in the work of the Commons. His popularity with his fellow members remained undiminished until 1626, when he refused to join in the attack on Buckingham and pressed too persistently for the passage of a subsidy bill. After 1626 his reputation declined rapidly, and three years later he himself was the object of an attack led by Sir John Eliot and his associates. For the greater part of his career, however, he was felt to be a loyal member of the House as well as a staunch and able royalist, and the respect accorded him was notable, if not unique. As Lord Clarendon observed, 'he carried himself so luckily in Parliament that he did his master much service, and preserved himself in the good opinion and acceptation of the House; which is a blessing not indulged to many by those high powers.'[30]

During the course of his career Sir Richard never sat for the same constitutency in successive parliaments. In 1601 he sat for Maldon, Essex, and in 1604–10 he represented Midhurst, Sussex. In 1614 he was returned as knight of the shire for his home county of Essex. In 1621 he sat for Arundel, Sussex, and in the parliaments of 1624–6 he represented three Cornish boroughs: Bossiney, Callington, and Bodmin. In the spring of 1628 he was elevated to the peerage as Baron Weston of Neyland and took a seat in the House of Lords.[31] That he served for so many different constituencies was not at all unusual, since parliamentary elections resembled a game of musical chairs during the first half of the seventeenth century. As Professor Neale has observed, the medieval practice of a man's representing the place where he lived and worked was rapidly dying out.[32] In the Elizabethan and Jacobean periods the gentry were so anxious to be returned that they were willing to stand in constituencies quite distant from their homes. It should be noted, however, that the support of a local patron was almost always necessary for election.

Until his health gave way in 1629 Sir Richard was a pleasant and agreeable man with a wide circle of friends. Affable and considerate, he was on intimate terms not only with Middlesex, who continued as Treasurer until 1624, and the Earl of Arundel, but also with Bishop Williams, Lord Keeper between 1621 and 1625, and Sir Edward Conway, who had bested him in the competition for principal Secretary of State. Especially useful was the friendship with Conway, who was willing to function as an intermediary between Weston and the favourite, between whom relations were often strained.[33] Since Gardiner's day historians have contrived to see Sir Richard as a 'creature' of Buckingham's, but a careful analysis of the record reveals something altogether different.

Weston's periodic difficulties with the favourite stemmed from his determination to maintain a measure of independence from him. Sir Richard's 'daring and boldness' were noted as early as 1621, when Bishop Williams warned against his appointment to the Exchequer.[34] Sir Richard was always ready to speak his own mind, if sometimes only in a circuitous way. But as Williams soon realised to his immense relief, Weston was a practical man who understood the realities of political life. Never disposed to fight losing battles, he knew that no one could advance or even survive without pretending to co-operate with the favourite; and not until 1627 did he propose a course that he knew to be in conflict with the Lord Admiral's objectives.[35] Yet throughout the period he served as Chancellor of the Exchequer, Sir Richard struggled to maintain a certain distance between himself and the favourite in order to keep from being branded as one of his 'creatures.'

During the spring and summer of 1623 the favourite was absent in Spain, where he had gone with 'Baby Charles' to woo the Infanta. While at the Spanish court Buckingham, who was made a duke during his absence, was informed that Weston had spoken ill of him and was, in general, being disloyal. Sir Richard felt compelled to defend himself and, in a letter of 17 July, he requested Buckingham not to 'depart from that [good] opinion you have hitherto conceived of me.'[36] Baby Charles and the duke returned to England in October, but Weston's relationship with the favourite improved more slowly than he hoped. After several weeks he felt obliged to seek Conway's assistance in clearing himself of the allegations of speaking ill of the duke. According to Weston,

> I know I have, in thought, word, and deed, been towards his Grace as I ought to be. It makes therefore no less impression in me, than it doth in his Grace, that any vain calumny should breed any distraction in him towards me, but I fear it not, for I rely no less upon his wisdom and goodness, than my own innocency, which I long to justify. Hitherto, in respect of his Grace's weighty affairs, I have foreborne to importune him with those particulars, but if . . . you [will] please to let me know when his Grace will give me leave to attend him, you shall add to the many favours I receive from you.[37]

Eventually Sir Richard recovered a measure of the duke's confidence, but only a small measure. When Middlesex was impeached in May 1624, he was the obvious choice to succeed him at the Treasury, but he was deliberately passed over, and the office was conferred on the aged Chief Justice of the King's Bench, Sir James Ley. Ley was married to one of Buckingham's nieces but was otherwise totally unqualified for the position. Sir Richard did not become Treasurer until July 1628, and even after his appointment the favourite continued to be wary of him. Had the duke not been assassinated within six weeks, 'he would have removed him and made another treasurer.'[38]

In view of this it is obviously erroneous to characterise him as one of the favourite's 'creatures.' Yet because of the duke's unquestioned supremacy until the last year of his life, Sir Richard was not prepared to antagonize him. Unwilling to pay the high price political opposition would entail and adamantly against trafficking with the King's enemies in parliament, he refused to speak out against the favourite even in 1626, when the House of Commons was bent on his impeachment. Had Weston and other officials shown more courage against a minister whose ruinous foreign policy was threatening to bankrupt the monarchy, they might have forced the King to part with him before it was too late. But because they knew their master would fight relentlessly to avoid sacrificing the duke, Sir Richard and his associates held back and failed to provide the evidence that alone might have ensured his overthrow.

Largely because of his sins of omission in 1626 Weston has traditionally been pictured as a 'timeserving courtier' and a creature of the duke's. Too deferential to those in power (and too intent on being deferred to once he became Lord Treasurer), he did in fact shrink from making a decision necessary for the stability of the regime that he himself favoured. Yet it should also be remembered that aside from Middlesex, Williams, and the Earl of Bristol, all of whom crossed swords with the duke and had their careers ruined for their pains, Weston followed a more independent course than any other official of the time. Certainly he was less subservient than Conway, Sir John Coke, and Sir Robert Pye, Auditor of the Receipt, who owed their positions directly to Buckingham's support and followed his instructions in all things. Thus Weston's independence of the duke was far greater than is generally realised. It would have been greater still had the King not insisted on unquestioning acceptance of his constitutional right to employ in office any man of his own choosing, regardless of how incapable or unsuited.

4 Chancellor of the Exchequer

Weston's contemporaries were in accord that he made an able and conscientious Chancellor of the Exchequer. Lord Clarendon maintained that he 'behaved himself well in this function and appeared equal to it'; and David Lloyd asserted that he was careful 'to perform all duties with obedience to his Majesty, respect to the Duke [of Buckingham], and justice to the particular parties concerned.'[1] Because popular opinion believed he was rendering honest service to the King, he was held in higher esteem than the average civil servant of the early Stuart period, many of whom were felt to be grasping and inefficient.

As Chancellor and Under-treasurer of the Exchequer, Weston occupied a post described by Lord Clarendon as 'an excellent stage for men of parts to tread . . . upon, and where they have occasion of all natures to lay out and spread all their faculties and qualifications most for their advantage.'[2] It was also a place of trust requiring long hours of tedious work. While serving in the post Sir Richard established himself as one of the chief workhorses of the central government, the most important associate of Lord Treasurer Middlesex, from whom he received valuable instruction in methods of revenue management. In his fine study of Middlesex's career, Professor Tawney praised 'the dogged labours of men like Weston' and acknowledged his manifold contributions in the period before he 'ran to seed.'[3]

During the years before the Civil War the Treasury had not yet emerged as one of the chief administrative departments, since its staff consisted of only a few clerks and secretaries who waited directly on the Lord Treasurer. It was not until midway in the reign of Charles II that the Treasury asserted its independence of both the Exchequer and the Privy Council, developed a large organisation with records of its own, and 'assumed something very like its later shape.'[4] The Exchequer was thus a more important institution during the 1620s and 1630s. It was beginning to atrophy, however, and its decay was hastened by the continuous disturbances of the 1640s and 1650s, from which it never recovered. During the period following the Stuart restoration, the Treasury emerged as an offshoot of the Exchequer, which has led a recent historian to describe the Exchequer as 'the Treasury's parent institution.' The leading authority on the subject has observed that 'to a very considerable degree, the growth of the Treasury came as a response to Exchequer decay.'[5]

During the first half of the seventeenth century the English financial system, of which the Exchequer was the undisputed capstone, was a rather inflexible and unwieldy system, one that could still function with a measure of efficiency when directed by honest officials but was likely to come to a halt whenever it lacked proper supervision. Theoretically the Exchequer supervised the collection and disbursal of all the royal revenues (except those handled by the Court of Wards and the Duchy of Lancaster) and audited the accounts of such major spending departments as the Wardrobe, the Chamber, and the Navy. In practice, however, the organisation and routine operations of the Exchequer, which consisted of an upper and a lower division and employed approximately 130 men, were so complicated that its officials had little time for the supervisory role that had been entrusted to them. Furthermore not all the royal revenues passed through the Exchequer, which made any efforts to supervise the main spending departments considerably more difficult, if not altogether impossible. As the seventeenth century wore on, an increasingly large percentage of the King's income by-passed the lower Exchequer, or Exchequer of Receipt, and went directly to individual royal creditors or to such administrative agencies as the Navy, the Chamber, and the Wardrobe.[6] This opened the door to a variety of abuses and particularly to the rapid growth of fraud and embezzlement. Many officials remained in possession of funds collected by them for six months or longer before releasing them to the assigned departments. During the interval between collection and release, such officials were in a position to use the unpaid cash balances for their own speculative purposes, often to the detriment of the crown.[7] Even worse, since payment was not made directly to the Exchequer, the possibility of conspiracies to defraud the King became appreciably greater.

The Exchequer's decreasing control over the financial system was compounded by the system of defalcations, which became more prevalent during the 1620s and 1630s. In essence, defalcations were little more than deductions made by revenue-collecting officials for local administrative expenses and other bureaucratic charges; as an important safeguard, however, it was an established rule that only standing charges could be 'defalked'. Moreover such outpayments had theoretically to be approved by the Lord Treasurer or the Chancellor of the Exchequer, or both, but they were sometimes made without the officials of the lower Exchequer having any notification of them. This provoked bitter complaints from the Auditor of the Receipt and the Clerk of the Pells, who insisted on being apprised of all transactions and would have preferred to see the King's entire revenue passing through their department.[8]

As an important member of the central government, the Chancellor of the Exchequer was invariably a member of the Privy Council, and it was commonly assumed that he would have a seat in the House of Commons whenever that body assembled. Just as the Lord Treasurer explained the King's financial policies in the upper House, so the Chancellor was trusted to outline royal policy in the Commons. Thus the dual post of Chancellor and Under-treasurer could hardly be entrusted to a peer, although Sir Richard held it briefly as Baron Weston of Neyland between April 1628 and the following July, when he became Lord Treasurer. During his seven years as Chancellor, Sir Richard helped to advance the prestige of his office relative to the King's other servants and officials. Certainly the position was of less importance in the 1620s than it is today, but it was more significant by the time Sir Francis Cottington received it in 1629 than it had been at the accession of James I.

The routine duties of the Chancellor and Under-treasurer were not precisely defined during the early seventeenth century. The extent of his responsibilities depended on his relationship with the Lord Treasurer and his willingness to devote long hours to bureaucratic routine. Among the tasks that he was normally expected to discharge were: (1) to approve the bills of the Usher of the Receipt; (2) to vouch for the fee claims of the officials of the Tally Court, a subdivision of the lower Exchequer; (3) to handle a portion of the work connected with the declaration of accounts by the two imprest auditors; (4) to sign warrants authorising outpayments from the lower Exchequer; (5) to help with the apportionment of funds for the yearly assignments to the Chamber, the Navy, and the other spending departments; (6) to counter-sign all leases of crown lands prepared by the Lord Treasurer and the Clerk of the Pipe; (7) to apply the Exchequer seal to all leases of crown lands of less than 40s. a year; (8) to witness the swearing-in of certain officials appointed by the Lord Treasurer; and (9) to handle any other matters of too little consequence 'for his Lordship to be troubled with' but which still required the attention of an officer of 'trust and discretion.'[9]

Among the most important perquisites enjoyed by the Chancellor was the right to appoint to certain positions in the upper Exchequer. Perhaps the most important office at his disposal was that of the Controller of the Pipe, an official whose main duty was to keep the copy of the Pipe and Treasurer's Rolls, now known as the Chancellor's Roll. Another functionary appointed by the Chancellor was the Clerk of the Nichills, who made a note of whatever revenues the sheriffs maintained they had been unable to collect. Other officers named by him included the Clerk of the Pleas, who served as prothonotary of the Court of Exchequer, and the Sealer and two appraisers of the same court.[10]

While Middlesex and Weston held office as Treasurer and Chancellor respectively, their relationship was a close and cordial one. Although Middlesex was a demanding superior who kept the reins of power tightly in his own hands, he was one of the outstanding officials of the early Stuart period, and his relations with Sir Richard were both pleasant and productive. This was largely owing to the personality of the latter, 'whose career was never ruined by the arrogance which brought down his chief and whose genial temper made him happy even to work with Middlesex.'[11] Much less can be said, however, of Weston's relationship with Middlesex's immediate successor, the Earl of Marlborough. Weston was resentful of Marlborough's appointment, which was arranged by Buckingham as a way of keeping him out of the office. Furthermore Weston was required to supervise all matters pertaining to the crown lands and to discharge many other routine duties for Marlborough, who was both an elderly man and totally inexperienced in details of Exchequer practice.

During the 1620s and 1630s the relationship between the Treasurer and the Chancellor was still rather loose and ill defined, and a great deal depended on the abilities and aspirations of the men involved. If the Treasurer was weak and the Chancellor strong, the latter would be in a position to exercise great influence. Such was actually the case between 1614 and 1618, when Suffolk often deferred to his Chancellor, Sir Fulke Greville, and again between 1624 and 1628, when Sir Richard's views carried considerably more weight than those of his incompetent chief. The reverse was naturally true when the Treasurer was a strong and capable individual. While Middlesex held the white staff between 1621 and 1624, Sir Richard exercised almost no initiative of his own. Similarly, Cottington enjoyed little independent power during Weston's term as Treasurer.

It was assumed, however, that the Treasurer and the Chancellor should be able to discharge one another's duties with little effort or notice. In April 1622, when Weston was appointed to conduct the peace talks at Brussels, Middlesex was made responsible for his routine duties at the Exchequer; and when Middlesex was impeached and confined in the Tower in May 1624, Sir Richard was directed to conduct the duties of his office until a new Treasurer could be appointed.[12] This flexible relationship continued throughout the remainder of the period preceding the Civil War. When Cottington was sent on a diplomatic mission to Spain in November 1629, Sir Richard was instructed to cover for him at the Exchequer; and when Weston accompanied the King on a progress to Scotland in May 1633, Cottington took over his duties as Treasurer.[13] By most observers, therefore, the Chancellor was regarded as the Treasurer's main assistant, although not necessarily as his heir-apparent. Of the seven Treasurers appointed during the first three decades of the seventeenth century, Sir Richard was the only one with prior experience as Chancellor.

During the early Stuart period the Chancellor was expected to attend occasional sessions of the Court of Exchequer Chamber, a tribunal that had acquired an equity jurisdiction during Elizabeth's reign and heard frequent appeals from the common-law Court of Exchequer. Whenever he was in attendance the Chancellor was required to support all courses that were 'to the King's most benefit and furtherance.' Weston was definitely present at a session of the court on 7 February 1622, when cases involving Sir George Goring and Theophilus, Lord Howard of Waldon, were heard. Also in attendance at that time were Middlesex, the Chief Baron, and three of the junior Barons of the Exchequer.[14] Unfortunately the records of the court, which were kept by the King's Remembrancer, do not reveal the personnel for every sitting, and it is impossible to determine just how many times Sir Richard was present during his term as Chancellor. Yet he clearly made an effort to be there whenever Middlesex was detained by business elsewhere.

Although his work as Chancellor took a healthy portion of his time, Sir Richard was not confined to Exchequer routine alone during the years 1621–4. At this juncture he was an active member of the Privy Council and belonged to a number of its committees and commissions. He was also included among an unofficial inner circle of administrators that consisted of Middlesex, the two principal Secretaries of State, Sir George Calvert and Sir Edward Conway, and the most experienced naval administrator of the period, Sir John Coke, who succeeded to Calvert's office shortly after the accession of Charles I. Sir Richard and these four men worked closely together and were largely responsible for superintending routine operations of government during the years 1621–4.

As the Treasurer's chief assistant it was natural that Sir Richard would play a prominent role in regard to commercial affairs. Even before becoming Chancellor he was directed in October 1621 to consider a petition of the Muscovy Company for a measure of governmental support, which the company felt obliged to request because of heavy trade losses incurred during the past few years. Shortly afterwards he helped with a survey of conditions in the outports that was undertaken because of declining foreign trade. Early in 1622 he and three others were instructed to consider the affairs of the Eastland Company, and in March 1623 he was named to a special committee to investigate all 'piraces, robberies, spoils, misdemeanors, and offences' committed on English soil or in English coastal waters since January 1619. From time to time he was involved with questions relating to the manufacture of soap, starch, glass, alum, and gold and silver thread.[15] During these years he continued to help with the regulation of naval affairs, although this was almost exclusively in a financial sense. Weston and his chief relied mainly on the customs duties as the principal source of revenue for the navy. At their command the naval Treasurer was to receive monthly payments of £1400 from the farmers of the great customs and the collectors of the impositions on imported silks. In 1623 the naval establishment also received a direct cash payment of £1200 from the proceeds of the tobacco duties.[16]

From time to time Sir Richard was called upon to give political advice to the King. During 1623–4 he was an active member of the Committee for Foreign Affairs, the most important standing committee of the Privy Council, which advised James on diplomatic matters. In so far as the crown was concerned, the main development of this period was the journey of Buckingham and Prince Charles to Madrid in 1623. This extraordinary affair, which lasted from March until October and imposed a crushing burden on the royal finances, was undertaken in order to win a Spanish bride for the heir to the throne. If only an Anglo-Spanish marriage could be arranged, Philip IV might agree to join a coalition for the restoration of the Palatinate. Should such a marriage occur, moreover, the dowry provided by the Spanish government would help to erase the debts of the English crown, which were now in the neighbourhood of £1,000,000. Unhappily these were vain hopes that were almost bound to be disappointed. Philip IV had no desire to see the Elector Palatine restored to his ancestral lands, nor was he anxious to see his sister, the Infanta Maria, become the wife of the heretic Prince of Wales. Only if Charles made a public announcement of his conversion to Catholicism would the Spanish King allow the marriage to take place, and even then he was unwilling to make any provision for the restoration of the Palatinate.[17]

Although only indirectly concerned with the embassy to Madrid, Sir Richard played a prominent role in the parallel negotiations held in England. Throughout the spring and summer of 1623 confidential talks took place between the English government and representatives of Philip IV and the Archduchess Isabella. These conversations, like those in Madrid, were intended to pave the way for a formal treaty between the two countries, which should include provisions for a marriage alliance and for future co-operation towards the restoration of the Palatinate. While most historians of the period concentrate on the *opéra-bouffe* journey of Buckingham and Prince Charles, the simultaneous negotiations in England were of equal importance, and certainly of greater dignity and substance.

Sir Richard took an active part in the London negotiations from the outset. The two Spanish Ambassadors received their instructions on 2 February, and within two weeks he was meeting with Isabella's representative, Ferdinand Boischot, with whom he had previously treated in Brussels. On 14 February Conway informed his fellow Secretary of State, Sir George Calvert, that Boischot's expenses were to be paid from London to Newmarket, where he was to confer with Weston and the Secretary and to present 'such papers as may concern the negotiation.'[18] Two weeks later Sir Richard was one of nine men commissioned to hold conversations not only with Boischot but also with Don Carlos Coloma, whom Weston had also known in Brussels. Associated with the Chancellor in this task were Middlesex, Calvert, Arundel, and the Marquess of Hamilton, or many of the same men believed by John Chamberlain to belong to the 'junta for foreign affairs.'[19] While involved in the negotiations with the two ambassadors, Sir Richard was issued large sums of money for purposes of secret service, which suggests that he was probably used by the King to channel bribes to Boischot and Coloma. As early as 28 January 1623 a royal warrant directed that £500 should be released to him by the officials of the Exchequer; and on 10 April the Auditor of the Receipt was instructed to pay him £4000 out of the receipts of the pretermitted customs. All but £200 of that amount was issued on 22 April, with the remainder being released to him some six weeks later.[20]

Throughout the early summer of 1623, English governmental circles were confident that a marriage agreement with Spain was about to be concluded. This optimism culminated on 20 July, when a treaty was signed in a public ceremony at Whitehall attended by Sir Richard, the other Lords of the Council, and the two Spanish Ambassadors. The marriage treaty stipulated that the Infanta would be permitted the free exercise of her religion once she took up residence in England and that she would be allowed the services of an archbishop-confessor and 24 priests. Of more practical importance, she would have the sole responsibility for the early training, religious and educational, of any children born of the marriage.[21] Once the terms of the treaty were announced, most of James's subjects, who had had a bitter hatred of Spain for more than forty years, were forced to conclude that the marriage would in fact take place. James himself was so confident that it would occur that he supposedly declared, ' "Now all the devils in Hell cannot hinder it." ' Furthermore he agreed to suspend the recusancy laws so there would be no Catholic petitions on the Infanta's arrival in England.[22]

The Spanish government had no intention of adhering to the marriage treaty and soon found ways to avoid doing so. When the death of Pope Gregory XV, who had granted a dispensation for the marriage, became known, Olivares stipulated that the Infanta could not leave her native land until a new dispensation had been received from Gregory's successor. Shortly afterwards Philip IV made the unreasonable suggestion that Charles remain in Spain until December, so the marriage could take place there rather than in England. Furthermore the Spanish authorities were now insisting that the Infanta continue in Madrid until delivered of a son, who would be reared at the Spanish court. To Buckingham these demands were both preposterous and dishonourable. He felt that the Spanish government was trifling with England and plainly told Olivares so. A bitter quarrel ensued between the two men, and Buckingham became *persona non grata* in Madrid. When events took such a sharp turn, the duke was able to convince 'Baby Charles' that nothing was to be gained by remaining any longer in Spain. The Prince signed a proxy for his marriage, and the two visitors and their numerous attendants set out on the homeward trip. Off the Spanish coast they were taken aboard a fleet commanded by Buckingham's father-in-law, the Earl of Rutland, and early in October they landed at Portsmouth, after an absence of almost seven months.[23]

There was great rejoicing throughout England when the Prince's safe return became known. The English people were delighted that their future King was back among his own people and had not been accompanied home by a Spanish wife. Church bells rangs out and bonfires were lit in all parts of the country in celebration.[24] During the autumn of 1623 Buckingham's popularity increased dramatically as reports of his quarrel with Olivares began to spread and he was credited with the 'satisfactory outcome' of the mission to Spain. For Buckingham the sudden development of a mass following was a heady experience. For the first time in his life he became acutely conscious of the growing force of public opinion and openly espoused the anti-Spanish sentiments of the English people. He put himself at the head of the war party and began to insist on a reversal of England's foreign policy. The journey to Madrid had given him first-hand knowledge of the declining power of Spain,[25] and the quarrel with Olivares had left him bitter and resentful. Enraged by his first real setback in public life, he began to cherish a desire for revenge, identifying England's national interests with his own reputation and personal feelings.

With firm support from Prince Charles, the duke was able to convince James to send new instructions to the Earl of Bristol, who was forbidden to surrender the proxy for Charles's marriage and directed to insist on the restoration of the Palatinate and the restitution of the electoral title to Frederick V as integral conditions of any marriage treaty with England.[26] But James was as yet unwilling to make a complete break with Philip IV. He had always favoured a policy of friendship with Spain, and for ten years his heart had been set on a marriage alliance, partly as a way of securing funds for the repayment of his own debts. In addition the King was somewhat less enchanted with Buckingham as a result of the journey to Madrid. Deeply concerned about the Prince's safety, he had objected to the plan for his heir to go in person to Spain. According to Clarendon, James held the duke responsible for the mission and never completely forgave him.[27]

With the duke's influence somewhat weakened, resistance to his views began to crop up in the Council. A number of the Councillors sided with the King and opposed any attempt to cancel the existing treaties with Spain. The official most emboldened at this stage was Lord Keeper Williams, who argued strongly against the duke's new policy and even attacked his personal chaplain, William Laud, Bishop of St David's.[28] It was the Lord Treasurer, however, who was the most persuasive critic of Buckingham's latest proposals. Middlesex was neither a pacifist nor an isolationist, but he argued convincingly that the crown lacked the resources to sever all its ties with Spain and enter directly into the war. Besides, the extent of the King's debts made it imperative that a marriage treaty with Spain be concluded.[29] Middlesex's position was supported by Weston, who had an equal grasp of the financial situation, and by Secretary Calvert and the Earl of Arundel. Of the remaining members of the Foreign Committee, four refused to commit themselves: the Duke of Lennox, the Marquess of Hamilton, the Earl of Pembroke, and Viscount Chichester. Only the Earl of Carlisle and Secretary Conway, the duke's closest associates, were willing to give active support to the new policy.[30]

During January 1624 the Foreign Committee met frequently and considered the alternatives of war and peace. With continued support from Prince Charles, the duke eventually triumphed and won the votes of the four uncommitted members. He also exacted a pledge of approval from the King, who was too old and emotionally dependent to risk losing the goodwill of 'Baby Charles and Steenie.' When it became clear how the sands were shifting, Sir Richard and Secretary Calvert fell into line and expressed grudging support of the duke's policy. Only Middlesex, Bishop Williams, and the Earl of Arundel had the courage to continue their opposition to the duke.[31]

Late in January James agreed in principle to terminate the negotiations with Spain, although it was still some months before he would take any action hostile to Philip IV. While preparing the country for a possible declaration of war, he naturally sought to arrange for meaningful co-operation with France and the United Provinces. Lord Kensington was sent on a special embassy to Paris, and a warm reception was provided the two new ambassadors from the States-General. More important than these initiatives was James's decision to hold another parliament. Despite misgivings about summoning the Lords and Commons at this juncture, he bowed to the views of Buckingham and the Prince and agreed on 3 January to send writs to the sheriffs. Except for a half-hearted attempt to exclude Sir Edward Coke and Sir Edwin Sandys, the King did little to influence the elections held two weeks later, and candidates who accurately reflected the will of the political nation were returned. John Chamberlain was impressed by the outcome of the elections and the way in which they were conducted. On 31 January he wrote to his friend Carleton: 'If I could expect good of parliament, I should hope well of this [one] because they are more careful than usually they have been in their choice of knights and burgesses, and have not that regard of great ones' letters and recommendations that they were wont [to have].'[32]

On 17 January Sir Richard was returned for Bossiney, one of the twenty-one Cornish boroughs that generally returned members in the crown's interest. Although he was unknown to the local voters, he had the assistance of William Roscarrock, escheator of the Duchy of Cornwall. Early in January Roscarrock received letters from the council of Prince Charles, who, as Duke of Cornwall, had extensive estates across the county and desired to see the return of thirteen candidates in as many different boroughs. Of the thirteen men nominated by the Prince and his advisers, only six were elected in addition to Sir Richard.[33] In the elections of 1624 a larger-than-average group of Councillors secured seats in the House of Commons. Besides Weston, the royal contingent consisted of the two principal Secretaries, Calvert and Conway, the Treasurer and the Comptroller of the royal household, Sir Thomas Edmondes and Sir John Suckling, and the former Secretary of State, Sir Robert Naunton, who was soon to become Master of the Wards.

Parliament opened on 16 February and remained in session until prorogued by the King on 29 May. Feeling was friendly on both sides, largely because James made a conciliatory speech from the throne and then refrained from interfering with the proceedings at Westminster. On their part, a majority of the members were determined to avoid another abortive session like the ones of 1610, 1614, and 1621. Compared to the other parliaments of the period, the one of 1624 was 'quite restrained.'[34] Because James was providing virtually no leadership, control of the proceedings was easily wrested from him by Buckingham and Prince Charles. Hoping to secure a declaration of war against Spain, the duke decided to take the members into his confidence by explaining the course of Anglo-Spanish relations during the past few years. When delegations from the two Houses assembled in the Great Hall at Whitehall on 24 February, he began his narration from the time Sir Richard departed for Brussels to conduct the talks for a preliminary suspension of arms. According to the duke, it was because of Weston's mission that the King became suspicious 'that there were no realities in the Treaties on that side.'[35] He then gave a long account of the journey to Madrid and maintained that the Spanish government had never intended to abide by a marriage treaty or to co-operate with England's efforts on behalf of Frederick V. He revealed that Philip IV had recently announced that the restitution of the Palatinate could not be regarded as an integral condition of a marriage treaty, as James was now insisting. Worse, the Spanish government had manufactured reasons to reduce the size of the Infanta's dowry, which could only be interpreted as an affront to the national honour of England.[36]

In his account of the embassy to Madrid, the duke minimised his own role and blamed his Spanish counterparts for the failure to reach an agreement. Indeed he described Olivares and the Council of State so scathingly that the two Spanish Ambassadors in London, Coloma and Inojosa, felt compelled to lodge a protest with James I. When word of this protest began to spread, the Lords leapt to Buckingham's defence by 'commending and thanking him for his industry, faith, and care in that negotiation,' which was equivalent to a vote of confidence.[37]

To report the duke's speech to his colleagues in the lower House, Sir Richard was selected. He was a capable speaker and respected member, and his own view of Spanish diplomacy had already been cited. Yet Weston must have had misgivings about performing the task now assigned him. As Chancellor he knew that the crown could not afford foreign war and had objected to the duke's proposals in January, when he had supported Middlesex's plea for continued co-operation with Spain. Since that time he had reversed himself and fallen in line behind Buckingham and his adherents, since he was not prepared to pay the high price political opposition would entail. Nevertheless he must have had reservations about advocating a course he knew to be dangerous and ill advised. Because foreign-policy matters were generally explained by one of the principal Secretaries, it was painfully apparent to his audience in the Commons that he had submitted to the will of the duke, who thus had recovered his control of an important but wavering subordinate.

There was a substantial consolation, however, that must have occurred to Sir Richard. Because of the known prejudices of the English people, a speech in support of Buckingham's policy would receive great public acclaim, and he craved popular esteem as much as any man. Just as he doubtless calculated, the reaction to his speech was an extremely favourable one. Early in March the English Ambassador at The Hague was informed by his nephew in London that 'Sir Richard Weston hath won much love and reputation by his carriage this Parliament, explaining the abuses of the Spanish party during his employment at Brussels.'[38]

Weston gave not only an account of his stay in the Spanish Netherlands but also a relation of the most important developments since that time, as recounted to him by the duke. He revealed that during the autumn of 1622 the Spanish government had promised to join with England in a war against the Emperor, should there be no other way of securing the restoration of the Palatinate. Yet when Charles and Buckingham arrived in Madrid and the Spanish government was asked to honour its pledges, Olivares declared it was monstrous even to suggest that his master should take up arms against his kinsmen, the Austrian Habsburgs. Weston also related how unceasing pressure had been exerted on Prince Charles to announce his conversion to Catholicism.[39] Once Sir Richard finished his narration, Sir Francis Cottington, the Prince's private secretary, gave his first-hand impressions of what had transpired in Madrid. Cottington criticised the actions not only of Olivares but of the Earl of Bristol, who had remained a firm partisan of the marriage alliance. After Weston and Cottington had both resumed their places in the House, the members were asked to decide whether the crown should be asked to terminate its negotiations with Spain.

The members were delighted by the invitation to speak out on foreign policy, which was so different from the treatment accorded them in the previous parliament. Sir Benjamin Rudyerd, an officer of the Court of Wards and a dependent of the Earl of Pembroke, set the tone of the discussion that followed by insisting that all treaties with Spain be broken off immediately. The Commons should realise that war with Spain was likely to follow and should be ready to vote sufficient funds 'to assure ourselves at home, to secure Ireland, to have ships abroad . . . and to assist the oppressed estate of our old allies in the Low Countries.' Such steps would serve to re-establish England's prestige in international affairs, which had fallen to such low levels in recent years.[40] After a succession of speakers had expressed their support of Rudyerd's views, the members voted in favour of breaking off the treaties. They also agreed to appoint a twelve-man committee 'to set down and collect their reasons' after consulting with a similar committee from the Lords. Sir Richard was named to help with this important duty as were such leading members as Sir Edwin Sandys, Sir Edward Coke, Sir Robert Cotton, and Secretary Calvert.[41]

Meanwhile the Lords and Commons had decided to send a joint petition to the King at Theobalds, advising him to sever all connections with Spain. At the Prince's suggestion, a special messenger was dispatched on 4 March to learn when James would be willing to receive the petition.[42]

Although parliament had made its wishes perfectly clear, the King was still reluctant to act. He was naturally hesitant to adopt a course that would lead to war until a subsidy bill had been passed and he knew how much money would be forthcoming. To forestall any misunderstanding of his financial position, he instructed Middlesex and Weston to address their respective Houses on 11 March. They should explain the main heads of expenditure since 1619 and show how the crown's debts had risen by more than £300,000, even though hostilities had not been declared. For the support of the Elector Palatine, Weston declared in his speech to the Commons, more than £325,000 had been issued, while the Prince's journey to Madrid had cost nearly £220,000. Mansell's campaign of 1621 against the pirates of Algiers had involved an outlay of almost £65,000, and within a few months £85,000 plus interest would be due to Christian IV of Denmark, whose campaigns in Germany the government had promised to subsidise. In his remarks to the lower House, the Chancellor also gave an analysis of the sums spent on naval and diplomatic affairs and for the maintenance of Ireland's defences during the past five years. At the conclusion of his address, several members expressed their unbounded joy at the prospect of a war against Spain.[43]

Still under the sway of his Treasurer, the King insisted on a grant of at least six subsidies and twelve fifteenths in order to prepare the country's naval and military forces for war. Middlesex was as strongly opposed to intervention in the conflict as ever and had persuaded James that parliament must be made to assume a fair share of the burden should hostilities be undertaken.[44] The Commons were amazed by the extent of the King's demands. He was requesting an unprecedented grant of taxation, and only a few members were willing to concede it.

The principal debate on supply took place on 19 March. Sir Benjamin Rudyerd called for the requested subsidies and fifteenths to be voted immediately but proposed that their collection be staggered over a period of several years, in order to afford some relief to the taxpayer. Rudyerd's suggestion was attacked by Sir Thomas Edmondes, Treasurer of the Household and a firm partisan of the duke. Edmondes maintained that the amount requested was so large it deterred the House and should be reduced by half. Only three subsidies and six fifteenths should be voted at present, although it must be understood that additional funds would be appropriated as circumstances required.[45]

Sir Richard was unable to concur with Edmondes's view and, in an important speech, urged that the full amount be granted. He acknowledged that the demand for six subsidies was indeed 'fearful' but declared that 'the greatness and goodness of the cause, the King's honour, and our safety require it.' Because an unprecedented sum was being requested, he suggested that conditions be attached to the grant. The entire sum should be voted in principle, but only a portion of it would actually be collected and made available for immediate needs. The remainder would be demanded of the taxpayer only as the situation required, and whatever was left to be collected would be cancelled upon the conclusion of a peace treaty. Sir Richard was so anxious for the whole sum to be voted in principle that he made two proposals having important constitutional implications, since they could only have enhanced the authority of parliament. First, he suggested that any funds granted be spent only with the concurrence of a committee appointed by and answerable to the lower House; and second, he called for the members to be consulted about the nature of the settlement to end the war.[46]

Despite the substantial concessions now being offered by the government, the Commons were reluctant to make such a sizeable grant. Several influential members, including John Pym and Sir Edward Coke, expressed misgivings and swayed the majority to their side. After heated debate over an extended period, the House voted in favour of a grant of three subsidies, three tenths, and three fifteenths, which should be collected from the taxpayer no later than May 1625. It was understood, however, that the King would be free to request additional funds whenever necessary and the members would be expected to comply. With Weston's suggestions of 19 March in mind, the Commons decided to attach specific conditions to the subsidy bill. All funds collected as a result of the grant were to be paid over to eight parliamentary treasurers and expended only on projects approved by the members. Furthermore the Commons made their grant only after receiving an assurance that another parliamentary session would be held in the autumn of 1624, when the two Houses would hear reports about the progress of the war and would be given an accounting of how the funds voted were being spent.[47] That James failed to honour his promise in this regard did incalculable damage to the cause of royal government. Bitterly disappointed, the members concluded it was dangerous to trust the King's word and appropriate funds on the basis of vague, unenforceable pledges. This hardening of attitude on the Commons' part was to cause a host of problems, psychological as well as practical, for James's son and successor.

Several days after the House decided on the terms of its grant, a delegation was sent to inform the King and secure a definite promise that the negotiations with Spain would be terminated. After listening to the Commons' message, James replied that a herald would shortly be sent to Spain to announce the cancellation of the treaties and that the English crown now considered itself free to adopt any course of its own choosing for the restoration of the Palatinate.[48] There was spontaneous rejoicing throughout the country when news of the King's decision began to spread. Just as when Prince Charles returned from Madrid, church bells rang out and bonfires were lit in celebration. The Spanish Ambassadors in London were so alarmed that they vainly sought to topple Buckingham from power.[49]

While resigning himself to the rapid drift towards war, James was taking steps to arrange for closer co-operation between England and the Protestant states of Europe. In mid-April he welcomed Count Mansfeld, the German mercenary, to London. He also revived the negotiations underway with the Dutch Ambassadors, which had lain dormant for several weeks. These talks led to the signing of a military alliance between England and the States-General on 5 June 1624, which prompted the departure of the Spanish envoys from London only two weeks later.[50]

Of the comparatively few Englishmen distressed by these events, Middlesex was far and away the most concerned. He knew that, even with parliamentary support, the crown was in no position to play an active role in the continental war and repeatedly warned James about the poor state of the finances. Yet the King was too weak to resist the entreaties of his son and his favourite, to whom increasingly more officials were reporting for their instructions. Everything was now being handled by the duke, whose adherents included even Weston and, to a lesser degree, Bishop Williams. Because of his isolation at the highest level of government, the Treasurer was so alarmed that he decided on a bold course which, should it fail, was likely to end his political career. The only way to avoid a rupture with Spain was to overthrow the duke and establish a new favourite in his place. Middlesex therefore began taking steps to stress the merits of his handsome young brother-in-law, Arthur Brett, whose sister Anne he had married in 1621 at the duke's suggestion.[51]

Arthur Brett had previously enjoyed considerable favour with the King and, while serving as a groom of the bedchamber in 1622, had received substantial financial rewards. On 8 February 1622 he was granted a lifetime annuity of £350 out of the Receipt, and on the 22nd of July following he was awarded a free gift of £300.[52] Although these grants were only a fraction of those being heaped on Buckingham, the latter was suspicious of Brett; and shortly before the favourite's departure for Madrid in 1623, he arranged for him to be sent on a minor diplomatic mission to Paris. During the following autumn Brett applied for permission to return to England, but the duke ordered him to remain indefinitely abroad. Once Buckingham's domination of the parliament of 1624 became apparent, Middlesex directed his brother-in-law to return, his arrival occurring about the end of Lent. Brett's subsequent reappearance at court was naturally viewed as a deliberate challenge to the duke.[53]

Unhappily for the Treasurer's cause, James refused to be a party to these intrigues. Taken aback by Brett's sudden reappearance, he insisted that he return again to France. Brett replied, however, that as a freeborn Englishman he had decided to reside in his native land, whereupon the King commanded him never to appear within the verge of the court and took steps to have his annuity stayed. It was not until June 1631, some years after James and the duke were both dead, that payment of Brett's annuity was resumed on an order signed by Weston.[54]

The Brett challenge caused Buckingham to decide on Middlesex's impeachment and overthrow. Just as when Bacon was ruined in 1621, now the Treasurer was to be cast cruelly aside. According to Clarendon, James was aghast when he learned what was in store for his capable minister. He summoned Buckingham and the Prince to an audience and denounced the moves they were making, which could only lead to a strengthening of the parliamentary opposition. To his favourite he declared, '"By God, Steenie, you are a fool and will shortly repent of this folly, and will find in this fit of popularity, you are making a rod with which you will be scourged yourself." ' Turning then to his son, James predicted that he 'would live to have his bellyful of Parliaments.' Once he was in possession of the sceptre, Charles would have good reason 'to remember how much he had contributed to the weakening of the crown by this precedent he was now so fond of.'[55] In the opinion of another seventeenth-century writer, James revealed an uncommonly clear understanding of the probable consequences. With prophetic insight he warned his heir 'that he should not take part with a faction in either House . . . and chiefly to take heed how he bandied to pluck down a peer of the realm by an arm of the lower House, for the Lords were the hedge between himself and the people; and a breach made in that hedge might in time perhaps lay himself open.'[56] It was a tragedy that James was unable to convince his son and Buckingham that they should not conspire in this way with the parliamentary opposition. Much future conflict might have been avoided had the King's views been respected.

Contemptuous of James's admonitions, Charles and the duke continued their plans full speed ahead. They allowed the Treasurer's enemies in parliament to know that he could no longer rely on royal support, which amounted to a veiled invitation to attack him. Because Middlesex had reduced royal expenditure by means of a campaign against pensions, he had made scores of enemies who were only too happy to back his impeachment. As in the Bacon affair of 1621, the attack began with the delivery of private petitions, which were amplified by the accusations of officials whose profits he had sought to limit. In the end the impeachment succeeded because Middlesex's associates, particularly those in the Court of Wards and Liveries, were disloyal and provided the duke's henchmen with enough evidence to convict him.[57]

In his campaign against the Treasurer, Buckingham utilised the services of a variety of men, including the Marquess of Hamilton, Lord Say and Sele, and the Earls of Pembroke, Montgomery, Carlisle, and Southampton. In the lower House he relied on Sir Benjamin Rudyerd, Sir Francis Seymour, and three of the most important opposition spokesmen: Sir Edward Coke, Sir Edwin Sandys, and Sir Robert Phelips. The most damaging testimony was given, however, by Sir Miles Fleetwood, Receiver of the Court of Wards, and by Sir Robert Pye, a prominent functionary of the Exchequer and the manager of Buckingham's personal finances.[58]

Weston's part in the proceedings was not clearly defined. Doubtless the duke hoped to secure his assistance, and, in the short run, it would have been politically advantageous for him to give it. But Sir Richard was moved by feelings of friendship for his chief and refused to join in the attack. Nevertheless he did less to defend Middlesex than he might have done, which has caused some historians to condemn him for disloyalty. Yet Mrs Prestwich and Professor Tawney both commend him for rendering even the slightest assistance. Among the charges against the Treasurer was an accusation that he had accepted a bribe of £1000 from the farmers of the great customs, which he persistently denied, insisting that the money had been offered in return for his surrender of several shares in the great farm. When questioned on this point Sir Richard corroborated the story and maintained that he 'remembered Middlesex telling him in the coach returning from Chelsea that he had just sold four shares in the Great Farm for £1000.'[59]

Despite the host of individuals clamouring to provide evidence, it proved difficult for the Treasurer's enemies to decide on their best course of attack. Middlesex was no more dishonest than the King's other officials – according to one observer his transgressions were 'not very heinous in these times.'[60] It is obvious that the impeachment was based on hypocrisy from the outset. Although he was charged with bribery and mismanagement of the royal revenues, he was actually being punished for opposing the duke and seeking to curb the King's bounty. His enemies had no desire to initiate an era of honesty and fiscal responsibility but were hoping to return to 'happier, more wasteful days.'[61] Unhappily Middlesex had weakened his own position as a reformer by enriching himself at the very time he was blocking the pleas of other men for grants and pensions. At least the duke had the virtue of consistency. While helping himself to as much as possible, he made no efforts to prevent others from doing the same.

On 5 May the King stopped over at Westminster on his way to Greenwich and made a last-minute effort to defend his capable minister. He compared Middlesex to the Duke of Sully, Comptroller-General of Finance to Henry IV of France, and declared that an honest Treasurer was bound to be hated. But James's speech was poorly delivered and made only the slightest impression on the members.[62]

A gruelling affair, the trial opened on 7 May and lasted a full week. Middlesex was exhausted by the proceedings and sent word by Sir Richard on the fourth day that he was ill and could not continue. The House was unwilling to countenance any interruption and sent six members and a doctor to investigate. Although they found him huddled in bed, they gave orders for him to appear that very afternoon 'to hear more of his iniquities.'[63] The Treasurer was charged with numerous offences, but four were of paramount importance. Not only was he accused of having accepted £1000 from the customs farmers, but he was said to be guilty of extortionate practices as Master of the Court of Wards and to have made excessive profits as Master of the Great Wardrobe. In addition he was charged with allowing a shortage of gunpowder to develop at the Ordnance office, which he had generally neglected. The Treasurer was convicted on all four counts.

After being commanded to pay a fine of £50,000 to the crown, Middlesex was stripped of all his offices and declared unfit for government service ever again. Like his brother-in-law he was ordered never to appear within the verge of the court and was forbidden to take his seat in parliament at any future time. In addition he was to be imprisoned in the Tower until James saw fit to release him. Despite its severity, public opinion did not regard the sentence as an unduly harsh one. Chamberlain remarked that it was 'marvelled they proceeded no farther to degrade him upon so many just reasons.'[64]

A week after the trial ended, Weston was authorised to perform all the duties of the Treasurership until a successor to Middlesex could be appointed.[65] At this stage there was some pressure for Sir Richard to be entrusted with the white staff in his own right. In a letter to Buckingham of 24 May, Bishop Williams observed of the Chancellor:

> I know of no fitter man in England for the office, if he come in as a creature of the Prince and your Grace's; nor unfitter, if he should take it without your likings. I think your Grace will remember that this fortnight, this hath been my constant opinion.[66]

Such an endorsement was of little value, however, for the duke's confidence in Williams had been so shaken by the events of the previous winter that any candidate proposed by the bishop was almost bound to be rejected.

During the remaining weeks of the parliament of 1624, which was prorogued on 29 May, Weston continued to play a prominent role. Indeed the King instructed him and Secretary Calvert to keep a watchful eye over 'the motions and proceedings of the House' and to prevent any discussion of such controversial topics as impositions, the privileges of the members, or any matter that might raise questions pertaining to the prerogative.[67] From time to time during the last few weeks of the session, there were complaints about the lenient treatment being accorded the English Catholics. It was widely felt that the recusancy laws were being allowed to rust and that this unpopular minority was being let off too easily. Chiefly for this reason James proclaimed his opposition to the granting of any additional concessions to them, even if a marriage treaty with Catholic France should soon be signed. Unhappily for the King, both Weston and Secretary Calvert were felt to be unduly sympathetic towards Catholicism; and even then pointed references were being made to the fact that Lady Weston and her six daughters rarely attended the services of the established church.[68] For this reason the King's statement did less to placate the critics of his religious policy than he had hoped.

By the end of May James had tired of the proceedings at Westminster and decided to end the session. On the last Saturday of the month he appeared before the Lords and Commons assembled together and expressed his appreciation for the subsidy bill, the proceeds of which he promised to use solely for a campaign on the Elector Palatine's behalf. He then gave his consent to a number of measures, including the famous Statute of Monopolies, which had been enacted to curb the grievance criticised so bitterly by earlier parliaments. He praised the conduct of parliament during the course of the session and ended by instructing the members to be ready to meet again on 2 November.[69]

Once the parliament of 1624 was prorogued, Sir Richard threw himself into the performance of his routine administrative duties. Hoping to distinguish himself through hard work and thereby procure the white staff, he wrote a confidential letter to the duke on 29 May, the very day the session ended. In this he first assured

Buckingham of the 'love and reverence' he felt for him and extended his thanks for the commission to serve as acting head of the Treasury. He then asked for advice concerning the assistance that should be given Middlesex's efforts to secure a substantial reduction of his fine.[70] This was a matter that involved him for almost a year and required a greater part of his time than he could possibly have anticipated.

5 Seven Months as Acting Lord Treasurer

Sir Richard doubled as Chancellor of the Exchequer and acting Lord Treasurer for seven months, until the white staff was entrusted to Sir James Ley on 20 December 1624. During this period he performed a number of services for his former chief, whose sad plight evoked his genuine sympathy. On 29 May he cautiously inquired of the duke how best to proceed under the existing circumstances.

> . . . I humbly beseech your Grace to direct me what to do. His Lordship sues for his inlargement, and I know desires to derive favours by your Grace's mediation. And I am careful to perform all duties in obedience to his Majesty; my respect to your Grace and my care of him (that relyeth upon me) being in affliction.[1]

Because the duke was ill and unable to take counteraction, Weston appealed for the earl's release from the Tower, which was effected only three days after parliament was prorogued. To Buckingham's annoyance, Sir Richard continued to serve as an intermediary between Middlesex and the crown, which led to speculations in some quarters that the ex-Treasurer might yet recover his position.[2]

Middlesex was primarily concerned to secure a reduction of his fine and continually urged Weston to labour towards that end. Parliament had set the fine at £50,000, which the King considered to be too high. James willingly consented to a reduction to £30,000, although the earl hoped that it might be remitted altogether. On 21 July Sir Richard was directed to confer with Middlesex, to inform him that his gains as Master of the Great Wardrobe would be treated as the principal offence, and to secure a detailed appraisal of his estate.[3]

Weston received these instructions while present at 'a noble and brave dinner' given by Lord Kensington in honour of the new

French Ambassador, the Marquis d'Effiat. The next day he travelled to the ex-Treasurer's house at Chelsea, where he reluctantly relayed the information conveyed to him. The earl was incensed that his Wardrobe gains were now under attack, for he was convinced that 'he had in no one thing ever done better service.' Concerning the all-important matter of Middlesex's wealth, Weston reported on 23 July that his lands produced no more than £4000 a year. Two annuities increased his yearly revenues by £2000; but because of a pressing debt of £12,000, his lease on the sugar farm was mortgaged for the next thirty months to Sir Peter Van Lore. Although the ex-Treasurer was still a very rich man, he himself calculated his obligations at approximately £30,000 and maintained that his annual income from all sources was only £10,000. Clearly sceptical of Middlesex's figures, however, Sir Richard ended with the sage observation that 'his personal estate and his debts will hardly be discovered but by himself.'[4]

Within a week Weston learned that the King was dissatisfied with his appraisal of the earl's wealth. Accordingly he scheduled another conference with him and attempted to secure additional information. Once again James was displeased with the findings of his Chancellor, who was informed on 27 August that the King 'seems to expect a more strict account . . . and will do so until you signify you can come no nearer to it.'[5] Throughout these months the ex-Treasurer was continuing to press for a further reduction of his fine; and early in November James agreed to lower it to £20,000, although he declared that he would not accept a penny less. Because of evasive steps by Middlesex, the King continued to be displeased and periodically called for more information. He was also concerned that there should be no unnecessary delays; and on 1 January 1625 Weston and his new chief, Sir James Ley, demanded immediate payment of the entire £20,000.[6]

From a friend Middlesex learned that Weston and the Earl of Holderness were genuinely sympathetic but lacked the influence needed to moderate the King's demands. The ex-Treasurer therefore concluded that he had no choice but to negotiate with Buckingham, which he did during the spring of 1625. To the favourite he offered to surrender his lease of the sugar farm and his house and estate at Chelsea. Eventually a compromise was arranged. In satisfaction of the entire fine imposed by parliament, the crown agreed to accept the surrender of Chelsea House and the lease of the sugar farm along with a cash payment of £5000. Chelsea House and the £5000 went to Buckingham, while the lease was granted on the same terms Middlesex had had it to the favourite's minion, Lord Goring. Initially then, the crown received not a farthing of the £50,000 that parliament had sentenced the earl to pay. These corrupt arrangements provoked a storm of indignation; and when the duke was threatened with impeachment in 1626, he hastily surrendered to the Household and the Wardrobe the £5000 he had received from the ex-Treasurer.[7]

Just as Buckingham and other royal favourites profited from fines imposed by parliament and the various law courts, private individuals were usually able to divert the receipts from the sale of crown lands into their own pockets. This was true even while Middlesex, the strongest Treasurer of the period, held the white staff. Middlesex had opposed any decrease of the landed wealth of the crown, but his views had not always been respected. On 8 February 1623 he and Sir Richard were directed to pay more than £4000 to Buckingham or his assignees from funds soon to be paid into the Exchequer for lands that had been sold to Sir Thomas Middleton and several others. In July 1623, and again in March 1624, the two officials were instructed to pay additional sums to the duke from the receipts of certain tracts in Yorkshire, Norfolk, and Northamptonshire, which had recently been purchased by the Earl of Northumberland and four others.[8]

As long as he remained in office Middlesex made strenuous efforts to prevent any further land sales, which would inevitably reduce the future revenues of the crown. When land sales, or land grants, could no longer be deferred, the Treasurer insisted that only small, outlying tracts be alienated, in preference to the larger and more valuable compact estates.[9] So little royal land was in fact alienated during the early 1620s that a reaction set in, which played no small part in bringing about his impeachment.

The depth of the average Englishman's hunger for land was not only grasped but also shared by Sir Richard, whose financial views carried great weight between May 1624 and his death in March 1635. Although Weston was in accord that only small, outlying tracts should be sold off, he saw no reason to insist that the crown should not dispose of any of its properties at all. Indeed the precarious state of the royal finances compelled him to advocate a programme of renewed land sales. Beginning in the summer of

1624 such a programme was in fact launched; and by the spring of 1635 tracts worth almost £30,000 a year had been alienated for a total cash gain of approximately £650,000. Because the crown lands had yielded receipts of slightly less than £84,000 in 1619, it can be inferred that during the eleven years he served as the King's chief financial adviser, the landed wealth of the crown declined by roughly 35 per cent. Archbishop Laud was alarmed by this development; and once the reins of power were in his hands, he refused to countenance the sale of any additional crown lands. Within five years, however, the rebellion sparked by his religious innovations in Scotland had led to such great demands on the Exchequer that a programme of land sales was reinstituted. During the troubled period between 1640 and 1660, so many tracts were sold off that the crown lands ceased once and for all to be an important branch of the royal revenues.[10]

By relying as heavily as he did on funds raised through land sales, Sir Richard was able to keep the crown from bankruptcy during a critical and often stormy decade. Of the approximately £650,000 raised in this way before 1635, almost £340,000 was used to satisfy loans secured in 1617, 1625, and other times from the City of London.[11] Unhappily how the other £310,000 was used is not so clear, although it seems likely that a large portion found its way into the pockets of Buckingham and other courtiers. During his years of greatest favour the duke received grants of more than £413,000 from the crown,[12] of which a sizeable proportion came from profits of land sales. Thus it can be concluded that Sir Richard's rather summary measures were prompted as much by the King's lavishness to his favourites as by the activist foreign policy counselled by the duke after 1623.

While relying on an intensified programme of land sales, Sir Richard was raising whatever funds he could by means of loans. Between 1624 and 1628 he and his new chief were able to borrow more than a million pounds, which was less than half of what the crown needed to fight the wars launched by Buckingham, however. During the first three years of Charles I's reign, the crown's extraordinary expenditures amounted to more than £2,250,000, of which only a small part could be provided by means of the ordinary revenue.[13] Thus the financial picture after Middlesex's fall was extremely bleak, particularly when it is remembered that the King's debts were in the neighbourhood of £1,000,000 in 1624.

It was chiefly for this reason that Sir Richard resorted to the methods of procrastination and delay for which he is so often criticised. Pensions and annuities owing to courtiers and officials had to be withheld, and the heavy obligations incurred by the crown during previous years were of necessity deferred, despite the justice of claims advanced by hordes of angry creditors. A good example of the way he was obliged to operate is afforded by the case of Arthur Brett, Middlesex's handsome young brother-in-law.

After the earl's impeachment Brett was banished from court and commanded never to be seen again within forty miles of the capital. The unfortunate man lodged an appeal with the duke but was naturally rebuffed, so he travelled to Wanstead to petition the King himself. James was startled when the man who had so brazenly attempted to capture his affections appeared before him and soon afterwards expressed his annoyance in a letter to Sir Richard. Because there was never enough money to satisfy the claims of pensioners, Weston quickly took the hint and withheld payment of all sums owing to Brett. When a manservant was unable to secure a satisfactory explanation, Brett himself appeared and demanded to know whether any command had been given for the stay of his pension. After listening angrily to Brett's arguments, Sir Richard snapped, 'No other command than want of money.'[14]

Brett was not the only suitor to approach Weston during the summer and autumn of 1624. Of the many men who sought his good offices at this time, the most prominent was Sir Francis Bacon, the former Lord Chancellor, whose career had been terminated by impeachment in 1621. On 7 July Sir Richard received an emotional appeal from Bacon, who explained how bitterly he disliked the prospect of being either a suitor or a 'shifter.' Yet he was in such dire need that he felt compelled to seek the crown's assistance. He closed his plea with the rather haughty words, 'I leave it to yourself [to decide] what you think fit to be done in your honour and my ease.' Apparently Sir Richard saw no reason to assist him, for on 9 October Bacon took steps to gain Buckingham's intercession.[15]

Although he was often guilty of dragging his feet, Weston acted with resolution whenever the King's private needs were involved. On 14 June he was instructed to send £100 to Greenwich for James's personal use. As there was not enough time to secure a warrant for the release of funds from the Exchequer, he decided to send £100 of his own money. Yet he was careful to remind the principal Secretary that funds for such purposes were normally a charge on the privy purse and not on the Receipt.[16] Just as moneys had to be withheld from courtiers and lesser government officials, the payment of royal debts was occasionally deferred for lengthy periods, lasting months and even years. This was particularly true of the expenses of James's late wife, Anne of Denmark, whose accounts were still uncleared almost fifteen years after her death in 1619.[17] Even the Duke of Buckingham had to wait patiently for large sums owed to him. In July 1627 the King instructed Marlborough and Weston to issue £39,835 16s. out of the Exchequer 'in satisfaction of the duke's attendance on us in 1623, on the journey to Spain, and for several jewels provided for our use at that time.'[18]

As acting Lord Treasurer, Weston made repeated efforts to maintain a careful husbandry of the King's revenues. He insisted on the receipt of properly drawn warrants before allowing the release of funds and took special pains to learn the true state of the finances. In October 1624 he directed the auditors to prepare a report showing all receipts from the crown lands; then he instructed them to compile another report giving details of all standing charges on the various branches of the revenue.[19] He was equally careful to restrict the size of outpayments whenever possible. Even before Middlesex's fall he had shown his concern for economy by striving, albeit in vain, to reduce the funds set aside for the care of an elephant and various other animals sent to James I by the King of Spain. During the summer of 1624 he used every resource at his disposal to limit his master's generosity to the new French Ambassadors who had arrived in London to witness the ratification of a draft treaty already signed in Paris.[20] On occasion he pressed noblemen and other powerful individuals to settle whatever debts they owed to the crown. On 13 September 1624, for example, he wrote a polite but unmistakably firm letter to the Earl of Salisbury at Hatfield.

> Whereas I understand that amongst others your Lordship is found indebted to his Majesty in several sums of money depending in charge against you upon record . . . And forasmuch as his Majesty's urgent occasions at this time do require speedy

payment, I have thought it fit both out of respect to your Lordship as also in discharge of the King's service to give your Lordship notice hereof by this my letter, hoping that accordingly you will take that order herein whereby his Majesty's occasions may be served and your Lordship freed of such other trouble which in case of default be made is likely to follow by the ordinary course of the Exchequer.[21]

While supervising the routine operations of the Exchequer, Sir Richard was carrying out a variety of official duties. He was able to excuse himself from a part in the initial proceedings against the Earl of Bristol, who was to be ruined because he had crossed swords with the duke, but he was periodically required to take a hand in the activities of the Court of Wards to see that the King's financial interests were not compromised. He was also instructed to oversee the work of the Great Wardrobe and help with a ruling on whether its officials could manage on the £10,000 annual assignment established for them by Middlesex. In 1624 Sir Richard remained active in regard to commercial affairs and from time to time expressed his views concerning complicated proposals for the better manufacture of soap and alum, of which his old associate, Sir Arthur Ingram, was usually the chief proponent. He was also concerned with matters pertaining to the Mines Royal, the Ordnance office, the manufacture of gunpowder, and the regulation of the rich Newfoundland whale fisheries.[22]

Owing to such a multitude of duties, the Chancellor felt compelled to resign his post as collector of the pretermitted customs in the port of London, which was then assigned to Abraham Jacob and his son John. As was often the case during the early Stuart period, Weston experienced certain difficulties when he attempted to clear his accounts as a customs collector. On 23 November 1624 he requested of the principal Secretary that

> . . . if there be a bill come to your hand, concerning the allowance of my fees, when I was collector of the pretermitted customs, you would be pleased to get that signed also; for the auditors stay my accounts only for the want of that warrant, though I have paid in all moneys due to the King long since.[23]

Weston's most important task in 1624 was clearly to negotiate a new lease with the farmers of the great customs. Because of the outbreak of hostilities with Spain, the old syndicate led by Sir John Wolstenholme, Abraham Jacob, Maurice Abbot, and Henry Garway was emboldened to demand a reduction of £12,000 yearly in its rent. This caused a rival syndicate organised by Sir Paul Pindar and Sir William Cockayne to advance an offer of £2000 more, or a grand total of £150,000 annually. Although the old syndicate quickly matched this offer, the contract was awarded to Pindar and Cockayne, who were required however to take Wolstenholme and Jacob, two of Weston's closest friends, into partnership with them. The two excluded men, Abbot and Garway, were bitterly disappointed and soon found a way to avenge themselves on the government. During the summer of 1625 they conspired with the parliamentary opposition to block the passage of a lifetime grant of tunnage and poundage to Charles I.[24]

Because it was no secret that the King thought highly of his work, rumours began to circulate that Sir Richard was about to be appointed Lord Treasurer in his own right. On 24 August 1624 John Chamberlain informed a friend that

> Sir Richard Weston hath bought or hired Winchester House in Broad Street, and is busy in tricking and trimming it up, whereupon the voice goes strongly that he shall be Lord Treasurer, Sir Robert Pye Chancellor of the Exchequer, and Sir Walter Pye Master of the Wards.[25]

Although this rumour soon proved false, Weston had in fact taken a lease on Winchester House, a large mansion at the corner of Broad and Threadneedle Streets, several blocks northeast of St Paul's Cathedral. Until 1624 he seems to have occupied a house in Holborn that had been bequeathed to him by his father; but as acting Treasurer he felt the need of a more impressive residence. Winchester House fulfilled his requirements easily. Built in the mid-sixteenth century by the Marquess of Winchester, who served as Lord Treasurer for twenty-two years, it was inhabited during the latter part of Elizabeth's reign by Gilbert Talbot, Earl of Shrewsbury. Sir Richard lived in the mansion for only four years, however, until he became Treasurer in the summer of 1628. Then he leased the even greater mansion of Wallingford House, which was located within a short distance of Whitehall, on the site of the present-day Admiralty Building.[26]

Once he had settled his family in Winchester House, it was

again reported that he was about to be named Lord Treasurer. Doubtless he hoped to become so at this juncture, but whether he was promoted or not would depend on the attitude of Buckingham, whose creature he had consistently refused to be. Indeed throughout his term as acting Lord Treasurer, he annoyed the favourite not only by supporting Middlesex but also by resisting the duke's attempt to dispose of lesser posts in the customs service, which was one of the chief perquisites of his own place.

Only a few days after the parliament of 1624 was prorogued, Sir Richard complained to Secretary Conway about the favourite's efforts to grant offices to his own followers without the acting Treasurer's knowledge. Although willing to assist the duke in most ways, he felt compelled to insist that all the privileges of his position be respected and that no nominations be passed without his own 'consent and approbation.'[27] This courageous protest was deliberately ignored, and several months later he sent another letter of complaint to the Secretary. Again he outlined the proper procedure for filling vacancies in the customs house and insisted that waiters could be appointed only on the recommendation of the Treasurer or the Chancellor. This second protest achieved the desired result, and within a week he was informed that Buckingham would henceforth defer to him in the filling of vacant places.[28]

Unhappily for Sir Richard, his victory over the duke was a costly one, as it all but destroyed his chances of becoming Treasurer. He himself was aware of this and turned for reassurance to Conway, who informed him early in October that he was still the leading candidate for the position. On 16 October he thanked the Secretary 'for the good offices you have done me with the Duke and I beseech you to continue them.'[29] Conway's efforts were of no avail, for the favourite had already begun to press for the nomination of Sir James Ley, who, a Londoner reported, 'will go shortly to Royston to receive the white staffes, for the King cometh not hither till Christmas.' Yet the Treasurership was not formally conferred on Buckingham's candidate until 20 December.[30]

The delay in confirming Ley's appointment was caused by James's reluctance to consent to the nomination. Doubtless the King preferred Weston to the septuagenarian judge who was now being thrust upon him. Although a respected lawyer, Ley was well past his prime and had no particular knowledge of public finance, which is what prompted Professor Aylmer's description of him as 'an ineffectual old man, incapable of serious efforts to raise more revenue or to reduce expenditure.'[31] Ley had one indisputable advantage over Sir Richard, however. When nearing his seventieth birthday, he had married a niece of Buckingham's, a young girl of seventeen, which not only prompted a number of crude jokes but gave promise of 'administrative inertia and political compliance.'[32] And to most observers in the capital it was obvious that the duke wanted someone in the position who would not object to being treated as a rubber stamp.

The two men were able to work effectively together, largely because Ley deferred to many of Weston's opinions, while Sir Richard was determined to make the best he could of a trying but probably temporary situation. That the Chancellor had to discharge many routine duties for his new chief can be seen in regard to the management of the crown lands. A responsibility usually falling to the Treasurer or to the Treasurer assisted by the Chancellor, the crown lands were now a province reserved almost exclusively for Sir Richard. The most important matters were invariably referred to him; and it seems clear that he had to instruct the Treasurer on the proper procedure for handling even the most minor problems.[33]

Although it was inevitable that he would be nothing more than a figurehead, Ley did make a few attempts at active participation in Exchequer affairs. In November 1625 he directed his secretary to keep a watchful eye over the proceedings of the Auditor of the Receipt and the Clerk of the Pells, which caused the Auditor to complain to a friend that 'my Lord Treasurer doth now intend to take all into his own and [his] secretary's hands, and endeavoureth the Chancellor should do the like . . . He will blindfold me if he can.'[34] Ley also called periodically for administrative economies and, possibly at Weston's urging, brought pressure to bear on the King to curtail the flow of pensions, free gifts, and other grants. Because of this pressure James sent more restrictive instructions to the Lord Keeper, the Lord Privy Seal, and the two principal Secretaries on 9 February 1625.[35]

Unhappily this gesture at greater financial control was like locking the barn door after the horses had already bolted. During the preceding month James had been unusually extravagant. He had granted a lifetime annuity of £2000 to Bishop Williams and a free gift of £5000 to Lord Walden, and had given orders for the release of a whopping £50,000 to Buckingham.[36] Even worse, the King was too weak to adhere to his own instructions of 9 February. Before the end of the month he had bestowed a free gift of £12,000 on the Earls of Carlisle and Holland, who had just returned from a diplomatic mission to Paris. Within a few more days he was showing exceptional favour to the widow and children of Ludovick Stuart, third Duke of Lennox, who had died in 1624. In March 1625 he granted the widow a free gift of £3350 out of the revenues of the Court of Wards, 'towards the payment of her husband's debts.' In addition he established an annuity of £2100 in her name, which was to revert on her death to her son James, the fourth duke, or, in default there, to his younger brother Henry and his male descendants. Furthermore the King granted the fourth duke a 21-year pension of £1400 in addition to a free gift of £700.[37]

Perhaps James realised that his days of dispensing such largesse were almost over. Nearing his fifty-ninth birthday, he was now in rapidly declining health and only a shadow of his former self. Afflicted with arthritis, he fell ill with a 'tertian ague' about the beginning of March and suffered violent convulsions every two or three days thereafter. By 21 March he was convinced his end was near and asked to receive the sacrament, which gave him some spiritual satisfaction. The physicians were unable to provide a comparable measure of physical relief, so Buckingham and his mother decided to administer potions suggested by John Remington, a country practitioner of Dunmow, Essex. This well-intentioned move backfired, for it led to no improvement in James's condition and prompted later charges in parliament that it had hastened his death. The King died about twelve noon on Sunday the 27th of March. He was attended in his last hours only by Bishop Williams, the Earl of Arundel, and a few other Privy Councillors. They attempted to make him as comfortable as possible, but 'a terrible dysentery carried him away and he died in filth and misery.'[38]

The accession of the new King was immediately proclaimed at the main entrance to Theobalds. Shortly afterwards Charles repaired to Whitehall, where an impromptu gathering of all the Councillors, peers, and bishops then in the capital took place early the next morning. During the course of that meeting, the principal Secretaries arrived with instructions for all but a few of James's Councillors to remain in office and take the proper oaths.[39] While the transition to the new order was taking place, Ley and Weston decided to make another plea for fiscal responsibility. Several weeks earlier they had complained to the duke that the revenues for the current fiscal year were already fully anticipated. Now they hoped to make an impression on the new King's mind and get his reign off to a good start.[40]

At first it appeared that the views of the Treasurer and the Chancellor might carry real weight with Charles. He was a stickler for routine and hoped to stamp out the jobbing and corruption that had characterised his father's court. Because he had no intention of curbing the easy access enjoyed by them during the previous reign, Ley and Weston had frequent conferences with him. Indeed Lord Clarendon maintained that 'the principal officers of the revenue, who governed the affairs of money, had always access with the King, and spent more time with him in private than any of his other servants and councillors.'[41]

During the spring of 1625 Weston and his chief, who was soon to be created Earl of Marlborough, performed a useful, if not absolutely necessary, service for the King by arranging a loan of £60,000 from the City of London at 8% annual interest. As security for this loan Charles pledged crown lands worth more than £216,000, although there was of course no way for the corporation to foreclose should he unexpectedly default. The King also promised to abide by a rigorously inflexible repayment schedule. By June 1626 he would repay not only the interest but also the principal on the loan now being contracted. In addition he gave his word that the £86,066 13s. 4d. still owing on a loan advanced to his father in 1617 would be repaid by December 1625. Unhappily there was no possibility that the crown would be able to adhere to such a demanding time-table, and both loans were still partially unpaid many years later, when Marlborough and Weston were both dead. It has been calculated that even after the outbreak of the Civil War in 1642, 'there still remained £12,500 of the principal and £13,074 of the interest to be repaid to the lenders of 1617, and £24,300 and £5980 interest to those of 1625.'[42] The rash and ill-considered promises made by the King in 1625 led to inevitable doubts about his financial responsibility. During later years Weston sought to repair the damage done at this juncture by insisting on the regular payment of royal obligations, but he was only partly successful.

Although Charles had the wisdom to retain Sir Richard and other experienced advisers of his father's, he did not have the abilities normally associated with a successful leader of men. Short of stature and cold of temperament, he was more interested in aesthetic matters than in problems of politics and government. Furthermore his outlook was rigidly moralistic, for, as he once boasted, he could never ' "defend a bad, or yield in a good cause." '[43] More harmful than this inflexibility was his almost total independence on Buckingham. Older and more experienced than Charles, the duke wielded even greater power after the new King's accession than he had before the death of James I. His optimism and self-assurance were an inspiration to Charles, who had long suffered from an inferiority complex and debilitating self-doubts. It was comforting to know that all matters could be entrusted to one who was not only a loyal servant but also an intimate friend. As a consequence Buckingham's influence was felt in all areas of government, and there were virtually no limits to his power. In a letter of 6 May John Chamberlain noted how he 'was never in greater favour and all things pass by him.'[44] Three weeks earlier the Tuscan Ambassador had given an unusually perceptive analysis of the favourite's position.

> The Duke of Buckingham, although deeply grieved by the loss of the late King, his ever-liberal master, may feel assured that the countenance and favour of the new King will be extended to him to a greater degree, if it be possible. This is already shown by the most transparent evidence. He is with his Majesty all day, he sleeps in a room contiguous to the royal chamber, he has been confirmed in all his offices, and he has also been made Gentleman of the Bedchamber, and has received the Golden Key, and the emblem of his office, so that he can, whenever he pleases and at any hour, enter that chamber as well as any other part of the palace occupied by his Majesty. In fine, nothing is done without him.[45]

Because of the duke's overweening influence, any attempts by Marlborough and Weston to initiate a period of fiscal responsibility were almost bound to fail. Royal extravagance continued as before, and funds were spent as if there would never be an accounting. Naturally no expense was spared for the funeral of James I, which took place on 7 May and was described as 'the greatest indeed that was ever known in England.' Arm-bands and mourning cloths were distributed to more than 9000 persons, and the hearse was said to be 'the fairest and best fashioned that hath been seen, wherein Inigo Jones did his part.' The obsequies cost in excess of £50,000, the payment of which had to be deferred for years, since the Exchequer was completely barren.[46]

Neither was there any change in the direction of England's foreign policy. Co-operation with France and war against Spain remained the officially declared policy of the English crown. On 15 June 1624 the late King had adhered to a league of friendship already established by the French and Dutch governments; and on the 11th of November following, he agreed to the betrothal of his heir to the fifteen-year-old sister of Louis XIII, Henrietta Maria. Charles and his French bride were married by proxy in the Cathedral of Notre Dame on 11 May 1625.[47] Meanwhile England's relations with Spain had completely deteriorated. The two Spanish Ambassadors left England on 21 June 1624. Six weeks later James's envoy in Madrid delivered an ultimatum breaking off all treaties between the two countries, which was tantamount to a declaration of war.[48]

During the same period the English crown was incurring extremely heavy expenditure. More than £128,700 was issued to put the navy in readiness, and £121,000 was advanced for the support of English volunteers in the Low Countries and for the payment of Christian IV and Count Mansfeld, who had been promised monthly subsidies of £30,000 and £20,000 respectively. For the Ordnance office, the armoury, and 'secret service,' nearly £33,000 was released. Large sums were also required for border defences and for installations to safeguard the Irish coasts. The greater part of these funds came from the subsidies granted by the parliament of 1624, which had produced a net revenue of £253,140 by 30 June 1625.[49] Because such lavish expenditure could not continue without additional parliamentary assistance, it quickly became apparent to observers that another session was in the offing. Indeed the first major political decision made by Charles after his accession was to summon a new parliament as quickly as possible.

The day after his father's death, Charles had an important

conversation with Lord Keeper Williams. After appointing him to deliver the eulogy at the coming funeral, the King asked that parliament be called into session for the purpose of granting subsidies. Since the last parliament had been prorogued rather than dissolved, he saw no reason to waste time on the holding of new elections. Dismayed by such ignorance of the constitution, Bishop Williams explained that the death of his father automatically dissolved the previous parliament and made new elections necessary. Annoyed by this, Charles insisted that no time be lost and called for writs to be issued to the sheriffs at once. Again the bishop felt compelled to object. If the elections took place before the elegible Councillors had a chance to find seats, the strength of the royal party in the lower House, and thus the success of the King's programme, would be seriously jeopardised. Charles refused to accept Williams's counsel, however, and retorted that '"it was high time to have subsidies granted for the maintaining of a war with the King of Spain, and the fleet must go forth for that purpose in the summer."'[50]

Writs were issued to the sheriffs on 2 April, and parliament was scheduled to open on 17 May. Happily for the King, the elections, which were held in late April, did not bear out Williams's prophecy of a political setback. The experienced Master of the Rolls, Sir Julius Caesar, lost his bid for a seat, and the staunch royalist, Sir Henry Wotton, was defeated in the campaign waged for him at Canterbury. But Sir Richard and five other Councillors were successful at the polls; so the royal party in the Commons was about the same size as in most other parliaments of the 1620s.[51]

Because of advice from the Council, the opening of parliament was deferred until 18 June.[52] During those last remaining weeks almost no steps were taken to ensure that the session would be a harmonious one. Still elated by the success they had enjoyed in 1624, Buckingham and the King were confident that the members would do exactly as instructed. Within a brief period their optimism was rudely shattered.

6 Proceedings in Two Parliaments

When the first parliament of Charles I opened on 18 June 1625, the government had two primary objectives it wished to accomplish: the passage of a lifetime grant of tunnage and poundage to the new King and the appropriation of a large grant of supply, amounting to at least six subsidies, for the support of Buckingham's foreign policy. In the pursuit of neither objective was the government successful. Charles and the duke were much too long in taking the members into their confidence, owing to a natural reluctance to admit the magnitude of the sums likely to be required for the war. Furthermore they had made inadequate preparations for the session, since neither was experienced in the techniques of parliamentary management. Although six Councillors had acquired seats in the Commons, neither Secretary of State was present there. Morton had been returned by the electors of Kent but was engaged on an embassy abroad, while Conway, who had recently been raised to the peerage, was now a member of the Lords. The three active Councillors in the lower House, Weston, May, and Edmondes, were anxious to provide a sense of direction but were never accepted as government spokesmen because Buckingham obviously refused to confide in them and utilise their services.[1]

The unsatisfactory lead provided by Charles and his favourite was compounded by parliamentary doubts about their ability to direct England's foreign policy. Even now reports were arriving from the coast concerning their support of Cardinal Richelieu's efforts to subdue the rebellious Huguenots of La Rochelle. Despite the widespread fears in England of the cardinal, Buckingham was so anxious to pave the way for an Anglo-French alliance against Spain that he had promised naval assistance to the French crown in March 1625. The royal ship *Vanguard* and seven merchant vessels were placed at the disposal of Louis XIII for a period not to exceed eighteen months. Under the captainship of John Pennington, this squadron could be used for any purpose that did not hinder or impede the commerce of Englishmen. Although the duke expected them to be directed against Genoa, the English ships were ordered to proceed against the Huguenots of La Rochelle, which caused Buckingham to realise his policy was bound to be attacked in the coming parliament. To prevent this he contrived to exploit the injured religious feelings of the crews, who did not relish the idea of fighting against fellow Protestants. By the beginning of June so much dissatisfaction had been provoked that the ships ignored their directions and sailed back to England. When 'commanded' to return to Dieppe the following month, the sailors aboard the *Vanguard* mutinied. Not until the first week of August were all eight ships actually in French hands.[2] It was against the background of these events that the first parliament of Charles I met at Westminster and was asked to give unquestioning support to royal policy.

Sir Richard played only a minor role in the first session of 1625, which lasted from 18 June until 11 July. Within two weeks of the opening of parliament, he had been named to three committees of the House, one to consider criticisms of certain Exchequer procedures, another to discuss proposals relating to 'secret officers and inquisitions,' and a third to examine the provisions of a bill against 'the procuring of judicial places & against [the] giving and receiving of bribes.' He was also active in arranging the delivery of a petition to the King for a general fast. This matter required much of his time between 22 and 28 June and necessitated his attending several conferences with delegations from the Lords.[3] Despite his contributions in this regard, Weston's record in the first session was an undistinguished one, for he had no instructions to explain the government's objectives as a way of winning support for a subsidy bill.

The question of supply was raised on 30 June, when Sir Francis Seymour suggested a grant of only one subsidy and fifteenth. This beggarly proposal was criticised by Sir Benjamin Rudyerd, who maintained that the amount suggested was 'too little in respect of want and his [Charles'] reputation.' Although not a Councillor and without the benefit of precise information, Rudyerd attempted to convince the House that a larger grant should be made by listing the main expenses confronting the government. He alluded not only to James's funeral and the coming coronation of Charles and Henrietta Maria but also to the costly entertainments of foreign ambassadors and the sending forth of naval and military expeditions in support of England's continental allies. After his remarks, which would have had a greater impact if delivered by Weston, debate became heated and lasted for several hours. Ultimately the House voted in favour of a grant of only two subsidies and fifteenths, which were expected to produce £160,000 but in fact yielded slightly less than £127,000.[4]

Once the question of supply was raised, the matter of tunnage and poundage came under consideration. The new King had authorised the collection of the customs duties only four days after his accession;[5] but because earlier rulers had invariably received lifetime grants of them from their first parliaments, he had every reason to expect parliamentary approval of his action as a matter of form. Unfortunately for Charles, the political situation at this juncture was a difficult one. Parliament, and especially the lower House, was conscious of its rapidly growing strength and assertive of its rights. Moreover, during the session of 1625 the leaders of the opposition were determined to establish the principle of parliamentary control over the pretermitted customs. The crown maintained that they were a prerogative matter, but the opposition contended that the authorisation of the Lords and Commons was necessary, thereby opening the door to conflict. It appears that the discontented elements in 1625 were spurred on by two wealthy London merchants, Maurice Abbot and Henry Garway, who had recently been ousted from the syndicate that managed the great farm of the customs.[6]

When debate on the tunnage and poundage bill opened on 5 July, the feeling of the House was immediately apparent. Sir Walter Earle moved that such a measure be passed for only one year rather than for the King's lifetime, until the question of the pretermitted customs had been settled. Earle's motion was seconded by Sir Robert Phelips, but the Solicitor-General, Sir Robert Heath, voiced cogent objections. Debate continued until 7 July, when the Commons authorised the collection of tunnage and poundage until 27 March 1626, the first anniversary of Charles's accession.[7]

When a one-year bill was passed Buckingham and the King saw

their error in not guiding the deliberations of the lower House. After supper on 7 July, the duke hurried from Hampton Court to Westminster, where he met with the most important members of the court faction about midnight. Plans were laid for a compaign to secure additional supply, the main responsibility being entrusted to Sir John Coke, an officer of the Court of Requests who was not yet a Councillor. In the words of a recent authority, 'the fact that May, Weston, and Heath were all passed over and the motion entrusted to Sir John Coke is proof in itself that Buckingham's ablest followers disapproved.'[8]

Shortly after the subsidy bill was passed on third reading on 8 July, Coke rose to address the House. Summarising the King's most pressing obligations, he maintained that Charles would soon require at least £69,000 for Ireland and the navy, which did not include the £47,000 needed for the Ordnance office and for castles and other fortifications throughout England. For the immediate support of troops in the Low Countries, £99,000 was required. In addition the crown was obligated to Christian IV and Count Mansfeld, to whom monthly subsidies of £30,000 and £20,000 had been promised. The King's ordinary revenue was already 'exhausted and overcharged with expenses,' and the supply just voted by the House would yield no more than £160,000 at most. In a commendable flush of patriotism, Charles and his closest associates had made use of their own private funds to finance the country's wartime needs. 'Shall it be said,' asked Sir John, 'that these men are left to be undone by their own readiness to public services?' The King did not require the introduction of a new subsidy bill, but Coke urged his listeners to consider whether they would be willing to 'relieve his Majesty in some farther proportion.' Unhappily this important speech, coming as late as it did, made a weak impression and fell 'terribly flat.'[9]

The question of additional supply was left pending until 11 July, when Secretary Conway delivered a royal message in the upper House. Charles was grateful for the funds already appropriated but considered them inadequate for his needs. A war on behalf of the Elector Palatine would require at least £700,000 annually, or the equivalent of eight subsidies and fifteenths granted each year. The principal Secretary then proceeded to explain the King's financial commitments in order to rally support for another subsidy bill. He ended by announcing Charles's willingness to grant an adjournment, which both Houses had requested because of the widespread incidence of plague in London. Later that day Lord Keeper Williams declared to the Lords and Commons assembled together that the proceedings were to be suspended until 1 August, when parliament was to reassemble at Oxford.[10]

During the three weeks that followed, a frantic attempt was made under Buckingham's aegis to strengthen the court faction and recover the initiative. Old and experienced hands like Weston were consulted and assigned more active roles. But the damage caused by the first session was almost impossible to repair, and tactics that might have sufficed before were now woefully inadequate.

On Monday morning the 1st of August the new session began at Oxford. The lower House met in the Divinity School, while the upper chamber convened in the Convocation House. At first the members concentrated on religious issues, as they debated the case of Richard Montague, an Arminian cleric whose recently published treatise, *A New Gag for an Old Goose*, expressed theological views distasteful to the majority. A dedicated high churchman, Montague was becoming known for his advocacy of a modified theory of good works, which was heresy to Puritans convinced of the Calvinist doctrine of predestination.

After three days of harangues over the dangers posed by Arminianism, Speaker Crew announced a summons to attend the King in Christ Church Hall on 4 August. In a characteristically brief address, Charles reminded parliament that the treaties with Spain had been broken off at its urging. That a war against Philip IV would soon follow had been the common assumption and desire in 1624. Promises of financial support had been made that the Houses now seemed inclined to forget. The two subsidies and fifteenths granted during the previous session were totally inadequate, but the government was determined to persevere with its plans. It would be better to send out a few ships than to keep the entire fleet bottled up in port, even if there was little likelihood of a successful campaign. Yet Charles felt that the members would want to make another grant of supply once they knew 'the whole particular of all expenses.' At the end of his speech, he called on Secretary Conway and Sir John Coke to explain the domestic and foreign situation in greater detail.[11]

When proceedings resumed in the Commons on 5 August, one member suggested a conference with the Lords before the lower House attempted to decide on an additional grant. But the majority were strongly opposed, and Sir George More, Chancellor of the Garter and a parliament man for more than forty years, declared that the Commons should decide for itself whether and how much to give before conferring with the upper chamber. More's view was seconded by Sir Francis Seymour, who contended there was no reason for another conference at the present time and proposed a grant of two additional subsidies and fifteenths. Seymour's remarks were applauded by Sir Humphrey May and Sir Thomas Edmondes, both Privy Councillors.[12]

Although many members were inclined to give, Sir Robert Phelips, the son of a former Speaker, was resolutely opposed. During the last few months, he maintained, 'there is a wrong done to us in levying the tonnage and poundage.' He charged that royal policy was often poorly conceived and executed, which could only be interpreted as veiled criticism of the favourite. 'In the government,' he declared, 'there hath wanted good advice. Counsels and power hath been monopolized. There hath been more assaults upon the liberties of the people, more pressures within this seven or eight years than in divers ages.' Before proceeding with another grant of supply, the House would do well to 'look into the right of the subject.' In conclusion Phelips urged the Commons to investigate the King's 'estate and government, and, finding that which is amiss, make this Parliament the reformer of the Commonwealth.'[13]

Phelips's allegations brought a rejoinder from Sir Richard, who sought desperately to weaken the thrust of his speech. At no other time, he maintained, had there been such need for close co-operation between crown and parliament. In his words:

> The King hath learned in Spain that nothing brought his father into so much contempt as the coldness betwixt him and his people, and that the contrary cause will have the contrary effect; and thereupon, like a happy star, led the way to the people in the last Parliament, when the best laws were made that divers ages have known.

Weston questioned why the House had, only a year earlier, supported aid for the Palatinate if it now intended to forsake the cause. He cautioned the members that they would forfeit all right to advise the crown should they fail to assume responsibility for their counsel. He then recounted the debts left by James I and the sums spent since the present King's accession. So much money had been required during the past six months that the ordinary revenues were anticipated, 'some till midsummer next, some till Christmas twelvemonth.' Weston concluded by supporting the motion for two additional subsidies and fifteenths.[14]

Despite the Chancellor's well-argued speech, Sir Edward Coke advanced stern objections to the proposal for additional supply. In his opinion sufficient funds had already been voted, and, because of the continued spread of plague and the disruption of England's foreign trade during recent years, the time was not ripe for heavier taxation. For longer than most men cared to believe, royal policy had been poorly directed by dishonest and incompetent officials. The King's revenues were being embezzled even now, and his household expenses were far too great. Coke's charges, the most serious made to date, were answered by remarks from Solicitor Heath and Sir George More, both of whom supported the call for additional supply. After prolonged debate the House adjourned for the day, without reaching a decision.[15]

On 8 August the Lords and Commons assembled together in Christ Church Hall to hear reports from Buckingham, Conway, and Sir John Coke. With the assistance of these two, the duke tried frantically to win support for a new subsidy bill. Once they finished the Treasurer made a rare speech and recounted the sums promised to Christian IV, Count Mansfeld, the States-General, the Elector Palatine, and other Protestant friends and allies. At the end of his address Marlborough announced that he, Sir Richard, and their subordinates at the Exchequer would gladly answer any questions concerning the King's financial commitments.[16]

Debate on the question of supply continued until 10 August. No decision was reached, however, because the members' attention was again diverted by religious matters. They were disturbed by reports that pardons had recently been granted to a convicted Jesuit and ten other Papists and that, on orders from Secretary Conway, a Dorsetshire woman had been exempted from taking the oath of allegiance. The House was outraged by such actions, which, it was declared, 'tended to the prejudice of true Religion, his Majesty's dishonour . . . and to the discouragement of the High

Court of Parliament.'[17] That the members were concentrating on religious questions rather than his own financial needs annoyed the King, who soon relayed important directions by Sir Richard.

On 10 August Weston reported that despite Charles's resolve to correct abuses, it should be obvious that 'this time is fit only for such matters as are of present necessity and dispatch.' Because of the continuing threat of plague, the King was concerned for the members' well-being and planned to end the session within a few more days. Immediate passage of a new subsidy bill was therefore essential. If the Commons would only do as Charles desired, he would redress their grievances at a safer and more propitious time.[18] Although the King was attempting to exploit the members' loyalty, the request relayed by his Chancellor was reminiscent of a promise made to the previous parliament. James I had given his word that a parliamentary session would be held in the autumn of 1624 to consider grievances and the expenditure of funds appropriated during the previous spring. But the late King had failed to honour that promise, which inevitably lessened popular confidence in the crown. As a consequence the message delivered by Weston made virtually no impression.

In a vain attempt to assist the Chancellor, Sir Robert Naunton advanced reasons why the House should pass a new subsidy bill; and Sir Humphrey May observed that James's first parliament had been much more generous than the present one, since it had granted three subsidies and four fifteenths. May's remarks were followed by a second speech from Sir Richard in favour of additional supply. He contended that all 'fears, jealousies, and disgusts' should be disregarded, at least momentarily, while an expedition to the continent was being planned and dispatched. The House had no reason to distrust the King's promise to redress grievances in a future session, since those evils complained about of late had not occurred during the present reign. At the conclusion of his address Weston implored the members to decide once and for all whether they would grant additional supply at the present time.[19]

Weston's second speech had no more impact than his first, for only a few members were willing to appropriate additional funds on the vague assurance that abuses would be corrected at some future time. To explain his own opposition to a new subsidy bill, Sir Robert Phelips made a broad appeal to history. In his opinion the national assemblies of France, Spain, and other European kingdoms had declined and all but disappeared because of their failure to insist that grievances must precede a vote of supply. England was the only monarchy in Christendom that had preserved its 'original rights and constitutions.' To ensure that this would continue, traditional procedures must be adhered to, and Phelips urged the appointment of a committee 'to prepare an answer for his Majesty, and reasons why we cannot [now] give.' Swayed by Phelips's arguments, the House decided that a grand committee should meet the following day to devise a reply to the King's message as delivered by Weston.[20]

On 11 August the Commons endorsed a proposal that the motion for another subsidy bill be withdrawn, 'for it is a greater disgrace to be denied by a few than by all.' Once they had voted against further action for the present, the members drew up a declaration informing Charles that

> . . . we will be ready, in convenient time, and in a parliamentary way, freely and dutifully, to do our utmost endeavours to discover and reform the abuses and grievances of the realm and state, and in like sort to afford all necessary supply to his most excellent Majesty upon present, and all other his just occasions and designs.[21]

Once the Commons' declaration had been delivered by Weston and the other Councillors in the House, Charles realised there was no chance of additional supply from the present session. Furthermore he was angered by criticisms made of the duke during the course of the session; so on 12 August he dissolved parliament and sent the members home.

Although close to a total failure, the parliament of 1625 did not weaken the King's faith in his chief minister. On the contrary Buckingham's influence increased to even greater heights during the autumn and winter of 1625–6, which was as detrimental to the cause of efficient government as it was to his own reputation and career. In September 1625 the Venetian Ambassador reported that because the duke 'disposes of everything . . . the hatred of the magnates increases against him, and one may say that he stands ill with everybody.'[22] At this juncture Sir Richard was attempting to assist the rise of a wealthy young squire from Yorkshire, Sir Thomas Wentworth, a friend of his old associate Sir Arthur Ingram. On 7 November Ingram informed the anxious Wentworth that, 'on my creed you are much beholden to the Chancellor of the Exchequer, who hath done you good offices to the King, and will continue the same upon all occasions.' Unhappily Weston's efforts were offset by Sir Humphrey May, who often made slighting remarks about the Yorkshireman's abilities in Buckingham's presence. And as Ingram sadly observed of the duke, 'who he will advance, shall be advanced, and who he doth but frown upon, must be thrown down.'[23]

Because of pressure exerted by the favourite, several important changes of government personnel took place during the autumn of 1625. After the death of Secretary Morton in September, his important office was conferred on Sir John Coke, who had been associated with the duke for almost a decade. Coke's unrivalled knowledge of naval affairs was of particularly great value to a minister who 'was constantly dreaming . . . of winning popularity through successful naval feats.'[24] Coke's place in the Court of Requests was assigned to another dependent of the favourite's, Sir Thomas Aylesbury, who was, by chance, Lord Clarendon's father-in-law. Of greater significance than these appointments was the discharge of Weston's old supporter, Bishop Williams, as Lord Keeper. Williams had objected to the duke's new foreign policy during the winter of 1623–4 and had given almost no assistance to the government during the recent session of parliament. Furthermore he was the target of allegations being made by a dangerous enemy, William Laud, newly consecrated Bishop of Bath and Wells. On 23 October Williams was commanded to surrender the Great Seal and retire to his diocese of Lincoln.[25]

To succeed Williams, the Attorney-General, Sir Thomas Coventry, was promoted. Coventry had won Buckingham's favour by helping with the settlement of a paternity suit brought by the duke's brother, Viscount Purbeck, against Sir Robert Howard. In Lord Clarendon's opinion, the new Lord Keeper was a man 'of wonderful gravity and wisdom,' who had 'a clear conception of the whole policy of government both of Church and State.' Yet Coventry's influence was never great, for he refused to ally himself with a faction at court and would not make 'desperate sallies against growing mischiefs, which he knew well he had no power to hinder.'[26]

As long as his influence with the King remained unabated, Buckingham was able to continue his policy of active intervention in continental affairs. Without any intention of doing so, he allowed England's relations with France to deteriorate while he was planning a naval expedition against Spain on behalf of the Elector Palatine. Aware that co-operation with Catholic France was resented by the Puritans, the duke and his master decided to reimpose the recusancy laws as a way of showing their dislike of Cardinal Richelieu. In addition they radically altered Henrietta Maria's household by dismissing almost all her French attendants. Such action was in clear violation of the Anglo-French marriage treaty and was bound to provoke the anger of Louis XIII.

While the Queen's household was assuming the importance of a major issue, a more fundamental cause of tension was developing. In September 1625 several French ships were detained on suspicion of transporting contraband goods to the Spanish Netherlands. As Lord Admiral, Buckingham ordered the confiscation of any gold and silver bullion aboard and the retention of all other items at Plymouth. By the beginning of November more than twenty French ships had been captured, which inevitably prompted French reprisals. Early in December two English ships anchored at Rouen were taken captive on orders from the governor of Le Havre. Charles retaliated by demanding the return of the eight ships lent by Buckingham to the French government during the previous March. Even more ominous, he took up the cause of the beleaguered Huguenots of La Rochelle. Although Richelieu and Louis XIII hoped to keep the peace, diplomatic relations deteriorated even farther owing to the intransigence of the English crown. Late in March 1626 Charles withdrew his two ambassadors and began to prepare for war.

Because Anglo-French relations were now entering a critical phase, an attempt was made to promote closer co-operation with the United Provinces. Sir Richard and nine other Councillors were instructed to confer with the special embassy led by Albert Joachimi which had been in London since June 1625 to explore the possibility of an Anglo-Dutch alliance. The Anglo-Dutch talks culminated on 8 September with the signing of the Treaty of Southampton, which provided for a joint naval campaign by the two countries, with England furnishing four times as many ships as the States-General. England would launch an attack on the Spanish coast, while the Dutch were to establish a blockade of Flanders and the Spanish Netherlands. It was hoped that the

Protestant rulers of central and northern Europe would adhere to the Anglo-Dutch alliance.[27]

Early in October a fleet of eighty English ships set sail for Cadiz under the command of Sir Edward Cecil, who had been created Viscount Wimbledon in anticipation of victory. Although the attack on the Spanish coast had been planned since midsummer, little had been done to ensure that the ships were adequately prepared. The *St. George* was equipped with sails that dated back to 1588, and the *Lion* was in such poor condition that she had to be left behind at the last moment. Many of the ships were leaky, and the crews were ill clothed and fed. Launched too late in the season, the expedition was caught in a great autumnal storm in the Bay of Biscay, during which, in the words of one participant, 'many a gallant man perished.' When Cadiz was reached the treasure fleet was nowhere to be seen, since it had received adequate warning of the approaching danger. Under Wimbledon's leadership a council of war was held and a poorly conceived assault on the Spanish coast launched. It accomplished nothing but the loss of additional lives, which prompted the commanding officers to engage in rancorous quarrels among themselves. When they returned to England in December, they attempted to evade any responsibility for the outcome by blaming one another. Charles and Buckingham took no heed of the fiasco, which they ascribed to chance or misfortune. Already planning another expedition for the following spring, they did nothing to see that it would be any better led or equipped.[28]

Originally expected to cost no more than £300,000, the Cadiz expedition led to expenditures of almost twice that amount. Where were Marlborough and Weston to find such a staggering sum? They relied on the subsidies and fifteenths granted by the parliament of 1625 and on what had been paid of the Queen's dowry. But these funds were woefully inadequate, and they had to make use of anticipations and tallies of issue. As early as April 1626 the revenues for the current year were fully anticipated.[29] Sir Richard and his chief were also compelled to withhold courtiers' wages and pensions, which caused one of the King's grooms to write dolefully to a friend:

> I see you hear divers reports of our Court, where indeed more discontent than faction appears, the times being so penuri-

ous and hopeless that every man complains. No wages, pensions, or debts are paid, and hardly is money found to furnish the King's diet and his officers.[30]

Because funds were so scarce during the autumn of 1625, Charles and his ministers appealed to the King's wealthier subjects for loans. Any loans extended would be guaranteed by privy seals and redeemed within a period of eighteen months. How much revenue was raised in this manner is impossible to determine. Very little it would appear, for only a few individuals believed that the loans would ever be repaid, and most kept their purses tightly closed. The government also attempted to raise money by means of a stricter enforcement of the recusancy laws, a course recommended by the Council in mid-October.[31] That the crown would be able to raise sufficient funds by such means was never a serious possibility, and overtures were therefore made to the States-General for a loan of £300,000. Although London offered to provide the crown jewels as collateral, The Hague refused to advance the money. In 1625 an attempt was also made to collect the old tax known as ship-money from the ports and coastal towns, but it was no more successful.[32]

If Buckingham's foreign policy was to continue, the government had no option but to summon another parliament. Informed observers must have questioned, however, whether a new parliament would be any more generous than the previous one. The Cadiz expedition had destroyed the duke's image as a successful manager of the country's naval and military forces; and his policy of quartering returning troops on householders in the southern and eastern counties had prompted scores of complaints to the Council.[33] Thus there was little likelihood that a new parliament would provide additional funds for him to squander. When the members did meet again in 1626, they quickly showed that they favoured an activist foreign policy but would not grant a farthing so long as he remained at the helm. In effect Charles was asked by his second parliament to choose between the duke and his present foreign policy. That he refused to part with either was disastrous for the royal cause. Tension between crown and parliament became greater than ever, no funds were appropriated for the war, and royal bankruptcy could no longer be dismissed as a remote possibility.

The government was obviously weighing the chances of another session as early as November, when sheriffs for the coming year were selected. Because sheriffs were expected to remain in their counties and were thus ineligible to sit in parliament during their year of service, the chief opposition leaders were chosen for this dubious distinction. Sir Robert Phelips was selected for Somerset and Sir Edward Coke for Buckinghamshire, while Sir Francis Seymour was exiled to the countryside of Wiltshire and Sir Thomas Wentworth to his native Yorkshire.[34] This clumsy attempt to silence the opposition backfired. That several leading members were barred from attending on such flagrantly partisan grounds created a grave new source of discord. Furthermore the void caused by their absence was easily filled by members even more critical of royal policy. In 1626 the Commons were led by such fiery spirits as Sir Dudley Digges, John Pym, and William Noy. Of greater importance than any of these was a young squire from Cornwall, Sir John Eliot, who had previously been a client of Buckingham's. Although he had supported the favourite throughout the previous parliament, hoping for a reconciliation between Charles and the lower House, the near-failure of that assembly had destroyed Eliot's faith in Buckingham's political talents; and the fiasco at Cadiz had caused him to break with the favourite altogether. Eliot had some faith in the King's goodness and assumed that if his evil genius, the duke, could only be removed, concord would automatically prevail between crown and parliament. From 1626 onward, Eliot's overriding aim was thus to accomplish Buckingham's overthrow. But despite his oratorical gifts, Eliot was not a totally effective parliamentary leader, for he had little regard for the finer points of the law; and whenever he criticised the favourite for misguiding or misinforming the King, he was thrown off balance by Charles's admission that such was not the case.[35]

During the parliamentary elections, which were held in January, Sir Richard experienced some difficulty finding a seat for the first time in his career. Buckingham planned for him to sit for Hythe, but the town corporation held a snap election as soon as its writ arrived on 7 January, in order to guarantee its representation by Sir Peter Hayman. The popular Hayman had sat for the borough in 1621 and 1624 but not in 1625, when the duke nominated two other candidates. As the only way of ensuring Hayman's election, the corporation acted immediately and returned him along with

Basil Dixwell. When Buckingham's letter of instruction arrived on 11 January, the municipal officials were distressed to learn that they had effectively rejected a candidate of Weston's stature. Sir John Hippisley, the Lieutenant of Dover Castle, reported to the duke that they were all 'sorrowful men' for what they had done. In their own letter of apology they described Sir Richard as 'an honourable and worthy person whom we in due respect to your Grace would willingly have accepted of.' Eventually a seat was found for him at Bodmin, in Cornwall, where he was returned on 21 January.[36]

Despite Buckingham's efforts to influence the elections, there was again a notable lack of government leadership in the Commons. Of the six Councillors returned, Sir Robert Naunton and Sir John Suckling took almost no part in the proceedings, just as they had done a year earlier. Sir Dudley Carleton spoke on a number of occasions but was made a baron in May, which led to his removal to the upper House, where his services were less needed. Secretary Coke was ill for more than six weeks, during the critical period between 21 April and 6 June, and was naturally unable to appear. Thus the burdens of leadership fell mainly to two Councillors, Weston and Sir Humphrey May, who neither liked one another nor worked particularly well together.[37] The session began on a surprisingly cordial note, however, and the royal nominee for Speaker, Sir Heneage Finch, was elected without opposition. Had the government not made a succession of tactical errors during subsequent weeks, it might well have achieved a measure of success, despite the mounting feeling against the duke.

In 1626 Sir Richard played a more active role than at any time since 1621. He was named to a number of important committees, including a standing one appointed on 9 February to keep a watchful eye over the privileges of the House. He was also one of ten men directed to consider the provisions of a bill for the regulation of woollen products exported to the continent; but his chief duty was to help with the passage of an adequate, and speedy, grant of supply. It is therefore surprising that he lacked precise instructions from Charles, at least at first. Because of this he was woefully prepared when debate on the question of supply began on 23 February. Although Sir John Savile proposed that the Councillors in the House be allowed to speak first, neither Weston nor any of his associates came forward to take the floor. Amazed by their reluctance to debate such an important issue, one indignant gentleman commented that there was little reason 'to call up men who have no mind to speak.' After several members had expressed their views, Sir Richard rose and made a few cautious statements. He believed the King would not object to a discussion of past expenditure but warned that royal permission should be obtained first.[38]

More than two weeks elapsed before Weston was able to satisfy the members' desire for information as to the crown's financial needs. Meanwhile the House had seized the initiative in order to elicit information for itself. Early in March it summoned the advisory body known as the Council of War to appear and disclose how funds granted by James I's last parliament had been spent, and particularly if they had been used for purposes stated in the subsidy act of 1624. Because the members of the council maintained that they, as officials responsible only to the King, could not be required to answer questions addressed to them by the House, a constitutional confrontation lasting several days occurred. Precedents were cited, and a special committee was appointed to investigate. Ultimately the council presented a statement signed by all the members excepting one, which was purposefully evasive, however. If the Commons continued to insist, they would submit a summary of their chief expenditures during the past year, but the King had expressly forbidden them 'to render account of the details, and being sworn to the King's service they must obey their oath and bond of secrecy.'[39]

The action taken by the House prompted Charles to intervene. He called in the Attorney-General, only to be informed that parliament's questions were in order because of the unusually explicit provisions of the subsidy act of 1624. When he finally saw he had no recourse, Charles sent a message on 10 March by Sir Richard, who explained at length why the crown desired an immediate grant of supply. Unless funds were soon forthcoming there would be no way to prevent a mutiny on the part of England's poorly paid mariners. In addition, regiments stationed along the southern coast would have to be disbanded, and the fleet of ships now being readied for action would be unable to sail forth and confront the enemy. After referring to disorders that were beginning to threaten in Ireland, the Chancellor declared that 'his Majesty commandeth me to tell you, that he desired to know without further delaying of time, what supply you will give him for these present occasions, that he may accordingly frame his course and counsel.'[40]

When debate resumed on Monday morning a leading opposition spokesman, William Noy, was appointed to the chair, after which Sir Richard delivered a written account of Charles's message concerning supply. The court faction then made a concerted attempt to rally support for a new subsidy bill. At the conclusion of a lengthy debate the members voted to declare their love of the King and their intention of supporting him 'in such a way, and in so ample a measure, as they may make him safe at home, and feared abroad.'[41] A definite grant was postponed, however, and the subsidy bill remained a burning issue for the duration of the session.

Even before the question of supply was tabled, the members were giving much of their attention to grievances. They were especially annoyed by the case of Sir Edward Coke, who was unable to take his seat as knight of the shire for Norfolk because of his prior appointment as sheriff of Buckinghamshire. In a message delivered by Sir Richard, the King insisted that Coke be formally excluded and a new election held in the county. But the House refused to comply, because it was unwilling to forget that 'parliament men' had been selected as a way of silencing the opposition. Thus while Sir Edward was not allowed to take his seat, orders were deliberately withheld for a new election in Norfolk.[42] The members were also concerned with religious issues, particularly after Sir Benjamin Rudyerd criticised the behaviour of the rural clergy and denounced the activities of two Leicestershire ministers who managed an ale-house on week nights. A more serious matter was the case of Richard Montague, the Arminian cleric whose theological views had been attacked in the parliament of 1625. Montague had recently published a new book, *An Appeal to Caesar*, in which he maintained that the Roman Catholic Church was not in fundamental error but only superficially corrupted. Such an opinion was bound to be attacked by members with Puritan leanings, who equated the Pope with Anti-Christ, and Montague was assailed throughout the session of 1626. Charles eventually intervened to halt the clamour by appointing Montague and another Arminian minister, Roger Mainwaring, to serve as royal chaplains. That the King so openly sided with the high-church party did nothing to improve his relationship with parliament.[43]

Ordinarily the Lords could be expected to support the King in most altercations with the Commons, but in 1626 Charles's policies were resented by a majority of the peerage. The upper House was especially angry that several of its own number had been ordered not to attend owing to strained relations with the duke. The Earl of Bristol, England's Ambassador to Madrid in 1623, had been critical of Buckingham's dealings with Olivares and was in a position to undermine, if not totally destroy, his already sagging reputation. Although Bristol had given no indication of being disloyal, he was directed to remain at his house in Dorset, under involuntary restraint. Another member excluded by Charles and his favourite was Weston's old friend Bishop Williams, the former Lord Keeper. When he failed to receive his customary writ of summons, the bishop complained long and hard of the duke's prejudice against him. As a result a writ was eventually delivered to him; but rather than incur even greater displeasure, he remained disconsolately at his episcopal palace in the midlands.[44]

Early in March the crown took disciplinary action against one of the greatest peers in all of England, the Earl of Arundel. A long-time friend of Sir Richard's, Arundel was committed to the Tower for marrying his son and heir, Lord Maltravers, to Lady Elizabeth Stuart, a sister of the fourth Duke of Lennox. Charles had intended for Lord Maltravers to marry a daughter of the Earl of Argyll, as a way of strengthening his own connection with the head of the great Campbell clan of south-western Scotland. When the King's plan was wrecked, Arundel found himself imprisoned, which caused feeling in the Lords to run strongly against the crown. The upper House voted an immediate declaration of support on his behalf, and until he recovered his freedom it would abstain from all business.[45]

Because of the breach developing between Charles and the Lords, the lower House was emboldened to make an open attack on Buckingham. As early as 10 February Eliot had made criticisms of the duke's harmful influence and suggested an investigation of his administration of the navy. But such a move had been premature, for, in the words of one observer, Eliot's speech 'was not applauded.'[46] However, by the second week of March feeling against the government had risen to dangerous levels, and Buckingham was being denounced from all sides. He was blamed for the disastrous expedition to Cadiz and for the dangerous situation now developing with France. Furthermore he had engrossed too many offices unto himself. Not only was he Lord Admiral and Master of the Horse but he was also First Gentleman of the Bedchamber, Steward of the Manor of Hampton Court, Constable of Windsor and Dover Castles, Lord Warden of the Cinque Ports, and Justice in Eyre of all the Forests and Chases south of the River Trent. Through his control of the patronage, he was able to dominate numerous other offices as well. The most powerful man in England aside from the King himself, he was the natural focus for any overt attack on the government.

Bitter denunciations of Buckingham's influence were aired in the Commons on 11 March. Dr Samuel Turner, member for Shaftesbury and a follower of the Earl of Pembroke, declared that he was responsible for the kingdom's chief grievances. Turner submitted six questions concerning the duke's activities that he wished the House to consider, most of which related to his private conduct rather than to his official actions. Turner's remarks were followed by a speech from Clement Coke, son of the excluded sheriff of Buckinghamshire, who also contended that the duke was the chief cause of the public misfortunes. Coke argued that it would be better 'to die by an enemy than to [continue to] suffer at home.' Under such prompting, at once encouraged by remarks from Sir Dudley Digges, the House voted in favour of an investigation of the duke's overweening influence.[47]

Two days later Sir Richard relayed a message expressing Charles's great displeasure and insisting that Coke's seditious words be censured by the House. The King was also incensed by Turner's questions, which had been offered 'without any ground or knowledge in himself, or any offer of particular proof to the House.' It was Weston's contention that the King could not

> . . . suffer an inquiry of the meanest of his servants, much less against one so near him; and [he] wonders at the foolish impudence of any man, that can think he should be drawn to offer such a sacrifice, much unworthy the greatness of a King, and master of such a servant. He desireth the justice of the House against the delinquents; and he be not constrained to use his regal power and authority to right himself against these two persons.[48]

Believing the King's anger would soon subside, the Councillors in the House sought to arrange a compromise. Sir Humphrey May made the inevitable suggestion that a committee be appointed to look into Coke's inflammatory statements. Eventually a grand committee devised the formula that Coke's words, while not technically seditious, had been displeasing to the House and open to sinister construction.[49] As for the other delinquent, Dr Turner sought to justify himself by making an appeal to history. He had submitted his questions in the traditional manner of offering 'accusations against great persons by voice of fame,' the same method used in the fifteenth century on the occasion of the Duke of Suffolk's impeachment. Turner's arguments caused the members to suspend debate on the matter until the parliament rolls could be searched for appropriate precedents.[50]

The King's need for a substantial grant of supply caused him to adopt a more conciliatory stance and make overtures to both Houses. When debate began again on 23 March the principal Secretary gave a detailed account of the crown's most pressing obligations. For the Cadiz expedition more than £313,000 had already been issued, and numerous payments were yet to be made. To equip the fleet of ships now being assembled, almost £175,000 was needed. An additional £104,000 was required for regiments to safeguard the English and Irish coasts, which was in addition to the monthly subsidies promised to Christian IV, Count Mansfeld, and the States-General. At the end of his report the Secretary estimated that the crown would need £1,067,221 13s. 2d. for the naval and military operations of the coming year.[51]

Weston also attempted on 23 March to win support for the King. He announced that Charles was 'much comforted with [our] care to examine his estate' and had graciously extended permission for the Commons to investigate past expenditure. After several other courtiers had urged the House to proceed with a subsidy bill, the members gave renewed consideration to the question of tunnage and poundage. Within a few more days, moreover, they agreed in principle on the nature of their grant to the King. If no complications arose, he would receive three subsidies and fifteenths, which were to be fully paid at the Receipt by 1 April 1627.[52]

Once this action had been taken, the House resumed its attack on the duke. In a vehement speech Eliot charged that past failures 'were undertaken, if not planned and made, by that great lord the

Duke of Buckingham.' Because of the government's obvious ineptitude, the Cornishman maintained that the subsidy bill should not be passed on third reading until grievances had been presented and the King's reply announced. He then cited precedents from earlier reigns to show that parliament could withhold funds until previous grants had been accounted for and objectionable ministers removed. Swayed by Eliot's oratory, the members voted overwhelmingly to uphold his position.[53]

After 27 March the issue between crown and parliament was clearly drawn. In the words of the greatest student of the period:

> . . . it would be a mistake to suppose that either party in the quarrel was grasping at power for its own sake. Charles believed that he was defending a wise and energetic minister against factious opposition. The Commons believed that they were hindering a rash and self-seeking favourite from doing more injury than he had done already. If neither was completely in the right, the view taken by the Commons was far nearer to the truth than the view taken by Charles.[54]

During the remainder of the session, which continued until mid-June, Charles and the members were involved in a bitter tug of war. The King was attempting to secure final passage of the subsidy bill so that he could dissolve parliament and bring a halt to the proceedings against his favourite. The Commons were determined to withhold their grant of supply in order to forestall a dissolution and continue their attack, which they regarded primarily as a personal assault, despite its obvious constitutional implications. If they succeeded in impeaching Buckingham against the King's will, ministerial responsibility to parliament would be established in all but name, even though the most radical members of the Commons were unable to conceive of such a revolution at this juncture.

In this unhappy contest Sir Richard played a conspicuous, if not particularly influential, role. He delivered numerous messages between Charles and the members and laboured unceasingly to promote a reconciliation. He also sought to defend the duke and encourage action on the subsidy bill, which caused him to appear a stauncher royalist than ever. On 28 March Weston reported that Charles desired the members to attend him at nine o'clock the following morning: until then all proceedings in the House were to cease.[55]

When they assembled the next day, the members were addressed by the Lord Keeper, who denounced the attack on Buckingham as an affront to the present King and a slur on the memory of his father. Coventry also maintained that the supply tentatively granted by the House was not only insufficient but also unworthy of Charles, since it had been offered with conditions attached. If the members failed to give a better accounting of themselves within three days, they must be prepared to see the session ended. After these belligerent remarks from the Lord Keeper, Charles made a short and tactless speech of his own. Believing he could bully the members into submission, he reminded them that 'Parliaments are altogether in my power for their calling, sitting, and dissolution; therefore, as I find the fruits of them good or evil, they are to continue, or not to be.'[56]

At a subsequent conference between the Lords and Commons, Buckingham attempted to defend himself and his governmental record. He had conscientiously attended to the affairs of state since his return from Madrid in 1623, but his efforts had continually been thwarted by misfortune or the failings of others. Such a superficial argument convinced no one. Under Eliot's leadership the House decided on 1 April to draft a remonstrance stating its position to the King. The remonstrance declared the members' right to attack the duke or any other minister and justified the Commons' refusal to take stern measures against Dr Turner and Clement Coke. Once the remonstrance had been drafted and accepted by the House, a committee of thirty members was appointed to deliver it, with either Sir Richard or Secretary Coke designated to read it to Charles, 'as shall be agreed upon between them.'[57]

Late in the day of 5 April Weston announced the results of the audience that had just occurred at Whitehall. The remonstrance had been presented by Secretary Coke, to whom Charles angrily replied that he would not give an answer at present. Instead he sent an order for the House to adjourn at once for its Easter recess. The Commons were annoyed by the command to adjourn, which was put to a vote and passed by a majority of only 30, out of 270 members present.[58]

When the members reassembled after an eight-day recess on

13 April, Sir Richard declared that the King hoped they would 'lay aside all petty occasions of business, maintain his Majesty's cause at home, and [keep him] feared abroad.' The Commons had promised to grant ample supply, but the subsidies and fifteenths proposed so far were altogether inadequate.[59] Despite this speech from the Chancellor, the members were not at all disposed to pass the subsidy bill for a third time. Weston was therefore directed to deliver similar messages from Charles on the 18th and 20th of April. By the beginning of May his continuous appeals were beginning to produce results. After another plea on 2 May, the members agreed to consider whether a fourth subsidy should be granted. When the draft bill was finally presented by Serjeant Hitcham on 5 May, Sir Richard delivered yet another message from the King, who had instructed him to announce that a refusal to proceed with the bill would be viewed as 'not only a neglect of his affairs, but also of his person.'[60]

While the Chancellor was doing his best to prompt the House to action, the attack on Buckingham was proceeding under the joint management of Eliot and Digges. During April and May evidence was collected to substantiate as many charges as possible against him. Since Charles refused to recognise his incompetence, the duke had to be accused of base and even criminal offences. By 2 May the members had agreed on the general strategy they would follow. In an important speech that day Digges bewailed the decline of English naval power, the consequent loss of English honour, and the near-collapse of England's trade with the continent. The duke's stewardship was the fundamental cause of all these misfortunes, and the House readily agreed to the passage of a resolution affirming his culpability. Not only had Buckingham mismanaged the King's revenues but he had engrossed too many offices unto himself, accepted bribes in return for honours and distinctions, and allowed unworthy men to buy positions in both church and state. In his desire to amass riches for himself, he had oppressed the merchants of the East India Company, extorting a payment of £10,000 from them. His guidance of England's foreign policy had led to a series of tragic blunders, for he had failed to safeguard the Narrow Seas, supported Cardinal Richelieu's efforts to subdue the Huguenots of La Rochelle, and authorised the seizure of French merchantmen, which had prompted counter-measures from Louis XIII. On a more personal level, it was alleged that Buckingham and his mother had administered potions to James I in March 1625, thereby hastening the late King's death.[61]

While doubtless sympathetic to some of the charges, Weston was outspoken in the favourite's defence. To the accusation that his remedies contributed to James's death, Weston declared that Buckingham 'cares not whether in this any man speaks for him or not, but relies wholly upon his own innocency.' When it was charged that he often blocked access to the King, Sir Richard replied that 'out of my experience in parliament, I [can] believe such an unreasonable proposition as this might be made, but I cannot believe such an assembly will agree to it.'[62] Inevitably, perhaps, some of Weston's remarks were in fact a defence of his own service in an administration dominated by the duke. When Walter Long charged that Buckingham prevented able men from counselling the King and that the latter therefore received only 'the poisonous information of those vipers that do us so much harm,' the Chancellor took umbrage and lashed out against his too bitter colleague. Weston's injured feelings were soon soothed by Eliot, who maintained that Mr Long had not meant 'to lay any aspersions upon the King's good officers' and that 'there are many, and that honourable gentleman for one, that have done good offices.' Eliot was adamant, however, that the good offices done by some did not excuse the faults of others.[63]

Sir Richard made an especially important speech on 9 May, when the members were clamouring for Buckingham's imprisonment until the time of his trial. He first cautioned the House to consider the ramifications of 'what we are about to do: and what is proper for us.' He then insisted that the duke's previous reputation, although now besmirched, had been honestly gained and well deserved. But despite his closing appeal for the members not to lay 'a certain infamy upon him for an uncertain crime,' the House decided by a vote of 225 to 106 that Buckingham should be committed to the Tower until his trial began. Yet the leaders could clearly see the danger of proceeding any further without a gesture of support from the Lords, and a committee was thereupon appointed to request a conference with the upper chamber.[64]

Despite the defence of him made by Eliot, Weston's efforts on the duke's behalf led to a significant decline in the popularity he had always enjoyed with his fellow members. When he attempted to speak on the preamble to the subsidy bill on 19 May, it was nearly two hours before he was recognised and granted permission to address the House. Even after starting his speech, he was given scant attention, for the Commons had now heard his views dozens of times. Five days later he tried for three hours to assemble the committee appointed to draft the bill's preamble before giving up in frustration and despair.[65]

Typically, the government made a series of tactical errors during the attack on Buckingham. Although Charles gave formal permission on 29 April for the House to proceed with its inquiry, he staged a diversionary movement by pressing charges against the Earl of Bristol, who had defied the royal injuction not to take his seat in the upper House. That Charles was concentrating on the proceedings against Bristol seemed to prove that he would never give serious consideration to the charges against his favourite, which annoyed the peers and drove them into the arms of the lower House. Then Charles outraged the feelings of the latter by ordering the arrest of Eliot and Digges, the ringleaders of the impeachment. Digges was released after only five days in the Tower; but on 17 May Sir Richard sought to justify the continued detention of Eliot by declaring that he had been committed for 'high crimes done to his Majesty out of this House.' Stony silence was the reaction to this statement, which was so obviously false, after which a furious debate occurred on such parliamentary privileges as freedom from arrest and freedom of speech. Dismayed by the violent reaction he had provoked, Charles backed down and ordered the release of Eliot, who re-entered the House in triumph on 20 May.[66]

Although the Commons were angry about the numerous offices already held by the duke, Charles proceeded to confer yet another position on him: late in May he used the influence of the crown to have him elected Chancellor of Cambridge University. Intended as a mark of continued confidence in his favourite, this move could only be interpreted as a deliberate slap at parliament, as a clear sign of the King's contempt for its views. For several days the members were in an uproar, and Weston's services as a peacemaker were enlisted by both Charles and the lower House. Throughout this latest crisis the oft-used messenger sought to heal the troubled spirits and prevent hasty, ill-considered action. He was particularly apprehensive that the members might demand an explanation of the Vice-Chancellor of Cambridge, 'which is especially forbidden to us by the King.'[67]

By this juncture relations between Charles and the Commons had deteriorated beyond all hope of recovery. Weston continued to press for passage of the subsidy bill, but his efforts were all for naught. By 15 June the King realised there was no reason to prolong the session. He therefore ordered a halt to the proceedings and, as justification, issued a proclamation asserting his unquestioned right to prorogue, adjourn, and dissolve parliament. The proclamation also contended that he was 'not bound to give an account to any but God only, whose immediate Lieutenant and Vice-gerent he is in his realms and dominions by the Divine Providence committed to his charge and government.' After tracing the major occurrences since his accession, Charles threw all responsibility for the dissolution on the factious behaviour of the lower House.[68]

The parliament of 1626 marked an important turning point in Weston's career. Until this juncture he had been a popular and respected member whose views had always been received with interest. During Charles's second parliament, however, his unswerving support of Buckingham, and his constant pleas for action on the subsidy bill, cost him a serious loss of prestige. During earlier parliaments he had been able to function in a dual capacity, as a loyal servant of both the House and the crown, but now he seemed to speak exclusively for the latter. His inherent conservatism was more divergent than ever from the majority view, and he was beginning to share in the growing unpopularity of the royalist cause. After 1626 he never sat in the Commons again. In April 1628 he was elevated to the peerage as Baron Weston of Neyland and took a seat in the upper chamber. During the following year he was the object of a bitter attack organised by the same men who led the campaign against Buckingham.

Whether Weston should have joined forces with the duke's enemies in 1626 is a question that defies a simple answer. Doubtless he longed for the restoration of stable government, and doubtless he entertained thoughts that the kingdom would benefit from the favourite's overthrow. But he was as reluctant as the Lord Keeper to make 'desperate sallies against growing mischiefs, which he knew well he had no power to hinder.' An observant man, Sir Richard had a good understanding of the King's psychology and recognised how dependent he was on Buckingham. For Weston to have supported an attack on him would not have guaranteed his overthrow but might well have terminated his own political career. For, as Lord Clarendon later observed, Charles 'admitted very few into any degree of trust who had ever discovered themselves to be enemies to the duke, or against whom he had ever manifested a notable prejudice.'[69] Thus it seemed better strategy in 1626 to side with the favourite, to secure his confidence and gratitude, and to work for a change of policy from within. That Weston failed to modify Buckingham's policy before the latter's assassination two years later does not prove that his tactics were altogether mistaken. But those tactics did insure that once the duke's presence was removed, the Chancellor would be in a position to put his own, more realistic ideas into effect.

7 Desperate Measures and Ill Effects

By the summer of 1626 serious dissatisfaction had developed among various sections in England. Members of the political nation were disturbed that Charles's second parliament had been a greater failure than his first, while the peerage was uniformly critical of the imprisonment of Lords Arundel and Bristol on seemingly frivolous charges. Individuals with Puritan leanings were annoyed by the King's support of Richard Montague and other Arminian clerics, suspecting that the established church as they had known it might now be transformed. Of equal significance was the mounting irritation in the southern and western counties over the forced billeting of troops to carry out the duke's designs. Few Englishmen doubted that anyone but Buckingham was responsible for the poor management of the country's foreign policy. The attack on Cadiz had been a dismal failure, and nothing had been done to advance the interests of the Elector Palatine and the continental Protestants. During the past six months relations with France had deteriorated steadily, and a new war was on the verge of breaking out at any time.

In the troubled period now facing England, Sir Richard did not play a particularly prominent role. He was concerned primarily with administrative matters and proposals for increasing the King's revenues. Yet he occasionally departed from Exchequer routine to take part in political affairs, if not an especially influential one. He was still seeking to advance the prospects of Wentworth, from whom he received urgent entreaties. Wentworth was involved in a bitter struggle with his chief Yorkshire rival, Sir John Savile, a supporter of the duke's. But there was little Weston could do to help, and the office of *custos rotulorum* was transferred from Wentworth to Savile.[1]

Weston also received periodic appeals from Middlesex, who felt he might yet recover his former position. Sir Richard was moved by feelings of compassion for the fallen earl, to whom he was willing to render some assistance. But he was in a difficult position owing to the suspicious attitudes of Marlborough, who was alarmed by reports that Middlesex's influence might be reviving. By giving support to his former chief, Weston would doubtless incur the present Treasurer's wrath, if not his avowed hatred. Because Middlesex had made no move to support the duke's enemies during the spring of 1626, steps were eventually taken to pardon him. This was not welcomed by Buckingham, who answered rudely when the Chancellor made an appeal on his behalf, 'Harry him, old fool, let him take the course.' Although Sir Richard has often been criticised for trimming his sails to the prevailing wind, he showed real courage by attempting to help his former chief in 1626–7. After he himself became Treasurer in 1628, he continued to assist Middlesex, of whose unpopularity he was well aware.[2]

Weston was also involved with weightier matters during the aftermath of the parliament of 1626. In October he was one of nine men appointed to investigate the affairs of the Great Wardrobe, a department in dire need of regulation. Unhappily the commissioners were unable to enforce any meaningful economies; during the period preceding Michaelmas 1627, the Wardrobe's expenditures exceeded its annual assignment of £7500 by almost 35%.[3] Another commission to which Weston belonged was made responsible for supervising the affairs of the navy and submitting reports to the Council. To facilitate their work, the King empowered the commissioners to summon witnesses and hear testimony under oath. They could also subpoena records and take whatever steps they thought 'fit for our better service in the premises.'[4]

During this stage of his career Weston was beginning to develop an interest in the management of Irish affairs. He had first become concerned with Irish problems shortly before the death of James I: in September 1624 he helped with the drafting of an important agreement between the crown and the City which paved the way for the establishment of a new plantation in Ulster.[5] During the spring of 1626 Sir Richard was one of six men to whom a bitter quarrel between Lords Falkland and Loftus, the Lord Deputy and the Irish Chancellor respectively, was referred for settlement. He also became involved, much against his will, in the bitter wrangles between Lord Falkland and his estranged wife, a recent convert to Catholicism, for whom the King insisted that adequate financial arrangements be made. Somewhat later he was one of four referees appointed to decide a case pending between the Earls of Desmond and Ormonde. In January 1627 Weston was named to a select committee for Ireland that also included Buckingham, Marlborough, the Earls of Pembroke and Dorset, and three others. These eight men were directed 'to enter into a serious consideration of the present condition of our affairs in that kingdom' and to advise Charles 'of the best and easiest way to give supplies to the present pressing necessities and defects, and reformation of the several disorders and misgovernments.'[6]

The situation in England was even bleaker than the one in Ireland, for funds were continually demanded of the government that were almost impossible to find. During the summer of 1626 the Earl of Leicester pressed insistently for £600 that should have been paid him a year earlier. Apparently Leicester's pleas to Marlborough and Weston fell on deaf ears, for in February 1627 he appealed directly to the Council.[7] Another persistent suitor was Aquila Wykes, keeper of the Gatehouse prison, who had spent £2000 of his own money since December 1625 for the 'lodging, diet, apparel, and other necessaries of prisoners.' Because of irregular issues from the Exchequer, Wykes had had to borrow funds at great cost to himself. Weston and his chief had been directed to grant him a measure of relief but had failed to act. A poor man with only a small stipend from the crown, he would be ruined if the Council refused to intervene and see that funds from the Receipt were soon forthcoming.[8] In June 1627 an appeal was lodged by Viscount Wimbledon on behalf of the still unpaid men who had participated in the Cadiz expedition of 1625. The King had ordered the release of £10,000 to them, but not a penny of that amount had been issued. In addition the duke had instructed Sir Richard to pay Wimbledon's own salary for two years' service, which the Chancellor had not yet done. The Council gave order for the immediate payment of £3344 to Wimbledon, but it overlooked his plea for the arrears owing to his men.[9]

The demands of the common sailor continued to be ignored by a government dominated by the landed classes. As a consequence a mutiny took place at Harwich during the following October, the men simply abandoning their ships and departing for London to agitate for their back pay. On 21 October Secretary Coke addressed a frantic letter to Sir Edward Nicholas, secretary to the naval commissioners, who was implored to convince Marlborough and Weston to release funds sufficient to allay the discontent. Apparently he was able to do so, for there was no repetition of the events of a year earlier, when the Council had ordered the Lord Mayor of London to post a guard around the house of the naval Treasurer 'for the repressing the insolencies of mariners.'[10]

In desperation the government resorted to a variety of devices to raise additional revenue. In June 1626 Charles ordered the stricter enforcement of the recusancy laws: convicted recusants were either to pay the monthy fine of £20 established by parliament or be assessed an annual rental on two-thirds of their properties. Whatever funds were raised in this way were to be reserved for projects associated with the duke's foreign policy.[11] With the Council's blessing Charles continued to collect the customs duties, although parliamentary authorisation was of course lacking. On 25 July 1626 Marlborough and Weston were commanded to imprison any merchants who attempted to evade payment of the duties.[12]

The customs farmers were continuing to make large profits, so the government did not hesitate to solicit loans from them. In October 1626 an important agreement was negotiated with Sir Paul Bayning, a wealthy merchant and customs farmer who eight years previously had lent £2500 to James I at 10% interest. According to the calculations of Sir Richard Sutton, one of the imprest auditors, Bayning was owed not only the entire £2500 he had advanced in April 1618 but also £1677 1s. 8d. by way of interest. After a round of talks with the Treasurer and the Chancellor, he agreed to extend his loan of £2500, to which all the accrued interest should be added, the resulting sum being subject to 7% interest. He also promised to lend an additional £7500 to the crown at 8%.[13]

The government made brief use of the old assessment known as ship-money, which was reserved for the support of the navy. In June 1626 directions were sent to the corporations of nearly thirty coastal towns, instructing them to furnish a fleet of 36 ships to combat 'the vast ambition and malice' of the King of Spain. Precise specifications concerning the vessels to be supplied were established by the government. For example, Falmouth and nearby towns in Cornwall were directed to provide a ship of at least 200 tons, armed with twelve or more long-range guns and manned by a crew of 124 sailors or more.[14] In most localities the ship-money assessments were actively resisted, with local officials complaining that the burden was far too heavy. The citizens of Bristol, who had been instructed to furnish two ships, protested that they were being taxed at the rate of eight subsidies, while the inhabitants of the adjacent rural areas, who had been directed to contribute one-third of the total charge, were being taxed at less than a single subsidy. Moreover, the residents of such nearby cities as Worcester, Shrewsbury, and Cardiff had not been asked to contribute anything at all. The scolding letters sent out by the Council accomplished nothing, and the government had no choice but to allow the coastal areas to compound by paying only one-fourth of the estimated cost of the ships demanded of them.[15]

Late in the summer of 1626 Charles decided to sell certain royal lands falling within the surveys of the Exchequer and the Duchy of Lancaster; on 15 September he instructed Marlborough, Weston, Buckingham, and seven others to supervise the sales and insure that all funds raised were actually paid into the Receipt.[16] The commissioners wasted hardly a moment getting down to business. Within four months almost £9700 had been paid into the Exchequer from the sales of royal manors and woods. Considerably more lands were alienated during the three-month period ending on 30 April 1627, by which time more than £30,000 had been paid in. By the last day of July an additional £9400 had been raised, and during the last five months of 1627 the King's patrimony was reduced by a further £34,000. All in all, slightly more than £84,000 was raised in this manner during 1626 and 1627.[17]

Among those who took advantage of the bustling land market was Sir Richard himself. On 18 June 1626 he arranged to buy the manor of Holdenby in Northamptonshire, for which he agreed to deposit £666 13s. 4d. and to pay the King an annual rental of £178 15s. 10d. In addition he consented to the cancellation of the £500 annuity granted him in 1620 by James I, which still had fourteen years to run.[18] Only nine months later he contracted to buy a tract of more than 400 acres at Putney and Mortlake in Surrey, for which he obligated himself to pay £1598 10s. outright, along with a yearly rental of £14 12s. On this tract a few miles southwest of Westminster he planned to construct a new country home.[19]

The programme of land sales continued throughout the spring of 1628 in order to provide funds for the payment of the King's servants. First choice in the selection of lands was of necessity allowed to the corporation of London, which was on the verge of completing a complex and exceptionally far-reaching transaction with the crown. During the summer of 1626 Charles's ministers had approached the City with a request for a loan of £100,000. Because the crown had failed to honour its commitments of May 1625, its request for another loan was speedily rejected. In an individual capacity several aldermen agreed to advance £20,000 of their own on the security of the petty customs; but the corporation as a whole demanded more substantial security for any additional funds advanced, which led the King to offer his plate and jewels as collateral. Even this offer was rejected, since the City was bent on receiving land and made repeated proposals to that effect during the winter of 1626–7.[20]

Serious negotiations between the government and the City began in April 1627 and continued for the next eight months. Early in December an agreement was reached by Marlborough and Weston for the former and the City negotiating team led by Sir Thomas Middleton and Sir Martin Lumley. It was calculated that the crown owed a total of £229,897 2s. in principal and interest on the loans of 1617 and 1625. As repayment of this amount, and in return for a further advance of £120,000 from the City, the crown agreed to surrender lands worth £12,496 6s. 6d. annually, a sum reached on the assumption that the true value of royal lands and woods was twenty-eight times their annual return. The King's agreement with the City was probably the most complicated financial transaction of the early seventeenth century. Often misinterpreted by historians, it was not, in the opinion of one authority, 'a loan on the mortgage of royal lands, but a gigantic repayment operation.' Lands were conveyed to the municipal corporation as a way of repaying three separate loans, the last just now being concluded.[21]

In 1626 and 1627 Charles made several pleas to the States-General for a loan of £300,000. Although the Dutch government was unwilling to lend, wealthy burghers in Amsterdam agreed to advance £58,400 on the security of jewels pledged by Buckingham and the King. Charles also turned to the officials of the East

India Company, who, after much bitter wrangling, made £30,000 available.[22] French and Flemish merchants resident in London were almost commanded to make loans to the government. Thirty-eight merchants of foreign origin were assessed sums ranging between £200 and £2000, which they were asked to lend for periods of eighteen months. In this way more than £27,000 was raised for the Exchequer. Early in 1627 the servants of the crown, particularly the officers of the law courts, the Exchequer, and the Court of Wards, were asked to open their purses. Among those who agreed to advance substantial sums was Sir Richard, who provided £4000.[23]

Charles also appealed to his wealthier subjects throughout the kingdom. In 1626 and 1627 he attempted to raise £300,000, or the equivalent of five parliamentary subsidies, through privy seal loans, which were nothing more than a disguised form of political pressure. Charles was convinced that his second parliament should have granted him five subsidies, so he now demanded that the taxpayers contribute what they would have been assessed had the subsidy bill of 1626 been enacted. Unfortunately for the King, the forced loans now required of the upper classes provoked serious criticism, both within and without his government. Sir Randall Crew, Chief Justice of the King's Bench, openly questioned the legality of the course, for which he was suspended from his post, at Buckingham's instigation. This naturally aroused fears about Charles's willingness to respect the independence of the courts.[24] Men of Puritan views were almost universally critical of the loans, but those inclined towards the high-church party, whose very existence was dependent on continued backing from the King, advanced theological arguments in support of them. This led Charles to respond with a further extension of his favour to the Arminians, which heightened the doubts and resentments of those in the Puritan faction.

A pragmatic man with a deep understanding of politics, Weston had ambivalent feelings about the course now necessitated by the duke's foreign policy. Although he must have hoped the loans would raise a substantial revenue, he probably questioned the political wisdom of imposing them. Yet he knew that the Tudor monarchs had relied on such methods of raising revenue, and he himself had advanced £4000 – if he was willing to make a substantial sacrifice for the public good, why should other men not be asked to contribute a fraction as much? Certainly public opinion regarded him as a supporter of the loans, which helps to explain why he was coming to be identified as a thoroughgoing royalist, if not an absolutist.

Although Weston would not speak out against the loans, his friend Wentworth showed no hesitation about doing so. Despite his inherent conservatism and his desire to enter the King's service, Wentworth was vigorous against the exactions, which he absolutely refused to pay. Consequently he soon found himself committed to the Marshalsea. After several months in prison, he was transferred to a private house in Kent, where he was detained until early in December.[25]

By midsummer 1627 opposition to the loans had become so widespread that the King ordered the arrest of scores of men whose refusal to pay was endangering the success of the venture. Among those taken into custody were Sir John Eliot, Sir Walter Earle, Sir Thomas Darnell, Sir John Heveningham, Sir John Corbett, Sir Edmund Hampden, and Sir Harbottle Grimston.[26] Within a few months several of these men had secured writs of habeas corpus, which enabled them to challenge the King's right to hold them in custody without bringing charges against them. Their case, the famous Five Knights' Case, was heard before the King's Bench in November. The defendants maintained that they were guilty of no crime by refusing the demand for loans. As free-born Englishmen they could not be held under indefinite restraint, since they were entitled to a fair and speedy trial on any charges brought against them. The judges, over whom the subservient Sir Nicholas Hyde now presided, disagreed and ruled that habeas corpus was a writ not of right but of grace and, as such, could be withheld by the government. By extension the King was able to arrest and detain any subject without showing cause.[27] Charles was delighted by this decision, which seemed to vindicate his policies of the past year. Once the judges had declared their support of him, he threw open the doors of the prisons and released the defaulters. By the end of December most of them had returned to private life, in sufficient time, it should be noted, to stand in the parliamentary elections that were to be held in a few weeks' time.

Despite the widespread criticism of the loans of 1626–7, the government raised large amounts by means of them. By mid-

November 1627 more than £243,750 had been collected, of which the greater part was deposited in the Exchequer.[28] Largely because of the substantial revenue derived from the loans, Professor Dietz concluded that the financial policies of the government at this juncture were extraordinarily successful. In his words, 'great sums were garnered in during the year ended at Michaelmas, 1627. The total receipts of about £850,000 besides £154,000 assigned by tallies, represent a prodigious effort, equal to almost two years' income before the beginning of the war.'[29] Professor Dietz's appraisal must be rejected as an overly sanguine one, however. Much of the revenue collected came from land sales or from exactions so unpopular that it would be dangerous to resort to them again in the near future. The heavy reliance on borrowing caused a sharp decline in the government's credit position. Methods of deficit finance increased steadily, and by March 1628 the revenues for the current year had been completely anticipated. Although Weston and other ministers laboured as diligently as could be expected, considering that it was for a cause in which they did not believe,[30] they failed to finance the war out of current income, which was clearly the King's objective. The debts of the crown were now approaching £1,500,000, and the spectre of royal bankruptcy loomed ever closer.

The fundamental cause of the government's financial problems was of course the duke's adventurous foreign policy. Huge sums were required for the naval and military expeditions he was continually planning. By these campaigns he hoped to recapture the popularity he and Charles had lost since the latter's accession in 1625. During the spring of 1627 the favourite organised an amphibious operation in support of the Huguenots of La Rochelle, who were still being besieged by Louis XIII and Cardinal Richelieu. If the islands guarding the city's harbour could be captured, the siege might be broken, which would inevitably redound to the duke's credit. Because he had been castigated for not leading the Cadiz expedition of 1625, he now decided to go in person. Late in June he set sail from Portsmouth with a force of not more than 7000 men, which was much too small to accomplish the intended objective. The expedition was poorly organised and equipped, since Buckingham had no gift for administrative detail. Although he showed conspicuous gallantry during the campaign itself, his lack of any real military experience was an almost insurmountable handicap. The Isle of Ré was captured and briefly held, but nothing was accomplished for the starving Protestants of the city. Like the earlier assault on Cadiz, the expedition to La Rochelle was little more than a wasteful extravaganza.

To the Treasurer and the Chancellor fell the duty of financing this latest campaign. How the favourite's endless demands were to be satisfied must have caused Sir Richard and his chief chronic worry. Buckingham's hold on the King's affections was as strong as ever, and to oppose his designs openly was inconceivable. Yet funds were so scarce that the two officials decided to test the waters by ignoring his demands on the Exchequer. As soon as it was apparent that they were refusing to supply any additional money, strong objections were voiced by Secretary Conway and Sir Edward Nicholas, the secretary to the naval commissioners who doubled as the duke's private secretary. Even the King took note of the affair, and towards the end of July he sent a number of peremptory letters to Marlborough and Weston.[31]

On 1 August Charles sent a particularly angry missive to the two officials from Woodstock. Not only were they accused of shirking their responsibilities but they were threatened with the treatment accorded earlier ministers who had displeased their sovereigns.

> . . . if Buckingham should not now be supplied, not in show, but substantially, having so bravely, and I thank God, successfully, begun his expedition, it were an irrecoverable shame to me, and all this nation; and those that either hinder, or, according to their several places, further not this action, as much as they may, deserve to make their end at Tyburn, or some such place: but I hope better things of you.[32]

Thoroughly intimidated, Marlborough and Weston did what they could to scrape up funds for the duke. As a consequence Charles was soon able to inform his favourite that, 'I have made ready a supply of victuals, munitions, four hundred men for recruits and £14,000 ready money, to be brought by [Sir William] Beecher, who, by the grace of God, shall set sail within these eight days.'[33]

Funds continued to be impossibly scarce, however; and on 21 September the Auditor of the Receipt wrote to inform the duke 'how far his Majesty's revenue of all kinds is now exhausted. We are upon the third year's anticipation beforehand; land, much sold of the principal, credit lost; and at the utmost shift with the Commonwealth.' Disaffection was rife in all parts of the countryside and local officials were doing nothing to advance the cause. Because the situation at home was deteriorating so rapidly, Pye hoped the favourite would soon be in a position to return.[34]

In a subsequent letter early in October, Secretary Conway maintained that the government was doing its best to overcome all obstacles and that Sir Richard particularly was co-operating in every way he could: 'I may humbly say without wrong to any man, that the Chancellor of the Exchequer is not a spark but a flame of fire in any thing that concerns you, and therefore you have cause to give him thanks.'[35] Whether Weston had any faith in the mission at this juncture or was more concerned to safeguard his position for the future is an impossible question to answer. Probably the latter consideration predominated in his thinking, for if he could convince the duke of his loyalty and diligence, he might yet acquire the much longed-for white staff.

If this was in fact the Chancellor's strategy, he ceased to be quite so co-operative when Buckingham returned from the Isle of Ré in November. Probably hoping that the expedition's failure would convince him of the futility of the war, Sir Richard must have been bitterly disappointed to learn of his plan to lead another campaign the following year. The royal finances were in a shambles, and the sums demanded by the duke were nowhere to be found. The debts of the army and the Ordnance office were calculated at more than £251,000; and almost £4000 a week was required simply to feed and shelter the troops returning from France. An estimated £506,000 was needed for the payment of recent expenditures and for the preliminary expenses of Buckingham's new campaign. Was there any chance that sums of this magnitude could be found, even by officials as diligent as Sir Richard and his chief had been during the past year? The Chancellor therefore proposed a change of policy as cautiously as he knew how. England should leave the war and issue a declaration of neutrality.

Weston's suggestions were dismissed out of hand. Charles and his favourite were determined to continue the present policy, even if a new parliament had to be summoned. The members were bound to present a list of grievances, but the duke and his master were convinced that the two Houses could be persuaded to pass a subsidy bill. To determine the best avenue of approach, they sought the advice of Sir Robert Cotton, a well-known antiquarian with ties to the main opposition leaders. He agreed that funds needed during the present crisis should be obtained from parliament, and not through the extra-legal methods of the past year. Yet he was critical of the poor showing of English arms during recent campaigns and maintained that 'the waste of public treasure in fruitless expeditions' was the chief obstacle to a sizeable parliamentary grant. Cotton also discussed the mounting opposition to the government's religious policy, for which he attempted to throw all blame on the duke. Although he insisted on the need 'to remove or compose the differences between the King and subject in their mutual demands,' he was unable to propose how this might be accomplished. He could only suggest that Buckingham pose as a firm adherent of parliament as a way of rebuilding public trust.[37]

Two weeks later writs for the elections were sent out, and it was announced that parliament would open on 17 March. In the campaign that ensued, the crown made a determined effort to secure the return of friendly candidates. Secretary Conway intervened at Yarmouth, Newport, Andover, Evesham, Newton, and Southampton, while Sir Edward Nicholas made use of his influence at Cambridge and Dover and also in the county elections at Chelmsford, Essex. The duke himself remained in London, 'negotiating and working with all his might, so that the members returned for the Lower House might be on his side.'[38] Unhappily the government's efforts were considerably less successful than had been hoped. When Buckingham urged the electors of Sandwich to return his two nominees, they refused to comply and rejected as prominent a figure as Sir Edwin Sandys. Once the session began there were bitter criticisms of the crown's attempt to 'pack' parliament, and fifteen different returns were challenged.[39]

In the parliament of 1628 the opposition forces were led by such experienced politicians as Sir Edward Coke, Sir John Eliot, Sir Thomas Wentworth, Sir Walter Earle, Sir William Strode, Sir Harbottle Grimston, and John Pym. Many of these men had refused to pay the forced loans of 1626–7 and had been imprisoned without trial for periods of six months or longer. Now they were determined to place restrictions on royal power so a repetition of their unhappy experience would be impossible. To counteract this band of resolute men, only three Councillors were present in the lower House: Sir Humphrey May, Sir John Coke, and Sir Thomas Edmondes. Moreover, the most important of these, Secretary Coke, was absent after 17 May, when he was sent to Portsmouth to supervise the preparations for Buckingham's new expedition to La Rochelle.[40]

Weston's son Jerome was returned for Gatton, Surrey, but he himself did not choose to stand. The King had already decided to confer a peerage on him, so a seat would soon be at his disposal in the House of Lords. Why he was selected for this honour at this particular juncture can only be surmised. Perhaps Charles was anxious to strengthen the court party in the upper House, as Professor Stone has suggested;[41] but more likely it was because of the mounting popular feelings against him. During the parliament of 1626 he had refused to join in the attack on Buckingham and called too insistently for the passage of a subsidy bill. Since that time he had tacitly supported the forced loans and had not spoken out against the imprisonment of those who refused to pay, which did nothing to improve his standing in the popular mind.[42] With his long record of parliamentary service, he was much too valuable a minister to be cast summarily aside. It therefore seemed wiser to transfer him from the lower to the upper chamber, which he entered for the first time on 14 April, only a day after being created Baron Weston of Neyland.[43]

Once he became a member of the parliament of 1628, Lord Weston assumed his customarily active role. Unusually regular in his attendance, he did not miss a single meeting between 14 April and the prorogation on 26 June. As a senior member of the government, he was named on 17 April to a committee for the sale of royal lands, and during the course of May he was appointed to six additional committees. During June he was nominated to five more, including one for the drafting of a bill 'to enlarge the liberty of hearing the Word of God preached.'[44] On almost all the committees to which he was named his old friend and supporter, Bishop Williams, also served. In the work of the upper chamber the two men co-operated on every measure of consequence, their most important concern being to amend and weaken the Petition of Right.

Shortly after the opening of parliament the opposition leaders decided not to reopen the impeachment proceedings of 1626 against the duke. Charles was as firmly committed to the favourite as ever and would doubtless respond to a renewed attack with a dissolution or an adjournment. Thus another strategy would have to be followed if the objective of limiting royal power was to be accomplished. On 22 March Wentworth proposed that the most pressing criticisms of the government be stated in a petition or bill to be presented to the King. Not until Charles promised to alter his policies in accordance with its provisions would a subsidy bill be enacted, despite the objections of Secretary Coke, who insisted on a grant of supply before the presentation of grievances.[45] Work on the petition proceeded rapidly, and a preliminary version was ready by 3 April, when the members voted in favour of four resolutions stating their most deeply felt grievances: (1) that no free man should be imprisoned without cause shown; (2) that the writ of habeas corpus 'ought to be granted to every man that is committed, or detained in prison . . . he praying the same'; (3) that once the writ of habeas corpus was delivered, the prisoner requesting it should be allowed bail and set at liberty until his trial began; and (4) that every Englishman 'hath a full and absolute property in his goods and estate' and could not be taxed without 'common assent by Act of Parliament.'[46] To these original provisions of the Petition of Right were added complaints against martial law in peacetime and the compulsory billeting of royal troops in private households.

The Petition of Right was Buckingham's only enduring contribution to the development of English government. Had his ambitious foreign policy not necessitated the forced loans of 1626–7 and the arbitrary imprisonment of those who refused to pay them – had the expeditions to Cadiz and the Isle of Ré not led to the billeting of government forces in private households and the declaration of martial law in peaceful localities, which seemed so alien to the English tradition – there is no reason to believe that this limitation of royal power would have occurred at the time it did. Thus Charles was now reaping the bitter harvest of his allowing too much power to his favourite.

Debate on the Petition and the liberties of the subject continued on 4 April, when Secretary Coke and Sir Benjamin Rudyerd criticised the course adopted by the House and called for the immediate passage of a subsidy bill. On the urging of John Pym, who had not given up all hope of co-operation between crown and parliament, the members agreed to give some consideration to the King's financial needs. In view of the grave 'national peril,' they consented to a grant of five subsidies, or approximately £300,000. Yet the vote of 4 April was one of principle only, a promise of further action once the King accepted the Petition. Three days later Secretary Coke reported that Charles was pleased by the offer of five subsidies but considered such a grant totally inadequate for his needs.[47]

On 7 April the principal Secretary delivered a message requesting a conference between the Lords and the Commons on 'some ancient fundamental liberties of the kingdom.'[48] Held in the Star Chamber, this consultation was the first of many between the two Houses during the spring of 1628, since the lower chamber was anxious to secure the Lords' support for the Petition. Once Weston took his seat in the upper House, he was an active participant in these conferences, attending at least nine between 23 April and 31 May.[49] During the course of these sessions he considered not only the general phrasing but also the specific provisions of the Petition. It has long been known that he proposed modifications that were designed to convert it into an almost meaningless document. At one point he suggested the framing of all clauses in such a way that 'neither the King may lose of his prerogative nor the subjects their rights,' which must have caused the delegates from the Commons to look at one another in dismay.[50]

In his attempt to weaken the impending restrictions on royal power, the Chancellor was supported by Bishop Williams and several other members of the upper chamber, including his old friend the Earl of Arundel. Indeed a formula he wished to attach to the Petition was devised, apparently, by Lord Arundel. According to this, the Petition should be introduced by the sentence: 'We humbly present this petition to your Majesty, not only with a care of preserving our liberties, but with due regard to leave entire that sovereign power wherewith your Majesty is entrusted for the protection, safety, and happiness of your people.'[51]

The formula proposed by the Chancellor was welcomed by Charles, who pressed for its inclusion in the Petition. But the lower House refused to have any part of it, sensing the danger of conceding the King's 'sovereign power' in a document designed to safeguard the liberties of the subject. Because of the unyielding position taken by the Commons, the upper chamber eventually agreed to withdraw the formula. The Lords then accepted the Petition as framed by the lower House with only one slight change of wording. That the document was not introduced in the manner desired by Weston amounted to a 'significant defeat for the absolute prerogative, and a victory for the rights of the subject.'[52]

While work on the Petition was proceeding, Charles was not altogether idle. On 28 April he summoned both Houses to attend him in the Great Hall at Westminster, where parliament was implored by Lord Keeper Coventry 'to rely on his royal word and promise for the preservation of their rights and the liberties of his subjects, and to lose no further time in granting him the supplies they had voted.'[53] Although the Commons had made it perfectly clear that a final vote on the matter of supply would be deferred until the Petition had been accepted, Charles continued to assume that the members would give way and not require his assent to the document. On 7 May he sent another message urging them to trust him to redress their grievances after funds had been appropriated. When they refused once again, he threatened to proclaim an immediate dissolution, which prompted the House to return to the subsidy bill as soon as agreement on the Petition was reached with the upper chamber on 26 May.[54] But the members would not give way altogether and refused to pass the bill on third reading until the Petition had been accepted. Eventually Charles conceded that he had no choice but to allow its presentation. On 2 June he appeared in the upper chamber, where the two Houses had gathered expectantly. As parliament's spokesman Speaker Finch read aloud the main clauses of the Petition and requested the King's acceptance of them. Charles's answer was deliberately evasive.

> The King willeth, that right be done according to the laws and customs of the realm; and that the statutes be put in due execution, that his subjects may have no cause to complain of any wrongs or oppressions, contrary to their just rights and liberties, to the preservation whereof, in conscience, as well obliged, as of his own prerogative.[55]

On the following day the disappointed members debated the King's answer, which they rejected as unsatisfactory. They then resumed their discussion of grievances by attacking the sermons of Dr Mainwaring, whose views had attracted much unfavourable comment during earlier weeks of the session. Still believing he could have his own way, Charles pressed the House on 4 June for action on the subsidy bill and threatened to proclaim an adjournment on 10 June.[56] The members were just as stubborn, however, and refused to take any further steps until the Petition received a satisfactory answer.

In an attempt to break the deadlock, the Lords requested a conference with the lower House on 6 June. It was then decided that Charles should be asked to make another reply to the document, and a delegation was dispatched to Whitehall with the request. The King contended that his answer of 2 June had been completely satisfactory; but to please parliament and allay any misunderstanding, he would return to the upper chamber that afternoon and give a second reply. At four o'clock on Friday afternoon the 6th of June, Charles reappeared on the dais in the House of Lords. After the clerk of the crown had read the Petition aloud, the clerk of parliament announced his answer: '*Soit droit fait comme il est desiré,*' words that gave the Petition the force of a common law decision and made it a matter of record. Charles then gave a brief explanation of what he felt he had conceded.

> This I am sure is full; yet no more than I ganted you in my first answer; for the meaning of that was to confirm all your liberties; knowing, according to your own protestations, that you neither mean nor can hurt my prerogative. And I assure you that my maxim is, That the people's liberties strengthen the King's prerogative, and that the King's prerogative is to defend the people's liberties.
>
> You see how ready I have shown myself to satisfy your demands, so that I have done my part; wherefore, if the parliament have not a happy conclusion, the sin is yours; I am free of it.[57]

As soon as Charles completed his remarks, the members gave a 'great and joyful applause.' Whereupon he arose and swept out of the House without even a backward glance.

Once debate in the Commons resumed, the members fulfilled their end of the bargain by completing the subsidy bill, which they passed on third reading and sent up to the Lords on 12 June.[58] Yet they also continued to discuss grievances and demand additional concessions from the crown, which can only be viewed as an error on their part. Rather than exploiting their victory over the King, they should have made a gesture of co-operation and reconciliation, which was as much in their interest as it was to his. But the radical element in the Commons was in the saddle; and even before the King gave his second answer to the Petition, Eliot had taken steps to reopen the attack on Buckingham. In a long and violent speech on 3 June, he heaped ridicule on the duke's management of England's foreign policy and sought to convince his listeners that all the country's ills were a result of his dominance. After several days of intense debate, the House decided to state its complaints in a remonstrance of nine articles, the last of which was a general charge 'that the excessive power of the Duke of Buckingham, and the abuse of that power, are the chief cause of these evils and dangers, to the King and Kingdom.' A committee of nine members, including Selden, Wentworth, and Pym, was appointed to frame the remonstrance, which was formally presented to Charles on 17 June.[59]

Secretly informed of the likely contents of the remonstrance, the King had conferred with Sir Richard, whose influence had risen to new heights, to Buckingham's chagrin. In the manner of a modern speech-writer, Weston had assisted his master in drafting an address that systematically refuted the criticisms expressed in the remonstrance. Charles denied the charge that innovations in religion tending towards popery had been made by his government and denounced the antagonism towards the recent spread of Arminianism. Neither had an attempt been made to silence Puritan preachers, and it was totally wrong to maintain that 'new monasteries, nunneries, and other superstitious houses are erected, and replenished in Dublin, and other great towns of that our kingdom.' Probably at Sir Richard's urging, Charles declared that there was good historical precedent for the forced loans of 1626–7 and the compulsory billeting of royal troops in private households, which could not therefore be considered innovations in government. Yet he evaded the thorny question of whether it was legal for him to hold his subjects in custody without bringing charges against them.[60]

To the accusation that he was becoming known as 'a breacher of parliaments,' the King responded that this was owing to the irresponsible actions of his critics in the lower House. Concerning the firing of Chief Justice Crew and the threat to the independence of the courts, he maintained that, 'We would have all men know, that we will have no one officer, or other so to live under us, as that he may presume to disserve us at his pleasure.' The criticisms of Buckingham were dismissed out of hand, the King lauding his favourite and denying that excessive power had been entrusted to him. Yet Charles did make one attempt to appease the members. Towards the end of his speech he assured parliament that he would never sponsor innovations in government: 'We declare to our loving people, that we heartily love the old ways of the kingdom, whenever we find moderation and duty in them.' But he destroyed any good effects these words might have had by concluding his address on a defiant note. He had hardly expected to receive such a remonstrance after accepting the Petition of Right and would give it no more consideration than it deserved.[61]

In the dissension now developing between Charles and the members, the upper chamber was left far behind. Only a few peers were willing to support the position taken by the Commons, which was bound to provoke a dissolution or adjournment. Feeling in the Lords was considerably more restrained, for most of the peers were anxious to reach an accommodation with the King, if not completely on his terms. Among those who urged the need for a reconciliation was Lord Weston, who was as active as ever in the work of his House. On 16 June he was appointed to a select committee to draft two messages to Charles, one advising him to halt the collection of impositions and other taxes not granted by parliament, and the other petitioning for the suppression of tracts written by Dr Mainwaring, who had been censured by the Commons two days earlier. Couched in typically deferential language, these two messages were received far more politely by the King than the remonstrance of the lower House.[62]

By 23 June Charles had concluded that nothing was to be gained by prolonging the session. He therefore announced that parliament would be prorogued three days later, which prompted the radicals in the Commons to begin the preparation of a second remonstrance. For more than a week the members had been considering the merits of a tunnage and poundage bill, which Eliot and his colleagues still contended was necessary to legalise the government's continued collection of the main customs duties. If the prorogation took place on 26 June, they would have too little time to pass the bill. To dissuade Charles from his course, they decided to frame a remonstrance stating that no customs duties could be collected without parliament's specific approval. For the King to collect the duties without parliamentary authorisation was not only a serious violation of the fundamental liberties of the kingdom but also in direct conflict with his recent answer to the Petition of Right.[63]

If Charles should be criticised for deciding on the prorogation prematurely, without staying abreast of the work of the Commons, he must be allowed some sympathy in regard to this newest step taken by the lower House. To the King it must have seemed that the radicals had lost all sense of proportion and were bent on declaring all his courses illegal. It was a great misfortune that by the third week of June, tempers were so short and nerves so frayed that a harmonious relationship between Charles and the lower House was no longer possible. When he learned of the new remonstrance, the King decided to prorogue parliament at once, in order to forestall its presentation. On 26 June, several hours before the prorogation was scheduled to occur, he appeared in the upper House to end the session in person. Addressing his remarks primarily to the Commons, who had been hastily summoned to appear, he revealed his knowledge of the impending remonstrance 'to take away the profit of my tunnage and poundage, one of the chiefest maintenances of my Crown.' He then declared that

> This is so prejudicial unto me, that I am forced to end this session some hours before I meant, being not willing to receive any more remonstrances, to which I must give a harsh answer. And since I see that even the House of Commons begins already to make false construction of what I granted in your Petition, lest it be worse interpreted in the country, I will now make a declaration concerning the true intent thereof.

Because neither House had intended for the Petition to encroach on the prerogative, Charles maintained it was only possible to hold 'that I have granted no new, but only confirmed the ancient liberties of my subjects.'[64]

Once he concluded his address, the Lord Keeper announced the royal assent to the subsidy bill and several other measures. Coventry then ended the session, the most explosive one to date, by announcing that parliament stood prorogued until 20 October 1628.[65]

8 Treasurer at Last

Because of his attempt to weaken the Petition of Right, Weston acquired significantly more influence with the King during the closing weeks of the parliament of 1628. Not only did he help with the drafting of Charles's address of 17 June, but he also began to tender advice in regard to the most important naval and military matters. It was largely because of suggestions made by him that Secretary Coke was sent to the Channel coast in mid-May to take charge of the preparations for the coming naval campaign, which Buckingham had shown scant interest in supervising.[1] On the very day parliament was prorogued, the King's new chief adviser was appointed to a special Council committee to consider 'the most important points of our service' and to direct whatever measures necessary for 'the succouring of Rochelle . . . and the providing of our magazines and stores.' This committee, which Chamberlain might have characterised as 'the foreign junta,' consisted not only of Weston and Buckingham but also of the Earls of Marlborough, Manchester, Pembroke, Montgomery, and Dorset, Lord Carleton, and the two principal Secretaries.[2]

By the end of June serious misgivings about the costliness of the duke's foreign policy were being voiced by various members of the government. An official report indicated that £1,300,000 would be required for the coming campaign and the repayment of obligations incurred during recent years. The five subsidies voted to procure the King's acceptance of the Petition of Right might yield as much as £300,000, but that would still leave a million pounds to be raised by extraordinary means.[3] Another round of land sales would have to be initiated, and another desperate appeal would undoubtedly be addressed to high officials and members of the peerage. Weston and several others, including Montgomery, Marlborough, and a handful of the bishops, volunteered to lend the Crown £200 each. Pembroke, Salisbury, Dorset, and the wealthier nobles advanced £500 each, while Buckingham, the only real supporter of the current foreign policy, provided £2000. Altogether 28 individuals agreed to make loans totalling £9600, which was only a fraction of what the crown needed at this juncture.[4]

That the crown so obviously lacked sufficient funds for another expedition to La Rochelle prompted Charles to engage in some serious thinking. Despite his fondness for the duke, he could no longer afford to follow the courses charted by him. Saner policies must be adopted or the monarchy would be severely weakened, if not crippled. Since the royal finances were the crux of the problem, it seemed high time to remove the well-meaning but incompetent Marlborough, who was generally considered 'too dull and phlegmatic for his employment,'[5] and appoint a more vigorous man in his place. And who could that be except the Chancellor, who had been waiting patiently in the wings since 1624?

The prospect of Weston as Treasurer, which would doubtless be interpreted as a lessening of his own influence with the King, caused Buckingham to become a stronger partisan of Marlborough than ever. The current Treasurer must be treated honourably and not be made to suffer as a result of the proposed change. Because the Earl of Worcester had recently died, it was possible for Charles to transfer the Earl of Manchester to the post of Lord Privy Seal, which freed the Lord Presidency of the Council, a purely ceremonial office, for Marlborough. Charles made the move considerably more palatable for him by a free gift of £12,000.[6] In this manner the way was cleared for Weston's elevation: on 15 July he was at last named to the dual position of Lord Treasurer of England and Treasurer of the Exchequer.[7]

Although Weston had hoped to receive the white staff since the time of Middlesex's impeachment, he was aware that the office was not what it once had been. Clarendon thought that 'the extreme visible poverty of the Exchequer sheltered that province from the envy it had frequently created.' In 1628 there were three living ex-Treasurers, whose terms had averaged less than three years each. When one of them (Middlesex) was asked the best way to avoid an early death, he replied, 'Get to be Lord Treasurer, for none died in that office.'[8] However, the Treasurership was unquestionably one of the greatest offices of state, comparable in importance to the Lord Chancellorship and the two principal Secretaryships. Although the Treasurer's official salary was only £365 a year, he received many times that amount through fees and gratuities. According to Professor Aylmer, 'a Lord Treasurer who was watchful of his own interests but not technically corrupt was said to be able to make £7000 a year.'[9]

Weston enjoyed considerably more than the £7000 a year that was accepted as tolerable by his contemporaries. In 1634 his political enemies, led by Archbishop Laud, made a determined attempt to destroy his influence with the King by accusing him of bribery and corruption. Charles responded by ordering him to draw up a list of all his gains during the past six years. Weston admitted to total receipts of £44,000, or slightly less than £7500 annually, but the many items he neglected to report would have increased the total significantly. A fair estimate of his official income would be in the neighbourhood of £11,000 or £12,000 yearly.[10]

Although Weston had every intention of making as much money as he safely could, he was determined to reduce the level of government spending and limit the King's bounty to others. Such a programme would inevitably provoke resistance; and in order to secure as much political support as possible, he sent a memorial to Buckingham on 13 August. Weston was hopeful of working with the duke: if only he could secure his endorsement for a retrenchment campaign, the most powerful obstacles would be neutralised. Once payments to courtiers and royal officials had been reduced, the new Treasurer pledged to do everything possible to raise funds for Buckingham's purposes for he was firmly resolved 'to furnish your Grace with those moneys which are behind.'[11]

In a subsequent letter to the duke, Weston insisted that he had issued all the funds that could be spared for the fleet at the moment and asked that no additional demands be made on the Exchequer until provision had been made for the King's personal needs during the coming year. He longed to hear of the successful completion of the expedition to La Rochelle, for he wished to see the duke at home again, where he would be able to supervise the King's affairs with the diligence they required. In effect the Treasurer was stating the outlines of his programme in as subtle a way as he could. 'As little as possible for the war, nothing for pensions for the present, and an early peace sums up Weston's policy at this moment.'[12]

Buckingham was incensed. A year earlier Weston had been lax in finding funds for him while he was away with the fleet, and now he was stressing the need for strict government economy. Inevitably the duke began looking for excuses to remove him from office – as Lord Clarendon says, 'many who were privy to the duke's most secret purposes did believe that if he had outlived that voyage in which he was engaged he would have removed him, and made another Treasurer.'[13] Fortunately for Weston's career, Buckingham was assassinated on 23 August, while awaiting his departure for La Rochelle.

Once the duke's powerful presence was removed, several months of uncertainty elapsed before the political situation was stabilised and the identity of the King's new chief minister became known. At first it appeared that Charles was going to take the government into his own hands and personally direct the affairs of state. But within a few weeks his resolve weakened, for he had neither the patience nor the self-discipline required of a personal ruler. Public opinion then concluded that Bishop Laud would probably inherit the duke's mantle. Laud's political and religious views were in total agreement with his master's; there was a strong bond of sympathy between the two men; and the bishop had been able to offer Charles a measure of spiritual comfort during the aftermath of Buckingham's assassination. Certainly Laud did not hinder his chances by the forceful way he took charge of his new diocese of London and prepared to assume leadership of the entire church.[14] The competition was eventually won by the Treasurer, however. Because of his unrivalled knowledge of domestic and foreign policy, his willingness to undertake the arduous tasks of day-to-day administration, and his unquestioned skill in the arts of political manœuvre, he emerged as the leading figure in the government by the end of November. During the last week of the month Secretary Conway informed a friend that Weston 'hath now the helm in his hand'; and within a few more days the Venetian Ambassador was reporting to his government that the Treasurer 'now rules everything . . . no one dares oppose him, since everyone has to pass through his hands.'[15]

Although another witness later maintained that Weston 'steered the main course of all the great businesses of the kingdom,'[16] it would be wrong to exaggerate the extent of his power between November 1628 and his death in March 1635. He never enjoyed that total domination of public affairs which Buckingham had exercised, and his influence over the patronage was much less complete. He did wield a preponderant influence over naval, Irish, financial, and foreign policy, but religion and the church were always under Laud's firm control. The Treasurer had also to contend with the rapidly growing influence of the Queen over her husband. After the duke's assassination the relationship between Charles and Henrietta Maria ripened into genuine love, and there was no chance for a new chief minister to dominate the King in quite the same way Buckingham had done. The Queen assumed the role of principal confidante to her husband and frequently offered political advice, not all of which he ignored. Thus there were now three main factions at court: one led by the Treasurer, another dominated by Laud, and a third centring around the person of the Queen.

Only three days after Buckingham died, a special commission was appointed to supervise the arraignment and trial of John Felton, the duke's assassin. This commission consisted of the Treasurer, Secretary Coke, and the Earls of Pembroke and Dorset.[17] Shortly afterwards the King decided to put Buckingham's most important office, the Admiralty, into commission, so that its revenues could be used to pay the duke's debts, some £70,000. Late in December 1628 Weston, Pembroke, Dorset, Lindsey, Dorchester, and Secretary Coke formed a board to perform the duties formerly discharged by the Lord Admiral. Within a few years they became known as the Lords of the Admiralty.[18]

The Treasurer also had a hand in the arrangements for the duke's funeral. Charles originally intended for the duke's obsequies in the Abbey to be a great state occasion costing at least £40,000. Weston objected to the King's plan on two counts. In view of the popular feelings against Buckingham, there was a distinct possibility that the ceremony would be interrupted by the rabble; and second, it seemed more sensible to spend the money on a monument that would be a permanent memorial. Charles reluctantly conceded the wisdom of the Treasurer's views and cancelled the plan for a state funeral. After supper on 17 September the duke's body was quietly interred in the Abbey, without pomp or fanfare.[19] Once Buckingham was safely buried, Weston began to advance objections to the monument he himself had proposed on the grounds that there was not yet a monument to the memory of James I. Until Charles saw fit to honour his own father, it would be undutiful to delegate funds for one who had been only a subject and a friend. Besides, the Exchequer was completely barren, and needless extravagances should be postponed until a more fitting season.[20]

Meanwhile the Treasurer was helping to supervise the arraignment and trial of Felton, the half-crazed lieutenant who had stabbed and killed the duke at Portsmouth. On 13 September Felton was brought by water to the Tower of London, where he was detained until his case was heard before the King's Bench on 27 November. After openly confessing to his crime, he was sentenced to die at Tyburn on the following day.[21] Closely associated with Felton's trial were the proceedings against one Thomas Savage of Nottingham, who claimed that Felton had tried to bribe him to murder the duke. Savage was commanded to appear at Westminster on 17 September, when he was examined by Weston, Lord Keeper Coventry, the Earl of Dorset, and several others, who ruled that he was both a knave and a fool and should be turned over to the Star Chamber for punishment. Late in October that court directed that he should be publicly whipped, pilloried, and branded on the cheeks with the letters 'F' and 'A', that his ears should be cut off and he should be imprisoned in Bridewell for the rest of his life.[22] This merciless treatment of a poor man guilty only of some foolish boasting is what provoked numerous angry complaints in the next session of parliament concerning the increasingly harsh sentences handed down by the Star Chamber.

Weston was confronted with matters of much greater urgency during the autumn of 1628, and particularly with questions relating to the conduct and possible reorientation of foreign policy. As the King's most important adviser he was in regular communication not only with foreign ambassadors in London but with England's representatives abroad. Yet it was not until late November, by which time he had consolidated his position, that his views concerning the necessity of peace began to prevail. Consequently he was not strong enough to block the sailing of a fleet already mobilised for the new expedition to La Rochelle. This fleet put to sea on 7 September but was unable to prevent the surrender of the city on 18 October.[23]

During the next few months substantial progress towards peace was made, especially after the appointment of a new Secretary of State, Viscount Dorchester, whose views were indentical with

Weston's. The first tentative discussions between London and Paris took place, apparently, during Christmastime 1628, and early the next month a series of draft articles were received from Cardinal Richelieu. Almost immediately thereafter the Treasurer's son Jerome was sent over to explain those few points on which there was still disagreement. The Anglo-French negotiations proceeded smoothly, and by the first week of April a treaty acceptable to both sides had been completed. It was signed on the fourteenth of that month at Susa, a border fortress in the south of France where Richelieu and the French army were then encamped. The Treaty of Susa amounted to little more than a return to the *status quo ante bellum*: no frontiers had to be rectified or colonies returned, for none had been captured by either side. It was expressly stated, however, that Charles I and Louis XIII would be free to handle all their own subjects as they saw fit. This was an attempt to keep England from providing any further assistance to the French Huguenots and to prevent France from rendering support of any kind to the English recusants.[24]

Meanwhile steps were being taken towards the opening of peace negotiations with Spain. In January 1629 Endymion Porter, an important courtier sent to the continent by Buckingham, who had considered Weston's call for an Anglo-Spanish settlement just before he died, was back in London with the news that Olivares and Philip IV were also anxious for the resumption of peaceful relations. Yet it was not until the arrival of the painter-diplomat Peter Paul Rubens towards the end of May that substantial progress towards a treaty with Spain was made.

The negotiations with France and Spain were dictated by the continuing problem of the King's finances. Royal bankruptcy seemed so imminent during the aftermath of Buckingham's asassination that Weston ordered a stay of all pensions and annuities, which provoked a storm of protest.[25] This was only one part of his campaign for a substantial reduction of governmental expediture. Before the end of July 1628 he had secured Charles's approval for an order forbidding the lodging of courtiers at Whitehall or Denmark House during periods the court was away from London on progress.[26] In September a special commission was directed to the Treasurer, his successor at the Exchequer, Lord Newburgh, the two principal Secretaries, and five lesser officials to consider the whole problem of the royal revenues. Charles was particularly anxious to secure a greater return from the crown lands, either through more effective management or by disposing of them for as high a price as possible.[27]

Fortunately for Weston and his royal master, the extraordinary payments of the crown began to decline after the autumn of 1628, since no more naval and military expeditions were launched after that time. These payments had reached a high of £585,448 in that year, but by 1631 they had fallen to £217,356. Within two more years they had declined to £114,663, and by 1635, the year of the Treasurer's death, they had fallen to only £66,441.[28] This in itself led to an immediate strengthening of the King's financial position and made it possible for him to avoid the declaration of bankruptcy that seemed so imminent in 1628. It might well be argued that the reduction of the crown's extraordinary expenditure, which resulted from the government's withdrawal from the continental war, was Weston's greatest achievement as Lord Treasurer.

While Weston was trying to reorder the royal finances, a serious outbreak of merchant agitation occurred in London. During the autumn of 1628 Richard Chambers, John Rolle, Maurice Abbot, various members of the East India Company, and perhaps as many as 475 other merchants proclaimed that the continued collection of tunnage and poundage was contrary to the Petition of Right and refused to pay the sums demanded of them.[29] The most defiant stance of all was taken by Chambers, who was primarily concerned to protest a new duty of 2s. 2d. on each hundredweight of currants, which had been imposed in mid-August and could easily be interpreted as contrary to both the letter and the spirit of the Petition. Chambers and several other defaulting merchants were summoned to appear before the Council at Hampton Court on 28 September. According to the Attorney-General, who was to prosecute him in the Star Chamber at a later time, the fiery merchant did on that occasion

> . . . in an insolent manner . . . utter these undutiful, seditious, and false words, 'That the merchants are in no part of the world so screwed and wrung as in England: That [even] in Turkey they have more encouragement.' By these words, he the said Richard Chambers . . . did endeavour to alienate the good affection of his Majesty's subjects from his Majesty.[30]

Chambers later denied having spoken these words with any evil intent to the crown, intending them only 'to introduce his just complaint against the wrongs and injuries he had sustained by the inferior officers.' Regardless of how he meant his remarks, to say such things before the Council was foolhardy, and he soon found himself clapped in the Marshalsea, where he was detained until 23 October. Shortly after his release a large consignment of his goods was seized as security for the payment of all duties owed on them. In an effort to recover his property, he applied for a writ of replevin from Chancery, only to find it voided by an injunction of the Barons of the Exchequer to the sheriffs of London. Chambers then attempted to arrange a compromise by offering to advance security for the payment of all duties owed by him in return for the immediate release of his goods. At first the Barons rejected his proposal, but eventually they permitted the release of any remaining merchandise after goods double in value the duties owed had been stored in royal warehouses.[31]

How Weston felt about the threat posed by Chambers and the other defaulting merchants is obvious from his realisation that the crown could not survive the loss of this exceptionally important branch of the royal revenues. He regarded the current situation as one in which the government must stand firm, and he urged the King to collect all the duties to which he was legally entitled. On 30 September he applauded a royal decision to prorogue parliament, which had been scheduled to reopen in three weeks' time, until late in January 1629. In the midst of such unsettled conditions as these, it would be the height of folly to proceed with another parliamentary session.[32]

Possibly on Weston's motion, proceedings were instituted against Chambers in the Star Chamber in November 1628. Once again the pesky merchant was committed to prison, where he was held until the following May along with several older men who had refused to pay the customs duties.[33] Meanwhile the Court of Exchequer Chamber, of which the Treasurer was the *ex officio* head, was meeting to consider the steps already taken in regard to the defaulting merchants. On 27 November a decision of the court signed by Weston, Newburgh, and the four Barons expressed approval of everything done to date. It was held that goods belonging to John Rolle, George Moore, and several others were not repleivable by law and must remain in the safekeeping of the customs farmers until all duties owed on them had been collected.

The Treasurer himself argued that no attempt should be made at present to settle the more important question of whether tunnage and poundage could legally be imposed without parliamentary authorisation. A matter of such fundamental importance could only be resolved by the coming parliament, in which he was convinced there would be renewed harmony between King and subject.[34]

Weston was not the only member of the government to be hopeful about the approaching session. On 19 November Secretary Coke informed a friend that, although proceedings would not begin until 20 January, 'we hope then to settle our home affairs in unity and regularity, to which the wisdom and moderation of our new Treasurer will contribute very much.'[35] In order to prepare for the coming session, a series of well-calculated steps were taken. Men out of favour during recent years were invited to return to court, and gentlemen who had formerly opposed the crown were encouraged to join forces with the government. Because the King was chiefly concerned about an attack on his religious policy, his patronage of high-church clerics and toleration of known Catholics, the Arminian tract *An Appeal to Caesar* was called in three days before parliament was scheduled to convene. On advice from the Treasurer, Charles agreed to allow Archbishop Abbot, who had been in disgrace for more than a year, to reappear at court on 11 December, when he kissed hands and received permission to resume his seat on the Council. Weston and the King hoped that Abbot's return to favour would lessen dissatisfaction among the Puritans and that the archbishop would co-operate by restraining his brother Maurice, one of the ringleaders of the merchant agitation in London.[36]

The Treasurer continued to advance the prospects of Wentworth, who was as anxious as ever to enter the King's service. The Yorkshireman was invited to visit the country home Weston was building near Roehampton, Surrey, where he was doubtless asked to forswear all co-operation with the parliamentary opposition. Once Weston and the King were convinced of Wentworth's loyalty, the aged Lord Scrope, whose Catholicism had been denounced by the Commons in 1626, was removed from the Presidency of the Council of the North, in order to make way for the rigorously Protestant Wentworth.[37]

The Treasurer was now receiving urgent appeals from Sir John

Eliot, who was also hopeful of a high government position. Eliot has traditionally been pictured as a martyr for the liberties of the English people, since he was arrested at the close of the 1629 session and held in the Tower until his death three years later. But it is clear that the fervent opposition of his last few years was prompted, at least in part, by frustrated ambition. Originally a protégé of Buckingham, he had gone into opposition as a result of the disastrous expedition to Cadiz. After the duke's assassination, he felt that the greatest of all grievances had been removed and that it would be safe to solicit a government appointment. According to John Hacket, the disciple and biographer of Bishop Williams, he made several overtures to the Treasurer, one of whose closest associates, Sir James Bagg, was an old enemy of Eliot's and no doubt poisoned Weston's mind against him. In addition the Treasurer was probably influenced by the 1627 inquiry into Eliot's accounts, which revealed evidence of large-scale corruption and made him appear a poor risk as a government employee. All in all, Weston was content to assist the rise of Wentworth, the more capable man, which in turn aggravated the relationship between Eliot and the Treasurer. For as Hacket explained in a memorable passage,

> Sir *J. Eliot* of the west, and Sir *Tho. Wentworth* of the north, both in the prime of their age and wits, both conspicuous for able speakers, clashed so often in the House, and cudgelled one another with such strong contradictions, that it grew from an emulation between them to an enmity. The L. Treasurer *Weston* picked out the northern cock Sir *Thomas* to make him the King's creature, and set him upon the first step of his rising; which was wormwood in the taste of *Eliot*, who revenged himself upon the King in the Bill of Tonnage [in 1629], and then fell upon the Treasurer and declared against him, that he was the author of all the evils under which the kingdom was oppressed.[38]

To strengthen the court party and consolidate his own position, Weston persuaded the King that several other changes of government personnel were needed. The Earl of Marlborough, whose health was now precarious, was induced to resign the Presidency of the Council, which was conferred on Sir Edward Conway, the solitary defender of the duke's foreign policy. Weston preferred to see the Secretary transferred to a position where he would be unable to exercise any real power. As his successor the Treasurer arranged for the appointment of Lord Dorchester, who was both an old friend and a supporter of the peace negotiations already underway. In December 1628 the Treasurer also attempted to remove Lord Newburgh from the Exchequer and to procure that position for his friend Sir Francis Cottington. But there was no vacancy with sufficient prestige for it to be acceptable to Lord Newburgh, so he had to wait until April 1629 before he could secure Cottington's appointment as Chancellor and Under-treasurer.[39]

By the end of 1628 Weston must have viewed his work of the past few months with satisfaction. The confused period following the duke's assassination was over; the merchant agitation seemed to be on the wane; new agreements with the customs farmers were about to be signed; a general reduction of royal expenditure had been accomplished; and the preliminary negotiations for peace treaties with France and Spain were under way. The court party had been strengthened, Weston's position as chief minister of the crown was acknowledged on all sides, and a measure of political stability had been achieved. Preparations for the coming parliamentary session were proceeding smoothly, and many Londoners believed that recent changes of policy would appease those who had formerly criticised the government. Because of the duke's absence, it did not seem fanciful to think of making a completely fresh start. Perhaps Weston and his associates did not do enough to insure that the new session would be a success, but they do not deserve the scorn that Gardiner, Willson, and other Whiggish historians have heaped upon them.

At first it appeared that the government's optimism might prove well founded. On 21 January 1629 Secretary Dorchester reported to one of England's representatives abroad: 'Yesterday the Parliament met, and by the good appearance of both Houses and quiet and peaceable beginnings, we promise ourselves a very happy proceeding: which I beseech God to grant.'[40] Unhappily the King did nothing for several days to defend his policies of the past six months, and when the Commons proceeded to business, a series of complaints were voiced at once. John Selden was especially critical of the sentence imposed on Thomas Savage three months earlier. Selden declaimed against the way a poor man had 'lost his ears by a decree of the Star Chamber, by an arbitrary judgment.' Unless the House took strong action, all Englishmen would stand in mortal danger: 'Next they will take away our arms, and then our legs, and so our lives.' He urged the passage of a protestation to the King and ended by charging that the Petition of Right had been violated by recent actions of the customs farmers.[41]

The seizure of the merchants' goods assumed the prominence of a major grievance when John Rolle, member for Callington, proclaimed that his goods were among those detained for non-payment of the customs duties. The Commons responded to this revelation by charging that their fundamental rights had been infringed, since Rolle was definitely entitled to immunity for his goods. At Eliot's prompting the members voted to summon the customs officials to explain why they should not be charged with contempt of the House. Secretary Coke urged the members to be more conciliatory, but they refused to listen and named a committee to investigate.[42]

On 24 January the King attempted to repair the damage that had been done by addressing the two Houses in the Banqueting Hall. Charles stated his desire for a harmonious relationship with parliament and maintained that all legal problems would disappear as soon as he was granted tunnage and poundage for life. He wished to accept the duties as a loving gift from his people and not to collect them simply on the basis of his prerogative. Even during the previous session he had never claimed tunnage and poundage as a right but only out of pressing necessity. He concluded his speech by declaring that all obstacles to the granting of the duties had been cleared away and that he expected the two Houses to proceed with all deliberate speed.[43]

Although the response to Charles's speech was a favourable one, Secretary Coke's plea for the speedy passage of a tunnage and poundage bill encountered much bitter criticism. Selden maintained that the Secretary had attempted to introduce such a bill, which amounted to yet another infringement of the liberties of the House.[44] Before the members could give much thought to Selden's charge, their attention was diverted by religious questions, particularly the continuing spread of Catholicism. Francis Rous complained about 'how the See of Rome doth eat into our Religion and fret into the banks and walls of it – the laws and statutes of this realm.' He criticised the privileges accorded the Arminian faction, which he compared to a Trojan horse leading straight to popery and Spanish despotism. He concluded, significantly, that those who were responsible for the spread of popery were also guilty of violating the traditional rights and liberties of the realm. Thereupon the House decided to appoint a Committee of Religion to investigate the growth of popery and Arminianism and all incidents related to their spread.[45]

Contrary to the King's wishes, the members showed little inclination to grant tunnage and poundage until grievances had been redressed. Charles was naturally opposed to the argument that grievances should precede a vote of supply, and during the next few weeks Secretary Coke plied the members with numerous messages urging them to proceed with the most important business of the session. But their will was as resolute as the King's, and inevitably the breach between Charles and the members began to widen.

Religion and the seizure of the merchants' goods continued to be the issues of greatest concern to the House. Royal support of Arminian clerics and pamphleteers was hotly contested; the bitterest criticisms were levelled against John Cosin's liturgical innovations in Durham cathedral and the high-church convictions of Richard Neile, recently invested as Bishop of Winchester. For five days the members were in an uproar over revelations that nothing had been done to punish individuals associated with a secret Jesuit college in Clerkenwell, which had been discovered a year earlier. It was held that men charged with 'plain treason' had been released and that the government was guilty of shocking ineptitude.[46] So much time was spent on religious questions that Eliot cautioned the House on 29 January to avoid the error of considering itself a 'theological school.' The great radical was primarily concerned to punish the customs farmers for their actions and hoped to prevent his more religious-minded colleagues from being sidetracked by what he considered less important matters.[47]

Under Eliot's prodding the House returned to the question of the merchants' goods. Committees were appointed to interrogate witnesses, and much time was given to the matter of whether Charles had had prior knowledge of what had transpired. Sir Humphrey May contended that the King could not have known beforehand of the actions of the customs officers, which had resulted from some grave error or mistake. Yet Selden immediately re-emphasised that the seizure of Rolle's goods could only be construed as a violation of the rights of the House. Impressed by the great lawyer, the members voted that Rolle had indeed been privileged for his goods and ordered the summoning of all persons connected with their detention.[48]

The Commons then turned to the role of the customs farmers and the Barons of the Exchequer, whose part in the proceedings was severely criticised. Eliot maintained that the Barons were guilty of a serious judicial error which must be corrected so that the merchants would 'suddenly come by their goods.' William Noy, another Cornish member and an advocate for the Five Knights in 1627, urged the House to postpone consideration of a tunnage and poundage bill until the Barons' proceedings had been reversed and the merchants' property restored. He contended that the customs duties were an aid freely given by parliament and not an inherent right that could be claimed by the King. Noy proposed that any informations pending in the Exchequer or the Star Chamber be withdrawn, 'for if we do not right ourselves in these things, we shall but confirm the King in the right of such Tonnage.'[49]

Throughout the controversy over tunnage and poundage, the Commons preferred to assume that Charles had been misled by evil advisers. As additional evidence was considered, including the testimony of three of the most important customs farmers, Abraham Dawes, Richard Carmarthen, and Sir John Wolstenholme, it became increasingly difficult for the members to cling to such a view, although they were unable to conceive of taking direct action against him. Because they could not dispense with the constitutional fiction that the King can do no wrong, they could only press for the punishment of his chief advisers. And because the greatest minister of all, Lord Treasurer Weston, was specifically mentioned on a number of occasions and was felt to be inclined towards Catholicism, he was soon singled out for special criticism.

By the third week of February Charles was exasperated with the behaviour of the lower House. None of his plans for the session had succeeded, and the members seemed to be farther than ever from granting tunnage and poundage. For his part, Sir John Eliot was also disappointed with the results of the session. His tendency to slough over religious questions and to disregard the finer legal and constitutional points had provoked criticisms from Pym and his followers, and as a result he was on the verge of losing his leadership of the House. Eliot was therefore heartened when the King announced on 25 February that the proceedings would be adjourned until 2 March. Charles hoped that a brief recess would temper the members' mood, whereas the Cornishman felt it might be possible to use the interval to tighten his hold over the radical faction and secure its endorsement for a direct assault on the government.[50]

During the last days of February, while the King was making overtures to the Commons – evidence of a more conciliatory attitude on his part – the more radical members were gathering at the Three Cranes Tavern in Chancery Lane to lay their plans for 2 March. Present at the tavern were Eliot, Selden, Danzil Holles, William Coryton, William Strode, Sir Miles Hobart, and Sir Peter Hayman. Eliot was in charge and secured support for a series of resolutions he intended to present to the House. He proposed to blame the Treasurer and Bishop Neile for all serious grievances in church and state and to lay the groundwork for their impeachment. According to Hacket, Bishop Williams soon learned of the course devised and informed Weston of what lay in store for him. In vain Williams offered to arrange an interview between the two men, in order that they might be reconciled and Eliot recruited as one of the Treasurer's servants. More concerned to forestall the opposition plan, the government decided to order another adjournment immediately after the session reopened.[51]

Once the members were in their places and the usual prayers had been read, Speaker Finch announced a command to adjourn for eight more days. This provoked an angry response from all corners of the House. One member blurted out that 'it was not in the office of the Speaker to deliver any such command unto them,' since a decision to adjourn could only be made by the chamber itself. Other members asserted their determination not to comply until they had completed a discussion of all things 'fit and convenient to be spoken of.' Thereupon the Speaker prepared to leave the chair, but Holles and several other opposition members rushed down and held him in his place.[52]

Eliot then threw down a copy of the resolutions he and his associates had prepared. His paper was delivered by willing hands to the clerk of the House amid shouts that it be read. Once order was restored Eliot took the floor and inveighed against the Treasurer and Bishop Neile, whom he insisted were to blame for all the kingdom's major economic and religious grievances. It was because of their rightful fears of punishment that recent decisions to adjourn parliament had been made: 'they break parliaments lest parliaments should break them.' Eliot urged his listeners to observe 'how Arminianism creeps in and undermines us, and how Popery comes in upon us.' Neile himself was a convinced Arminian, and 'we know what he hath done to favour them'; but it was the Treasurer, 'in whose person all evil is contracted,' who was the greatest danger to the liberties of the English people.

> I find him acting and building on those grounds laid by his Master, the late great Duke of Buckingham . . . I find him the head of all that great party the Papists, and all Jesuits and priests derive from him their shelter and protection. In the great question of Tonnage and Poundage, the instruments moved at his command and pleasure; he dismays our merchants, and invites strangers to come in and drive our trade, and to serve their own ends.[53]

Eliot proposed that the House draw up a remonstrance against the Treasurer, while another Cornishman, William Coryton, called for the expulsion from the Council of all those who 'have been here noted to be ill Counsellors for the King and Kingdom.'[54] The Speaker attempted to block a vote on the proposed remonstrance, but his refusal to put the question provoked a sharp complaint from Selden, who contended that Finch had no right to ignore a command of the House. He was its duly elected servant, and Selden called for him to be punished so that his disobedience would not serve as a precedent to future Speakers.[55]

At length Jerome Weston rose to defend his father against Eliot's charges. He declaimed against the casting of such aspersions on so noble a man as the Treasurer, who had long served the crown with honour and loyalty. Eliot had failed to offer proof for any of his charges, which were patently untrue and should be acknowledged as such. Jerome's spirited defence of his father was received as a commendable expression of filial piety, but Clement Coke attacked his assertion that the Treasurer was a loyal servant of the kingdom. Anyone who encouraged the collection of tunnage and poundage without parliamentary authorisation was in fact an enemy of the kingdom, and Weston had supported such a course for several years.[56]

As finally presented to the House by Holles, Eliot's resolutions were passed by a resounding vote and stipulated that:

I. . . . Whosoever shall bring in innovation in religion or, by favour or countenance, seek to extend or introduce Popery or Arminianism or other opinions disagreeing from the true and orthodox Church, shall be reputed a capital enemy of the Commonwealth.

II. . . . Whosoever shall counsel or advise the taking and levying of the subsidies of Tunnage and Poundage, not being granted by Parliament, or shall be an actor or instrument therein, shall be likewise reputed an innovator in the government, and a capital enemy to this Kingdom and Commonwealth.

III. . . . if any merchant or person whatsoever shall voluntarily yield or pay the said subsidies of Tunnage and Poundage, not being granted by Parliament, he shall likewise be reputed a betrayer of the liberties of England and an enemy to the same.[57]

When Charles learned that the members were still sitting despite his instructions to the Speaker, he sent a command for the serjeant of the mace to leave the House, since no discussion could take place when the mace was absent from the table. But several opposition members restrained the serjeant, took the key to the door from him, and gave it to one of their own number for safekeeping. When this attempt to halt the proceedings failed, the King angrily directed Black Rod to go down and dissolve parliament. The Commons refused to admit the usher, however, and Charles thereupon resolved to use force. He summoned the captain of the palace guard and ordered him to break open the door. But just as the troops arrived, the members declared themselves adjourned, and, in the words of a participant, 'the rising of the House prevented the bloodshed that might have been spilt.'[58]

These events made a lasting impression on Charles and his ministers. They had approached the session in a spirit of optimism and reconciliation, and, while they had doubtless made tactical errors during the past few weeks, they had done nothing to justify the discreditable episode that had just occurred. The more radical members seemed to have lost all sense of proportion. They were claiming powers that traditionally belonged to the crown; a near-revolutionary situation had in fact materialised. The attack on Weston had neither merit nor justice to commend it, as several witnesses were quick to point out. In Hacket's opinion it was altogether wrong to blame the Treasurer for the failures of royal policy during recent years. 'Somebody must bear the burden as the Duke had done; yet this Lord was not like to be the man, who had been in his great place but about six months, unless he could conjure, and work miracles in a trice.' Sir Philip Warwick maintained that the widespread dislike of Weston was prompted chiefly by jealousy, for his elevation 'soon brought him into envy, which ever dogs new raised greatness.'[59] It was basically because Weston was now the King's principal adviser that the attack of 2 March was made on him – anyone else in the same position would probably have been attacked in the same way. Thus it would appear that Eliot and his associates, regardless of whether they were fully conscious of what they were about, were attempting to forge a new constitutional balance in which preponderant power would be held by parliament, and more particularly by the House of Commons. In these circumstances the King had no choice but to dissolve an assembly that had shown it would not co-operate until the crown accepted a long list of humiliating concessions.

Instead of destroying Weston's influence with the King, the events of 2 March strengthened his position as chief minister. Indeed most observers believed that he was primarily responsible for Charles's decision to rule without parliament for the next few years. Clarendon and David Lloyd both regarded him as the chief architect of the period of Personal Rule, which now opened and lasted for more than eleven years. Public opinion was also convinced he was responsible for the recent dissolution, and his previous popularity collapsed altogether. On 6 March the Venetian Ambassador reported that 'the kingdom is furious against the Treasurer, and bears the King very little love.'[60] To convince Charles that another parliament should not be summoned for some years, not a difficult task under the circumstances, Weston took the line that he only wished to preserve the traditional powers of the crown, irrespective of the claims of parliament. In the autumn of 1629 the Venetian Ambassador gave a correct reading of the situation when he reported that the Treasurer 'knows his fall is inevitable if parliament should happen to meet, and so he will do everything to keep the King from any idea of summoning it.'[61]

In fairness to Weston's memory, however, it should be noted that there is no evidence of any desire on his part to do away with parliament altogether. Never an absolutist, he had been a respected member of the Commons between 1601 and 1626, and until the very end of his life he continued to believe in the mixed constitution of Tudor times. Only when the radicals in the lower House began to threaten the established order did he encourage Charles to rule in a personal fashion for some years. Thus it appears that he merely envisaged an interval of twelve or fifteen years, during which the angry tempers revealed by the latest session would have a chance to subside. If such a cooling off period could be arranged, during which the government should be able to extricate itself from the corner into which Buckingham's policies had boxed it, younger and more tractable members might be returned at the next elections. Then a new spirit of co-operation between crown and parliament might arise, just as the government had hoped to make a fresh start in 1629.

With the benefit of hindsight it appears that Weston and his master were on the right track and that the period of Personal Rule might well have achieved the objectives set for it. During the 1630s several of the King's bitterest critics died, including Eliot and Sir Edward Coke; and by December 1643 John Pym, the mastermind of opposition to the crown in the Long Parliament, was dead. Had the next meeting of parliament been delayed until 1644 or 1645, the course of English history might have been appreciably altered.[62] The detailed study made by Messrs Brunton and Pennington of the membership of the Long Parliament, which assembled in November 1640, has revealed a significant age difference between those who were willing to support the King and those who opposed him. On the average the royalists at the beginning of the Civil War were 36 years of age, while the parliamentarians were 47.[63] How is this remarkable age difference to be explained? Younger men are usually the radicals, while older ones tend to be more conservative. In the 1640s it would appear that the parliamentarians were the young radicals of the 1620s grown older, while the royalists, who had come of age during the 1630s and had no first-hand knowledge of the failures of the Buckingham era, were in greater sympathy with the King.

Doubtless there were other changes in English society of which Weston and the King were unaware but which suggest to present-day historians that time was on their side.[64] If the period of Personal Rule had lasted only a few years longer than it did, the more malleable and conservative generation on the verge of maturity would have displaced its elders, who were sternly opposed to co-operation with the King. Weston and his master deserve real credit for devising this simple strategy, which came so close to achieving the objectives set for it. By the same token the Treasurer's great enemy, William Laud, an absolutist who, in his zeal to promote the interests of the church, extended the objectives set for the period of Personal Rule, deserves disapprobation for bringing the strategy down in ruins. As long as the Treasurer remained at the helm, successful efforts were made to avoid another crisis, either political or religious, which would require the summoning of another parliament. When Laud became the King's chief adviser in 1635, his uncompromising policy, epitomised by a blind demand that Charles bring all his kingdoms into religious unity, led straight to the consequences that the Treasurer had laboured so hard to avoid.

9 Foreign and Financial Policy

Once the crown had decided on its response to the turbulent events of 2 March, it was necessary to justify the dissolution of parliament and the resort to methods of personal government. Late that same day Charles issued a proclamation explaining that the Council had urged him to order the adjournments of 25 February and 2 March, which had been intended to promote 'a better and more right understanding . . . between Us and the Members of that House whereby this Parliament might have a happy end and issue.' Yet because of the irresponsible actions of a small group within the lower House, the crown had been forced to a dissolution. Those whose behaviour had necessitated this course would not be forgotten, for Charles promised that he would 'ever distinguish between those who have shown good affection to religion and government and those that have given themselves over to faction and to work disturbances to the peace and good order of our kingdom.'[1]

Accordingly the government ordered the arrest of the most important radical leaders, including Eliot, Holles, Valentine, Hobart, and Strode. It also kept watch over the activities of Sir Edward Coke, who was now living quietly at Stoke Poges; and it directed that books disputing the legality of the continued collection of tunnage and poundage should be suppressed. Both Weston and the King were convinced of the need for law and order, and steps were taken to break the resistance of merchants who were still evading payment of the customs duties. To this purpose Charles issued a declaration asserting that all his predecessors had collected tunnage and poundage from the first days of their reigns without waiting for specific authorisation from parliament. He had therefore done nothing more than earlier Kings had done, and he had used the proceeds for such purposes as the defence and good government of the realm. His predecessors had been voted tunnage and poundage 'readily and cheerfully' by the first parliaments of their reigns, and only the captious behaviour of a few disaffected members had prevented his own first parliament from doing the same. He was determined to collect the customs duties in the future just as other Kings had done in the past, and the merchant community should take heed not to oppose his designs.[2]

Opposition to the collection of tunnage and poundage declined steadily during the spring of 1629. Government firmness caused most of the merchants to end their resistance and submit to royal leadership in mercantile affairs. Because of the recent falling off of trade with the Low Countries, a number of merchants requested Council support of their efforts to sell English textiles abroad. And to the Treasurer's undoubted satisfaction, a group of men engaged in trade with France called for the English customs duties to be increased in response to recent advances ordered by Louis XIII and Cardinal Richelieu.[3]

Not all the merchants were willing to forget their past opposition so easily, however. John Langham continued to refuse payment of duties on large quantities of imported currants as did Samuel Vassell, whose arrears to the crown amounted to more than £460. Their cases were heard by the Court of Exchequer Chamber in June 1630, when Weston and three of the Barons ordered the defendants to show cause why they should not be held in contempt.[4] John Rolle, whose affairs had provoked so much discord in parliament, was just as defiant, though he was unable to recover his goods before February 1633, when his case was finally considered by the Exchequer Chamber.[5] The most troublesome of all the merchants was Richard Chambers, who had repeatedly denounced the new impositions on currants during the autumn of 1628. The government was determined to break Chambers' resistance, and judicial proceedings against him extended over a long period of time. They were still pending when Weston died in 1635.[6]

During the period the Chambers case was under review, Weston was especially active in the work of the Exchequer Chamber. The court generally held three terms a year: in January and February, in June and July, and during October and November. In each of these periods the court sat two or three times a week, with the Treasurer attending a majority of the meetings. Indeed the most important cases could not be settled unless he was there.[7] Many of the suits considered by the court involved the royal revenues and, more particularly, the customs duties. On 17 April 1630 the Treasurer and three of the Barons, Sir Thomas Denham, Sir John Trevor, and George Vernon, debated the merits of a petition submitted by several of the customs farmers, who were seeking an abatement of substantial sums owed by them to the crown. Because of recent trade reverses they complained of having suffered irreversible losses, and the court saw fit to allow them an abatement of £12,475 5s. 4d. In November 1630 a similar case was handled by Weston, Trevor, and Vernon, who granted an abatement of more than £2260 to the syndicate responsible for collecting the duties charged on seacoals shipped from Newcastle-upon-Tyne to London or transported out of England and Wales to other parts of the British Isles.[8]

Weston was from time to time concerned with other duties of a judicial nature. He frequently appeared in the Star Chamber, where he generally opted for moderate fines and reasonable sentences, his harshness in regard to the defaulting merchants notwithstanding. He also played a leading role in the Council's judicial work – as joint Lord Lieutenant of Essex from January 1629, it naturally fell to him to supervise the activities of the justices of the peace of his home county. Weston was by this juncture the most powerful member of the Council. Charles often conferred privately with him before the beginning of scheduled meetings and made important decisions on his recommendation alone. When the King's wishes were later revealed to the full board, only a few members had the courage to register dissenting views.[9]

The Council had no regular meeting place but almost invariably met on Wednesday and Friday afternoons. When in London it usually met in the Council Chamber at Whitehall; but because it followed the King on his progresses around the kingdom, it occasionally convened in such scattered locales as Greenwich, Windsor, Lambeth, Hampton Court, Oxford, Theobalds, Salisbury, Reading, and Southampton. Before the outbreak of the Civil War, a number of meetings were held in the Star Chamber, and a few in the Inner Star Chamber. While Weston remained at the helm, the Council sometimes met at Wallingford House, his London residence and the seat of the Treasury.[10]

In addition to his presence at regularly scheduled Council meetings, the Treasurer was expected to attend a series of committee meetings, since he belonged to all five of the Council's standing committees. During the period of Personal Rule there was a system of interlocking committee memberships, since the most important Councillors served on most, if not all, of the committees, an arrangement that naturally enhanced their power and enabled them to dominate the Council's work. In 1634 Weston and his good friend Arundel, along with the two principal Secretaries, sat on all five of the standing committees; Sir Francis Cottington belonged to four; and Laud and the Earl of Dorset served on three.[11] As the King's chief financial adviser, the Treasurer was naturally a prominent member of the Committee for Trade, which met on Friday mornings, usually at 8 a.m. He also belonged to two committees that were scheduled to convene on Tuesdays: the Committee for Ireland, which usually assembled before dinner, and the Committee for the Ordnance, whose deliberations occurred between dinner and supper. The fourth committee on which he served was the Committee for Foreign Plantations, which generally transacted its work on Wednesday mornings.[12] The last but not least important one to which he belonged was the Committee for Foreign Affairs, whose membership included the two principal Secretaries, Laud, and the Earls of Arundel and Holland. This committee had no definite meeting time or place but assembled when and wherever the King directed.

Weston had long been concerned with the conduct of English diplomacy, and once he emerged as the leading member of the Foreign Committee, he became unashamedly protective of his authority in this regard. When in 1632 Secretary Coke discussed a confidential matter with the Dutch Ambassador, the Treasurer reproved him for interfering in business that did not concern him.[13] Foreign ambassadors posted to London were not unmindful of his position and power. In April 1632 the Venetian envoy explained to his government why he had broached a certain subject to the Treasurer: 'It is always necessary to approach him before anyone else upon all matters, owing to the influence he possesses.' Accordingly most ambassadors were careful to pay their respects to him at Wallingford House, after which he would politely escort them to the head of the main staircase. On rare occasions he even accompanied them through the hall and courtyard to the doors of their waiting coaches.[14]

During the summer and autumn of 1629 Weston met on numerous occasions with the Flemish painter-diplomat, Peter Paul Rubens, who had just arrived in London from the continent. Rubens had previously made a visit to Madrid, to begin a portrait of Philip IV and confer with Olivares about possible peace negotiations with England. His view that the English government was ready to accept a settlement was confirmed by Endymion Porter, an important English courtier sent on a confidential mission to Spain in August 1628. Subsequent letters from Sir Francis Cottington affirmed that both Weston and Charles I desired 'a firm and honourable peace,' which prompted Olivares to dispatch Rubens as a special emissary to England.[15]

Rubens arrived in London on 25 May and procured lodgings for himself in the residence of Balthasar Gerbier, a Dutchman once employed as curator of Buckingham's paintings at York House. Almost immediately he was summoned to an audience at Greenwich, during which Charles acknowledged that he desired a peace treaty with Spain but was reluctant to conclude an agreement that did not include provisions for the restoration of the Palatinate. The King noted that his alliances with other states forbade him to enter into negotiations for a separate peace treaty and that he could not afford to forfeit them should a truce with Spain fail to produce a permanent settlement. He also insisted that the peace talks take place in Madrid and that Philip IV should give a solemn pledge that the Emperor and Maximilian of Bavaria, whose troops now held most of the Palatinate, would be represented. Although Charles agreed to eschew co-operation with France while the negotiations in Madrid were underway, Rubens was disheartened by the interview, since the King refused to participate in the talks until Philip IV surrendered any places in the Palatinate still being held by his forces.[16]

Before being dismissed, Rubens was directed to inform the Treasurer of all that had been said, which he did during the afternoon of the same day, after dining with the Earl of Carlisle. At the outset of his meeting with Weston, which was private except for the presence of Cottington, Rubens delivered a 'very kind' letter to the chief minister from Olivares and questioned whether much could be expected of the present talks in view of Charles's inflexible attitudes. The two officials replied that 'the King had been too hasty and they feared that if the matter came before the Council it would be rejected; for it was clear that to accept a part of the Palatinate was virtually to renounce all the rest.' These opinions did little to satisfy Rubens, who met again with Charles that evening and asked for a confirmation of everything that had been said during their previous meeting. To this request the King readily assented, and when Weston and Cottington later appeared in the royal presence chamber, he 'repeated and confirmed anew' what had just been said.[17]

On 27 May Rubens met with Secretary Dorchester, and on the following day he dined and conferred again with the Treasurer. On Sunday the 28th it was decided that he should consult yet another time with Weston at Wallingford House, along with Cottington and the Earl of Pembroke. On either the 29th or the 30th, he 'came and spent with them more than an hour.'[18]

During his stay in London Rubens was dismayed by the conflicting views expressed to him, for it was his impression that the English government was speaking with several different voices. In so far as he could tell, there was no unity of opinion between the King and his ministers, which led him to conclude that there was no intention of adhering to any particular course. Late in June he complained to Olivares about 'the instability of the English temperament. Rarely, in fact, do these people persist in a resolution, but change from hour to hour, and always from bad to worse.' Rubens was also critical of English diplomatic procedure in general. 'For whereas in other courts negotiations begin with the ministers and finish with the royal word and signature, here they begin with the King and end with the ministers.'[19]

Despite Rubens' criticisms, considerable progress was made towards the opening of formal talks, and on 12 July he was able to forward a memorandum containing the English demands. By this juncture Weston and the King had decided to send Cottington as Ambassador Extraordinary to Spain. Rubens was pleased by the choice of Cottington, who, on his part, did not welcome the responsibility now entrusted to him. Only recently appointed Chancellor and Under-treasurer, Cottington disliked the prospect of being away from England for a long period of time. Furthermore he was convinced that the peace party would suffer during his absence and 'the affair would run the risk of failure, through the weakness of the men who support it.'[20]

Cottington's departure for Spain, originally scheduled for 1 August, was delayed until 5 November because of a succession of difficulties. While he was preparing for his journey, Cardinal Richelieu attempted to secure the embassy's cancellation by sending messages intended to convince the Treasurer of his desire for friendship and co-operation between France and England. The Spanish government was in no position to effect the restitution of the Palatinate, but his own master had this within his power, for Louis XIII had undoubted influence with Maximilian of Bavaria. If England would only adhere to the coalition comprised by Savoy, the United Provinces, and France, Richelieu would do everything in his power to help Charles accomplish his most cherished objective. At this point the cardinal allegedly offered Weston a substantial bribe, 'either in capital or in the form of a pension, as he preferred.' But the Treasurer refused to countenance such an offer and presented the note in which it was made to the King. Charles 'simply laughed at it and said "he was well acquainted with the wiles and tricks of Cardinal Richelieu, and that he would prefer to make an alliance with Spain against France than the other way around." '[21]

Early in August Rubens travelled to Oatlands, where he revealed that an old friend of Weston's, Don Carlos Coloma, had been appointed the new permanent ambassador of Spain in England. Rubens then asked if Cottington was ready to leave for Madrid, 'since on our part we could do nothing before his departure.' Charles replied that the Chancellor would be unable to set out before the beginning of September but should be ready to depart shortly thereafter. Following his meeting with the King, Rubens paid a visit to the Treasurer's estate in Surrey, where the two men had a frank interchange of views. Weston boasted that the documents forwarded by Rubens on 12 July had been kept so confidential that 'neither the Ambassador of France . . . nor any other person knew anything about it up to the present.' But Rubens countered that nothing more could be done until Cottington arrived in Madrid, since the documents alluded to by Weston had been 'drawn up in terms both obscure and ambiguous.' To this assertion the Treasurer made a sharp retort, declaring that the documents had been perfectly intelligible and that in any event Rubens should be able to clarify any doubtful points in his dispatches to Olivares. After a discussion of various technical matters relating to the negotiations, Weston predicted 'that the arrival of

Cottington in Spain would settle the peace within one hour, or else it would never be settled.'[22]

That Coloma was being posted to England was deplored by the Venetian envoy in London, Girolamo Soranzo, who was convinced that Weston and Coloma were were intent on following courses harmful to the 'public cause' and would work together to 'hide the truth from the King and keep up his hopes.' Throughout these months Soranzo placed the worst possible interpretation on Weston's attempt to conclude a peace treaty. In September 1629 he informed his government that

> . . . it is certain that the Treasurer wishes to use the peace with Spain as the Achilles of his preservation, and will do everything in his power to bring it about, without regard to the King's honour or the Palatine's interest, and will go with his eyes shut to encounter every prejudice in the hope of saving himself. In this matter he no longer talks of keeping the King from expense, because the war with Spain does not cost a farthing, but only of providing for present needs by opening that trade, without recourse to parliament.[23]

Even before he was instructed to do whatever he could to impede the Anglo-Spanish negotiations and to encourage England's entry into the coalition led by France, Soranzo began to insinuate that the English crown should not expect to accomplish anything through its negotiations with Spain. He also insisted that England stood to profit from the continued campaigns of France and Savoy in northern Italy and the military triumphs of the Dutch.[24]

Late in October the Venetian decided to state his arguments directly to Weston at Wallingford House. After he had insisted that Cottington's embassy to Madrid would inevitably arouse the suspicions of the Dutch, the Treasurer replied curtly that his associate was almost ready to set out and that the embassy could not be cancelled at the last moment. Although Weston himself had some doubts about the mission's chances, he maintained that, should it succeed, the results would be beneficial to all. And if it should fail, as Soranzo, his French counterpart, and several others were so loudly predicting, England would be free to undertake some course for the enhancement of her own reputation and the promotion of the 'public good.'[25]

While Cottington was absent in Madrid, the Foreign Committee continued to play an active role in London. Whenever important questions arose, Charles invariably referred them to it. During the spring and summer of 1630 the committee met frequently with the new Spanish Ambassador, who arrived in London shortly after the beginning of the year and was warmly received by Charles and Henrietta Maria in a ceremony in the Banqueting House.[26] The Treasurer was now making concerted efforts to retain the good will of the French. He supported an Admiralty decision to return French prizes to their rightful owners and agreed that priests and convicted recusants should be placed in the custody of the French Ambassador, the Marquis de Châteauneuf, who was allowed to arrange for their transportation to the continent. Yet because of his insistence on the necessity of peace, Weston refused to consider Châteauneuf's proposal for an alliance with France against Philip IV and the Austrian Habsburgs. When it became clear he would never support a pro-French policy, the ambassador took steps to meet with the other members of the Foreign Committee, to whom he suggested that London and Paris co-operate 'for the restoration of the Palatinate and the liberation of Germany from the oppression of the House of Austria . . . Everyone knows he is doing this and discusses it openly in the public squares and streets of London.' In time the Treasurer developed an intense dislike of Châteauneuf, whose recall he demanded in 1630.[27]

Meanwhile Cottington was hammering out the preliminary terms of a peace treaty with Spain, a draft copy of which he forwarded to London during the summer of 1630. In a meeting with the King at Theobalds, Weston and his associates on the Foreign Committee, who had expected to make peace on the basis of the *status quo ante bellum*, compared the articles now referred to them with the provisions of the Treaty of London of 1604. It was immediately noted that there were several important differences 'and some of such consequence that they could not be admitted without much prejudice to his Majesty both in honour and profit.' There were two points to which the Foreign Committee took particular exception. First, in the draft treaty it was specified that English trade with Spain and her colonies in the New World was to be limited not to where it had been prior to the outbreak of war in 1624, nor to where it had been in 1604, but to those few areas that had been open to English traders in 1575; and second, the preliminary articles stipulated that all prizes taken more than six months after the conclusion of the treaty must be returned to their rightful owners. On the first point Weston and his colleagues won a substantial victory, compelling a return to the commercial arrangements established by the Treaty of London; but concerning the second point, they had to settle for a compromise formula. The English wanted the acceptance of a twelve-month period between the signing of the treaty and the time when prizes could no longer be taken and retained by either side; they ultimately consented to a transitional period of nine months between war and peace.[28]

During his stay in Madrid Cottington sought to keep Olivares from ignoring the problems of the Elector Palatine by making veiled threats of renewed British intervention in the war. But in London Weston assured Coloma that his master was ready to sign a peace treaty regardless of what arrangements were made for the Palatinate. The Treasurer understood the danger of making a peace settlement dependent on Spanish support of Frederick V and did more than anyone else to shape the outcome of the negotiations, although Cottington is regarded by most historians as the principal architect of the treaty. The Treaty of Madrid was signed on 5 November 1630, exactly a year after the Chancellor set sail from Falmouth. Because of Weston's determination to arrange a settlement at this juncture, Philip IV and Olivares were able to avoid a commitment in regard to the Palatinate and to give only a vague assurance that England would be allowed to mediate any future disputes between Spain and the United Provinces.[29]

The Treasurer's enemies hoped Cottington might feel wronged by the decision to undercut his efforts to secure more satisfactory arrangements concerning the Palatinate. When the Chancellor returned from Madrid in March 1631, they attempted to create a gulf between the two men by exploiting the latter's injured feelings and suggesting his appointment as Secretary of State. After securing a promise of the Queen's assistance, Weston's enemies proposed that Dorchester be made Lord President of the Council and that Cottington be given the Secretary's seals. But Dorchester balked at taking a position with no real power, and Cottington declared that he did not intend to accept a new office without his mentor's blessing.[30] Thus Weston's enemies were unable to make use of the negotiations to separate him from his most capable associate.

Although foreign policy required much of his time in 1629 and 1630, the Treasurer was chiefly concerned with the continuing problem of the royal finances. The extraordinary expenditure of the crown was beginning to decline, but the corner had only just been turned and the financial situation was still a bleak one. It was to remain so throughout the 1630s, despite Weston's efforts to curb government spending and develop new sources of revenue. Because of the costly naval and military expeditions of 1625–8, large sums had to be earmarked each year for purposes of debt reduction. By the time the Treasurer died in 1635, more than £340,000 had been issued towards the repayment of loans contracted since 1617, but the crown still owed more than £1,160,000.[31] Thus whatever funds were available had to be put to the most efficient use possible, and a series of cheese-paring economies were absolutely essential.

Unfortunately for the Treasurer, his royal master had little regard for such matters. Charles's attitude towards economy was one of princely disdain: why should he be overly concerned with getting and saving when so much more pleasure was to be derived from spending? In this his views coincided exactly with those of his leading nobles. Professor Stone, in his study of the fortunes of such aristocratic families as the Cecils and the Howards, observed that 'the maximization of profits was far from being in the forefront of the minds of many of the leading members of this highly restricted group. They were, for the most part, more concerned with expenditure than with income, and it was only if the latter was failing in its duty to support the former that attention was shifted to means of increasing revenue.'[32] How true this was, not just of the King's greatest subjects but of the King himself! Because James I had shared such attitudes, the English court had become grander and more elaborate with each passing year since Queen Elizabeth's death. By the early 1630s it had become so extravagant that Professor Trevor-Roper has characterised it as 'the last of the great Renaissance courts . . . the most brittle, most overgrown, most rigid court of all.'[33]

An indication of what had happened is afforded by a report compiled during the winter of 1626–7 by Marlborough, Weston, and several others. Although chiefly concerned with proposals for increasing the King's revenue, this report included a comparison between current levels of expenditure and those of Queen Elizabeth's day. It revealed, for example, that the £200 granted to huntsmen each year before 1603 had since swollen to almost £3000 a year. The great Queen had been served by eight footmen at an annual charge of £320; there were now eighteen footmen at a yearly cost of £960. In former times less than £2000 had been issued for musicians and falconers, servants who were now being paid more than £6500 a year. By reducing the number of royal physicians and surgeons, as much as £3000 a year might be saved. If the palace guard were decreased by only 40 men, from 200 to 160, an annual saving of £2500 would result.[34]

Unhappily little was done to implement the recommendations of 1626–7, and the court remained as elaborate and costly as ever until the upheaval of the 1640s. The nineteen palaces and castles belonging to the crown required enormous amounts to staff and maintain. Purchases of tapestries, paintings, plate, and furniture consumed a large proportion of the royal revenues, as did the renovations that occurred from time to time. In the spring of 1632, £2000 was spent on the conversion of a tennis court at Denmark House into a private chapel for the Queen's use. Although Henrietta Maria had her own separate establishment, for which £15,000 a year was provided, large sums were additionally required to satisfy her needs. In the summer of 1631, a total of £2800 was spent on new furnishings for the royal nursery and bedchamber.[35] Lavish arrangements were naturally made for the many children born to the royal couple. Shortly after the birth of the heir to the throne in May 1630, a separate household was established for him at St James's Palace, which was staffed by a governess, two physicians, an apothecary, a lawyer, and between 200 and 300 ordinary servants. When the Prince of Wales reached his sixth birthday in 1636, his household was reconstituted and made even more elaborate. Similarly, great sums were lavished on the Princess Royal and the Duke of York, born in 1631 and 1632, respectively. Nor was any expense spared for the King's journey to Edinburgh in May 1633, when he was at last to be crowned by Scottish rites. Between 8 January and 10 April 1633, almost £13,000 was issued by the Exchequer just to prepare for his departure. Because of this Lord Clarendon was later to maintain that Charles's progress northward 'was made from the first setting out to the end of it with the greatest magnificence imaginable.'[36]

It was with this expensive and complicated system that the Treasurer had to contend. Not only did he have to find funds for the ordinary operating expenses of the government and the repayment of its past expenditure but also for the unceasing demands of an extravagant King and Queen, who saw no reason to scrimp on the arrangements made for themselves, their children, or their relatives in exile at The Hague, who were now costing the English government in excess of £20,000 a year.[37] In the Treasurer's eyes Charles's refusal to economise was the height of irresponsibility, although he was in no position to tell him so. Weston was indeed the leading financial officer of the kingdom, but his power was subject to definite limits and he had no illusions about being irreplaceable. Moreover, he was responsible in both a practical and a theoretical sense to the Privy Council, which kept a close watch over the royal finances during the early Stuart period. Without the Council's permission he could not dispose of a single acre of royal land, nor could he make binding agreements with the customs farmers until it had been apprised. The Treasurer's influence over taxation was also restricted, since he had no power to authorise the use of new revenue-producing measures, for which the approval of parliament was required after 1628. Neither could he order the implementation of basic financial changes: any policy of retrenchment or reform had to be discussed with the King and his other Councillors, regardless of whether it was the Treasurer, the Chancellor, or some other minister who provided the initiative for it.

Fortunately for Weston, his master's confidence in him never wavered, he remained the dominant figure on the Council, and he was able to exercise broader powers than his great predecessor, the Earl of Middlesex, whose role had always been limited by Buckingham. It would be misleading to portray Weston as either a reformer or a moderniser – he was content to operate within the limits of the existing system and exploit whatever opportunities it provided – but he did make a series of administrative changes during the early 1630s. Many of the great spending officials were required to prepare their accounts for audit, and beginning in July 1630 the weekly reports of Exchequer transactions, a regular feature of Queen Elizabeth's time, were reinstituted. Secret service disbursements were reduced; frauds in the royal stables were exposed and punished; the annual issues to the Office of Robes were limited to £5000; and new procedures were established to assist the Household in curbing its expenses. Such officials as the Master of the Robes, the Master of the Great Wardrobe, and the Cofferer of the Household '. . . actually kept within their assignments in some years, and received but small extraordinary issues in others.' Efforts were also made to keep the officers of the navy within their annual assignment, which was set at £27,905 in 1632.[38]

Weston was as determined to reduce pensions and annuities as he was to control expenditure. During the first three decades of the seventeenth century, the percentage of the King's income used for this purpose had risen steadily, requiring one-fifth of the ordinary revenue, or almost £125,000 a year by 1630, which was considerably more than was devoted to them during the later Hanoverian period. Although royal income increased rapidly during the century after the Civil War, the King's pension list averaged only £95,447 annually between 1721 and 1780. Thus it was essential to make an attack on this item of expenditure if Charles's budget was ever to be balanced. As was no doubt expected, the Treasurer's retrenchment campaign was an unpopular one, and bitter complaints were voiced from time to time. Yet by the year of his death, the royal pension list had been reduced to £80,000 annually, or by more than 35%. The saving of £45,000 that resulted must be accounted one of his most notable achievements.[39]

During the early 1630s Weston was successful in raising the King's income in a variety of small ways. He increased the yields of clerical tenths from £8000 to £14,000 a year between 1630 and 1635; and in 1630 he negotiated a new lease on the alum farm at an advance of £1500 in the annual rent. Three years later he helped to secure the adoption of a proposal to require licences for the sale of tobacco, which produced more than £18,000 for the crown by the end of 1635. Monopolistic privileges were conferred on the manufacturers of playing cards and dice, in return for which they agreed to pay an annual royalty. The fines assessed on new buildings in the capital, which he urged Charles to collect, yielded £9552 during 1634 and 1635. Even Ireland began to show a profit for the first time in nearly a decade, owing largely to the efforts of the new Lord Deputy, Sir Thomas Wentworth. In 1633 slightly more than £4750 was received from Ireland; in the next year,

£4692; and in 1635, £5352. During the same period the revenues of the Court of Wards showed a comparable increase, although they fluctuated by as much as £10,000 from one year to the next.[40]

Despite his alleged sympathy for Catholicism, the Treasurer had no scruples about steeply increasing the recusancy fines, which were collected from those who failed to attend the services of the established church. In 1630 the recusancy fines produced slightly more than £5000, but by 1633 their yields had risen to £11,000. In 1634, the last full year of Weston's life, they produced a total of £26,000 for the crown. It was largely because of the dramatic increase of the recusancy fines that he never enjoyed the support of the English Catholics. In Clarendon's words,

> . . . he never had reputation and credit with that party, who were the only people of the kingdom who did not believe him to be of their profession. For the penal laws . . . were never more rigidly executed, nor had the Crown ever so great a revenue from them, as in his time.[41]

While Weston was at the helm there was also an increase in the fines imposed by the Star Chamber and the High Commission, but this was not owing to his efforts and was of less importance than the rising yields of the recusancy fines.

A revenue-producing measure in which the Treasurer took a special interest was the proposal to assess fines on well-to-do gentlemen who had failed to apply for the order of knighthood at the time of Charles's coronation. This measure was suggested by John Borough, who had been instructed in January 1628 to search through the records of the Tower to discover what projects of earlier periods might be applicable to the financial problems of Charles I's government. Once Borough had reported, a special commission was appointed in April 1629 to make a detailed study of the proposal. This commission consisted of Weston, Lord Keeper Coventry, the Earls of Arundel, Manchester, Pembroke, Dorset, Salisbury, and Exeter, the two principal Secretaries, and ten others. They had completed the necessary preliminary work by the end of the year, and on 28 January 1630 another royal commission, with virtually the same personnel, was instructed 'to compound with persons who, being possessed of £40 per annum in lands or rents, had not taken upon them the order of knighthood.'[42]

The fines were actually assessed by local officials and ranged between a high of £100 and a low of £10, with the national average falling between £17 and £18, which was considerably less than the fees charged when a man was knighted. An attempt was made to assess them in relation to wealth and income, but this was of necessity rather crudely done. The fines tended to be heaviest in the northern counties and lightest in the midlands. Although most of the men fined could easily afford to pay the sums demanded of them, there was an alarming outcry when the first fines were imposed. A hurried resort to the Court of Exchequer was therefore made. In a series of decisions handed down between August 1630 and February 1631, the Barons held that the government's course was completely legal.[43]

All sums deposited in the Receipt as a result of the knighthood fines were channelled through a single teller, Edward Carne, who was directed by the Treasurer to be especially careful in his book-keeping. It is nevertheless unclear how much money was raised in this manner. W. R. Scott maintains that £167,315 was collected between 1630 and 1633; but Professor Dietz contends that only £165,000 had been received at the Exchequer by 1635. Neither of these sums corresponds to the figure given in a manuscript in the British Museum, which indicates that a total of £173,537 was raised through the knighthood fines.[44] It is apparent, moreover, that not all the money collected was transported to London and paid into the Receipt. For example, the collector of knighthood fines in Hertfordshire, Sir Edward Bashe, was instructed in 1631 to issue £250 from his collections to the Earl of Salisbury as remuneration for work supervised by him at Theobalds. In the same way Sir Thomas Wentworth was directed to withhold a portion of his receipts for the payment of certain administrative expenses in the counties under his jurisdiction as President of the Council of the North. Altogether Wentworth paid £24,800 into the Receipt and retained £3395 19s., the greater part of which he used for improvements to the King's Manor at York.[45] In both cases tallies were struck so that Bashe and Wentworth received credit for the sums withheld and disbursed by them; but whether those sums were noted by Scott and Dietz is, again, unclear. If not, the total receipts from the knighthood fines may have been somewhat greater, perhaps as high as £180,000 or £190,000.

More important even than the proceeds of the knighthood fines were the receipts from the customs duties, the largest single item of the King's ordinary revenue. Clarendon believed that once England withdrew from the continental wars, her foreign trade recovered from the prolonged depression of the 1620s, the receipts from the customs duties increased, and both Charles and his subjects enjoyed greater levels of prosperity and contentment.[46] Clarendon was not alone in believing that the decade of Personal Rule was an era of growing financial stability. Because of the return to more settled conditions, the prospects for invested capital appeared unusually bright, and in June 1630 a new company for trade with Africa was chartered. The East India Company was allowed to export bullion and soon began to show greater profits, as did the Greenland Company and various other mercantile organisations.[47]

With the return to peace England's economy was certainly healthier than that of her continental neighbours, but present-day historians dispute whether the return to prosperity was as sudden or as widespread as Clarendon suggested. England's foreign trade experienced only a minimum level of recovery between 1629 and 1631, but in 1632 something of a boom did at last occur, which led to a dramatic increase of imports as well as exports. In successive years trading conditions remained unsteady, with some branches of the economy prospering and others lagging behind. The output of coal rose impressively owing to the increasing demands of Londoners, who were becoming more numerous with each passing year. But the cloth industry continued to languish, and in 1640 only 45,000 undressed cloths were exported by way of the capital, in comparison with the 120,000 pieces sent abroad in 1606.[48]

As both Treasurer and *ex officio* chairman of the Committee for Trade, which met on Friday mornings, Weston could not have been unaware of the unsettled trading conditions that persisted until the end of 1631. It was doubtless because of his knowledge in this regard that he agreed to continue, at least for the present, the annual leases on the great farm of the customs, which had been initiated in 1628. By 1632, however, England's foreign trade had improved to such an extent that he was able to persuade the farmers to accept a three-year lease at an annual rental of £150,000, which was the same amount they had paid each year since 1629 but £10,000 more than they had paid in 1628. The lease of 1632 was renewed in 1635 at no increase of rent; but when it was renegotiated for a second time in 1638, Archbishop Laud and the new Lord Treasurer, William Juxon, Bishop of London, required the farmers to accept an increase of £22,500 in their yearly rent, even though trading conditions continued to be uncertain.[49]

From time to time Weston was obliged to confer with the farmers of the petty customs, who managed the duties charged on French and Rhenish wines and on currants from the Levant. Some years earlier, before the death of James I, the three petty farms had been leased for an annual rental of £44,005 to a syndicate dominated by Henry Garway and Nicholas Salter. Although three separate leases had been signed, they were considered part of a single contract, which was to remain in effect until 1632. On the expiration of that contract, Weston and the King decided that the three petty farms should be consolidated and managed as a unit bearing a yearly rental of £60,000. A new lease was accordingly drawn for seven years, and in July 1632 the now-unified petty farm was granted to a syndicate directed by Sir Paul Pindar, John Harrison, Thomas Dawes, and Sir John Wolstenholme the Younger, or the same men who dominated the great farm of the customs, which could not have been a coincidence. The consolidation of the petty farms into a single farm, whose personnel was then merged with that of the great farm, was to facilitate the government's efforts at a later date to resume direct management of all the customs duties. Such a step was never considered by Weston, however, and it was not taken until he had been dead for more than thirty years. Weston was strongly opposed to the idea of trading the certainties of customs farming for the uncertainties of direct management, and as long as he remained at the helm there was no chance that he would sponsor such a fundamental change of customs policy.[50]

10 Family and Factions

While employed as the King's chief minister, Weston was the recipient of numerous marks of his master's favour. In January 1629 he and the Earl of Warwick were appointed joint Lords Lieutenant of Essex, and three months later he was inducted into the Order of the Garter. In 1631 he was named to four related ceremonial positions: Lord Lieutenant of Southampton, Lord Lieutenant of Hampshire, Captain General of the Isle of Wight, and Governor of Carisbrooke Castle. The last of these offices he arranged in 1633 to be transferred to his son Jerome, who held it until ousted by parliament for his royalist sympathies in 1642. In his capacity as Captain General of the Isle of Wight, the Treasurer doubled as Governor of the newly rebuilt Sandown Castle, where he took steps to have his coat of arms carved over the mantelpiece in the Great Hall.[1]

Like other important members of the government, Weston could expect to receive occasional grants and awards from the crown. The King's ministers at this time were paid only a fraction of the real value of their services and necessarily depended on their master's bounty as a supplement to their official salaries. The Treasurer was no exception to this rule and periodically benefited from the most tangible expression of Charles's appreciation. In July 1629 he was awarded a portion of the profits to be derived from the sale of lands that had formerly belonged to Sir John Carroll, a convicted recusant. Three months later he and Cottington shared between themselves a seven-year grant of 'all fines and sums of money due to his Majesty upon licences and pardons of alienations and upon all fines and recoveries of all manors, lands, and tenements within this realm of England.' In 1630 the Treasurer was awarded the proceeds of all alienation fines in Chancery. In June 1631 he and several associates were authorised 'to work and make saltpetre and gunpowder by themselves or their deputies within the realms of England and Ireland and dominions thereof'; and in March 1632 he was granted the 300-ton prize ship *St. Claude*, which he could use 'for the fetching of Masts from Scotland or otherwise as his Lordship shall think good.'[2]

In an oft-cited passage Clarendon maintained that 'the King was pleased twice to pay his debts; at least, towards it, to disburse forty thousand pounds in ready money out of the Exchequer.'[3] There is no evidence in the Public Record Office or the British Museum to substantiate this charge. In a report submitted to the King in October 1634, Weston acknowledged receipts of £10,000 from the crown since being entrusted with the white staff, the greater part of which had been camouflaged under the heading of secret service money. Unless other payments were made to him of which the King was either unaware or prepared to dismiss completely out of hand, it must be concluded that he received far less in the way of direct cash awards than Clarendon averred. Yet Charles did present an unusually generous wedding gift to one of the Treasurer's many daughters. When Anne Weston became the wife of Basil, Lord Feilding, she received £3000 'as his Majesty's free gift.'[4]

During these years Weston was again an active speculator in the land market, in an effort to increase the size of his estate. In 1632 he took part in a complicated series of land transactions in Lincolnshire, Cambridgeshire, and the Isle of Ely, in which he was associated with his son Jerome, the Earl of Bedford, and several other courtiers. The Treasurer gained possession of two manors near Cambridge, Whittlesey St Mary's and Whittlesey St Andrew's, while Jerome, who was a partner in Bedford's project to drain the fens of East Anglia, received a grant of certain lands in Lincolnshire. Somewhat earlier the Treasurer had by himself arranged to purchase the manor of Appleby in Lincolnshire, which remained a Weston property for only a few years, however. In the autumn of 1635 this large tract was alienated for £12,000, or nearly twice what had been paid for it. Weston made a valuable addition to his lands in Essex through the acquisition of Blunts Hall, a large property noted for its handsome manor house, which was located midway between Chelmsford and Maldon.[5]

While enlarging his estate, which was now worth almost £6000 a year, Weston was giving much time and attention to the construction of a new family estate in Surrey. Charles frequently went on progress and expected his ministers to maintain residences large and grand enough to receive the court. In January 1628 he had in fact instructed the officers of the Exchequer to 'provide themselves with great houses and furniture in all points requisite . . . to be always in readiness for the service of his Majesty and his Kingdoms as there shall be cause.'[6] Thus it was essential for the Treasurer to build a country home nobler and more elaborate than the family seat at Skreens, which was little more than a simple timber building. Since the tract known as Putney or Mortlake Park which he had purchased from the crown in 1627, was only a few miles southwest of Westminster, he decided to build his new house there and seems to have set to work immediately. By the autumn of 1628 the mansion was taking shape, and during the summer of the next year a number of illustrious figures, including Rubens, the Marquis de Châteauneuf, and both Charles and Henrietta Maria, were entertained in the house.

Little is known about the mansion, since it was demolished midway in the reign of George III after being damaged in a great storm. It must have been a large and imposing structure, however, for Charles II was a frequent guest at Putney Park during the 1660s and 1670s, when it was owned by the Dowager Countess of Devonshire, who presided over a distinguished circle of poets, wits, and philosophers.[7] Clearly the Treasurer lavished great amounts upon it, and it was principally for this reason that he left obligations of nearly £21,000 behind him. Such profuse expenditure was typical of the Elizabethan and early Stuart periods, when men born into the gentry and middle class suddenly found themselves raised to the peerage. Such men were expected to live up to their rank and spend on the same extravagant scale as the Manners, Howards, Sackvilles, and the other great families of the time. So prodigal was the English aristocracy that Rubens observed to Olivares in 1629: 'All the leading nobles live on a sumptuous scale and spend money lavishly, so that the majority of them are hopelessly in debt.'[8] Because of his long-time interest in problems of financial management, the Treasurer showed more restraint than many of the *nouveaux arrivés* of his generation; and with his combined income of £17,000 or £18,000 a year from land and office during the early 1630s, he could well afford to build an imposing country home.

In the selection of the interior appointments for his new

residence, Weston procured the services of Balthasar Gerbier, a Dutchman who had once been associated with Buckingham and was now the accepted arbiter of fashion in the capital. Gerbier made suggestions concerning the design of mantelpieces and balustrades and recommended the hiring of craftsmen, painters, and sculptors. It seems likely that he was responsible for the selection of Bernardo Zucchero, scion of a distinguished family of Roman painters, to decorate the ceiling of the mansion's chapel with a fresco of the Last Supper. Work on the ceiling had been completed by 26 May 1632, when the chapel was dedicated in a ceremony conducted by Laud, to whom the Treasurer made occasional friendly, albeit unsuccessful, gestures.[9]

Gerbier also assisted with the layout of Weston's garden and served as an intermediary between him and Hubert Le Sueur, who was commissioned to cast an equestrian statue of Charles I. Sealed in January 1630, the contract specified that the Frenchman should cast a work in bronze, the King's figure being 'proportionable full six feet' and his steed 'bigger than a great Horse by a foot.' He was to receive a total of £600 for the statue, which was one of the highest prices paid for a single work of art during the 1630s.[10] For some reason not yet discovered Le Sueur's statue was never erected in the garden at Putney Park: it remained stored away in his studio, which was within a short distance of St Bartholomew the Great in West Smithfield. When the Civil War broke out in 1642, the statue was seized by parliament; and in 1649 it was sold to a London brazier, John Rivett, who was given strict orders to break it up. Rivett made a pretence of complying with these instructions but actually buried the statue in the cellar of his house. After the Restoration in 1660, Jerome Weston learned of its continued existence and made several unsuccessful attempts to establish his claims to it. For more than ten years it remained in the possession of Rivett, who eventually presented it to Charles II. In 1674 it was at last erected at Charing Cross, to become a familiar and much-loved spectacle of the London scene.[11]

Weston's children were now coming of age, and arrangements had to be made for their education, marriage, and advancement in life. In October 1629 he secured a licence for three years' foreign travel for Jerome and Thomas, his two eldest sons by his second wife.[12] The Treasurer had high hopes for his son Jerome, whom he wished to see appointed Secretary of State or Master of the Court of Wards and Liveries, and he was bent on a great marriage for him. As early as 1630 it was rumoured that Jerome was engaged to marry 'one of the Blood-royal of Scotland, the Duke of Lennox's sister, and that with his Majesty's consent.' Yet it was not until 25 June 1632 that his union with Lady Frances Stuart, a sister of the fourth Duke of Lennox and a cousin of the King himself, was solemnised. The ceremony took place in the newly consecrated chapel at Putney Park, with Bishop Laud again officiating. Charles and Henrietta Maria, accompanied by large numbers of the court, were in attendance. The King is said to have given the bride a present of £10,000, and with 'extraordinary favour' he even agreed to give her away.[13] Ben Jonson wrote the ode for this joyous occasion.

> See, the Procession! what a Holy day
> (Bearing the promise of some better fate)
> Hath filed, with *Cacoches*, all the way,
> From Greenwich, hither, to Row-hampton gate!
> When look'd the yeare, at best,
> So like a feast?
> Or were Affaires in tune,
> By all the Spheares consent, so in the heart of June?
>
> What Beautie of Beauties, and bright youth's charge
> of Summers Liveries, and gladding greene;
> Doe boast their Loves, and Brav'ries so at large,
> As they came all to see, and to be seene!
> When look'd the Earth so fine,
> Or so did shine,
> In all her bloome, and flower;
> To welcome home a Paire, and deck the nuptiall bower?

On a more down-to-earth note, the Venetian Ambassador reported that the marriage negotiations succeeded only because of the King's intervention.

> The thing that has astonished everyone is that they say, to remove all objections to the marriage, in other respects a very unequal one, the young duchess being very much above him in fortune and birth, that the King himself desired to act as the mediary and manager by his personal interposition.[14]

The marriage was also assisted by the Earl of Arundel and his heir, Lord Maltravers. Arundel was an old friend of the Treasurer's, and Maltravers, who was on intimate terms with Jerome, was a brother-in-law of the prospective bride. The marriage ultimately proved to the Howards' financial benefit, since it was to be the descendants of Lady Elizabeth Stuart and Lord Maltravers, who succeeded his father as third Earl of Arundel, that the bulk of the Weston lands passed when the direct line became extinct in 1694.[15]

Next the Treasurer entered into negotiations for a union between his daughter Anne and Basil, Lord Feilding, heir apparent of the Earl of Denbigh, the current Master of the Great Wardrobe. Their nuptials took place shortly before Christmas 1632, for the wedding supper occurred on 23 December.[16] As to the Treasurer's other children, Catherine became the wife of Richard White of Hutton, Essex, while Frances was betrothed to Philip Draycote of Paynesley, Staffordshire. Weston's son Benjamin, who was granted the freedom of Poole in 1630, took as his wife Anne Villiers, dowager Countess of Anglesey. Ben's older brother Thomas, the last of the Treasurer's descendants to inherit his titles, remained a bachelor for many years but was ultimately married to Anne Butler, daughter of John, Lord Butler of Bramfield and widow of Mountjoy Blount, Earl of Newport. For the support of his son Thomas the Treasurer devised a generous settlement out of 'natural love' in March 1634. The younger man was granted the family estate of Skreens and a host of nearby properties in Chelmsford and Dunmow hundreds, Essex.[17]

The Treasurer's decision to confer Skreens on a younger son was doubtless prompted by the illness and impending death of his namesake, Richard, the only son by his first wife, Elizabeth Pincheon. Except for the fact that he helped to collect the knighthood fines in Staffordshire, little is known about the younger Richard Weston's activities during the early 1630s. He was never knighted and there is no evidence that he took a wife. It is clear, however, that he was suffering from a mental or emotional disorder by this time, for in May 1634 Sir Thomas Wentworth learned from a friend in the capital that the Treasurer's eldest son, 'who was mad and kept at Coventry, is lately dead.'[18] When the younger Weston's collapse and commitment occurred is impossible to determine, although by 1632 his half-brother Jerome was being hailed as the Treasurer's heir apparent. Furthermore when the latter was created Earl of Portland, the honorary title of 'Lord Weston' was accorded the second rather than the eldest son.

Weston's elevation to the Earldom of Portland took place on 17 February 1633, with the King himself bestowing the sword and mantle, the insignia of his new rank. To celebrate this happy occasion Ben Jonson composed a short poem 'To the Envious.' Those guilty of any jealousy towards the Treasurer were enjoined by the poet:

> Looke up thou seed of envie, and still bring
>   Thy faint, and narrow eyes, to reade the *King*
> In his great Actions: view whom his large hand,
>   Hath rais'd to be the *Port* unto his *Land*!
> WESTON! That waking man! that Eye of State!
>   Who seldom sleepes! whom bad men only hate!
> Why doe I irritate, or stirre up thee,
>   Thou sluggish spawne, that canst, but wilt not see!
> Feed on thy selfe for spight, and shew thy *Kind*:
>   To vertue, and true worth, be ever blind.
> Dreame thou could'st hurt it, but before thou wake,
>   T'effect it; Feele, thou 'ast made thine owne heartake.

Although described by Jonson as one 'whom bad men only hate,' there was mounting resentment against him on the part of his own neighbours in Essex, and it was undoubtedly for this reason that Charles decided against creating him Earl of Chelmsford, as some observers had predicted he might do. The Treasurer was recognised as the chief proponent of several of the government's most unpopular policies, including the knighthood fines that were currently being assessed on the gentlemen of his home county. During the years 1631–5 some 121 Essex gentlemen were required to pay sums ranging between £10 and £32 10s., a total of £1529 being extracted from them.[19] The fact that the Treasurer was felt to share his second wife's sympathy for Catholicism was also resented by the inhabitants of a county that was predominantly Protestant.

By 1633 the Earl of Portland, as he must now be called, was the most controversial member of the government, with scores of enemies and detractors as well as friends and supporters. Clarendon disliked him for personal reasons and charged that 'all the honours the King conferred upon him . . . could not make him think himself great enough.' In Clarendon's opinion, the Treasurer was a man of 'mean and abject spirit,' who, after Buckingham's assassination, quickly 'threw off his old affectation to please some very much and to displease none . . . [and] found himself to succeed him [the duke] in the public displeasure and in the malice of his enemies, without succeeding him in his credit at Court or in the affection of any considerable dependents.'[20]

Clarendon's judgment was an extremely harsh one, influenced in part by the views of a man he held in high esteem: William Laud, the Treasurer's chief enemy. Clarendon's hatred of Portland must thus be balanced against the attitudes of others, who were invariably more sympathetic towards him. Sir Philip Warwick, a Secretary of the Treasury after the Civil War, thought him to be 'a Gentleman of serious thoughts, and good parts, and verst in the chief employments at home and abroad'; and in the wedding ode for Jerome Weston and his young wife, Jonson described the elder Weston in flattering terms.

> *Weston*, their Treasure, as their Treasurer,
> That Mine of Wisdome, and Counsells deep,
> Great Say-Master of State, who cannot erre,
> But doth his Carract, and just Standard keepe
> In all the prov'd assayes
> And legall wayes
> Of Tryals, to worke downe
> Men's Loves unto the Lawes, and Lawes to love the Crowne.

It is undeniably true that the Treasurer was never as powerful as Buckingham, but he was far from careless about political matters and periodically attempted to bolster his faction. His relations were invariably friendly with the Earl of Denbigh, father-in-law of his daughter Anne, and the Earl of Dorset, Lord Chamberlain to the Queen; and he was particularly mindful of the need to cultivate the good will of the Earl of Carlisle, to whom he made repeated overtures after 1628. In December 1631 Carlisle was reported by a Londoner to be 'very great with my Lord Treasurer, and a most diligent waiter at court.'[21] Portland's most reliable associates, however, were his old friends the Earl of Arundel and Bishop Williams of Lincoln. Arundel had a powerful following of his own and was able to render invaluable assistance – the support of so sincere and discriminating an aristocrat was in itself a tribute to the Treasurer's character. But as a result of his low-church views, Bishop Williams was hated by Laud and was more of a liability than an asset. Portland could also count on the assistance of Lord Dorchester, with whom his relations were always cordial, and Sir Francis Windebank, who was nominated principal Secretary after Dorchester's death in February 1632. Although a friend of the Treasurer's for some years, Windebank was appointed to the office largely because of Laud's campaign on his behalf. Once in possession of the seals, however, he revealed his intention of cooperating with Portland and his most important administrative associate, Cottington, to the bishop's chagrin.

Several men formerly associated with the parliamentary opposition were among those advanced by the Treasurer. In November 1630 a reversion to the Mastership of the Rolls was granted to Sir Dudley Digges, one of the most outspoken critics of royal policy during the previous decade. Another opposition leader brought into the government through his efforts was William Noy, who was named Attorney-General in August 1631. The chief minister naturally reserved places in the royal household for his followers. Sir John Savile, a prominent Yorkshireman who had once been a client of Buckingham's, was made comptroller of the household; and shortly after receiving the post of cofferer, Sir Henry Vane was characterised as 'a great creature of my Lord Treasurer.' The most important individual sponsored at court by Portland was of course Sir Thomas Wentworth, who had been named President of the Council of the North in December 1628. A year later Wentworth was sworn of the Privy Council, again largely because of the Treasurer's efforts.[22]

While working to create as strong a following as possible, Portland kept a careful watch over the patronage, which he was naturally tempted to exploit for his own financial advantage. Before James Maxwell was nominated Clerk of the Court of Wards and Liveries, he found it necessary to make a payment of £1000 to the Treasurer. An equally sizeable sum was required of Thomas Fanshawe prior to his appointment as Clerk of the Crown in the Court of King's Bench. Because he refused to curb his own profits while restricting the King's generosity to others, Portland became the target of much abusive comment. Clarendon was especially critical of the way he manipulated the patronage and complained bitterly about his refusal to remain 'within the verge of his own province.'[23]

The mounting chorus of dislike for him was reinforced by his erratic and unpredictable behaviour towards others. He was now in his mid-fifties and plagued by recurrent stomach trouble, which tended to make him irritable and short tempered. In July 1629 Rubens reported to Olivares that Weston was 'suffering from gallstones, so that one must excuse him for the moment.'[24] The Treasurer was actually afflicted with a kidney condition, but Rubens' statement is the first reliable evidence of the chronically poor health he endured during the last years of his life. In July 1631 he himself referred to his condition as 'my wonted indisposition'; and in May 1633, while attending the King on his progress to Edinburgh, he suffered a serious 'fit of the stone, not without some aguish distemper.' At the time he was a house guest at Worksop, where he had been invited by Arundel to spend a few days, while Charles and his train were being entertained at Welbeck by the Earl of Newcastle. Happily, the physician William Harvey, the discoverer of the circulation of the blood, was also a house guest at Worksop and was able to take charge of his case, and within a few days he was ready to resume the journey to Scotland.[25] Because he was often uncomfortable if not in severe pain, Portland tended to be rude and snappish even with such dependable associates as Cottington. In March 1634 the latter informed a friend:

> My Lord Treasurer hath of late had very little health, and at this time is worse than I have ever known him. Before his sickness he grew very dry towards me, insomuch as in some days together he would scarce speak to me.[26]

Most historians have failed to realise how sickly Portland was during these years, which has caused them to misinterpret his personality and to misunderstand the difficulties confronting other ministers who worked closely with him.

Yet Clarendon was undeniably correct in holding that he had a high sense of his own importance. Like his royal master, Portland placed great stress on decorum and insisted that others show proper deference for his exalted position. Except with the members of his own circle, his manner tended to be formal and excessively reserved. Whenever petitioned by others, he insisted on a correct, and usually prolonged, consideration of the matter, which is what prompted Gardiner's criticisms of his 'ponderous inertia.'[27] Suitors soon realised that he had to be treated gingerly and with extreme care. When in March 1634 Wentworth sent his brother George on a mission to London, he gave careful instructions concerning the best way to approach him.

> In any case I would not advise you to seem to importune my Lord Treasurer too much for your dispatch; only put yourself sometimes in his eye, and now and then gently let him know you wait his good pleasure without troubling him with mere words, unless himself give you the occasion of further discourse.[28]

It should not be forgotten, however, that whenever feeling well, Portland could be charming and highly obliging to his friends and supporters. Generous and warm-hearted by nature, he was invariably helpful to those he liked and trusted. He had a keen sense of humour and was not unwilling to laugh at himself, which is amply proved by an episode concerning Sir Julius Caesar, the aged Master of the Rolls.

In 1630 or 1631, when one of the Six Clerks in Chancery was about to retire, Caesar, who had an unquestioned right to make all appointments in that office, made it known that he intended to name his own son Robert, then a Clerk of the Enrolments, to the position. Upon learning this, the Treasurer intervened and persuaded Charles to forbid the nomination until a statement of the royal will had been issued. He then proceeded to extract a cash payment of £6000 for the government's use from William Carne, who was rewarded with the place originally intended for the younger Caesar. Once this action had been taken, Sir Julius complained long and hard and rallied the support of his friends and sympathisers. As a consequence Weston was obliged to promise that when another of the clerkships became vacant, it would be conferred on Robert Caesar, even if his father had died in the meantime. The Treasurer also pledged to secure 'some declaration to that purpose under his Majesty's sign manual.'

As he did on numerous occasions, however, Weston procrastinated, for which he was reprimanded by the Earl of Tullibardine, to whom he replied that he had simply forgotten about the matter and was heartily sorry. He then requested the earl to put a few words on paper as a reminder for him to discuss the subject with the King that very afternoon. Tullibardine obliged by writing the two words 'Remember Caesar' on a sheet that the Treasurer put into 'that little pocket where, he said, he kept all his memorials which were first to be transacted.' Yet some weeks elapsed before he discovered the note among his other papers, at which time he was unable to remember the meaning of the command to 'Remember Caesar.' After a worried discussion with several of his closest friends, it was decided that the injunction could only be interpreted as a warning to avoid crowded places where he might be struck down. He was advised to remain safely at home, feigning illness if necessary, and only to admit persons of 'undoubted affections' into his presence. That night Weston forbade the porter of Wallingford House to open the gates for any reason whatever and directed his household servants to maintain a close watch until the following morning. Towards noon of the next day Tullibardine arrived to inquire if the Treasurer had in fact remembered Caesar, which caused him to recollect his earlier promise and enjoy a hearty laugh that he was happy to share with his friends and servants, even though the joke was on himself.[29]

Because Weston occasionally encroached on the appointive rights of other officials, and because of various other irritants, such as his campaign to restrict pensions and his aloof and sometimes rude behaviour, there was much wishful thinking during the early 1630s concerning his possible overthrow. His power was far from absolute – he was more like a first among equals than a modern Prime Minister – and the King had a number of influential confidants, who included not only the Queen and Bishop Laud but also the Earls of Carlisle and Pembroke and his two Scottish favourites, the Duke of Lennox and the Marquess of Hamilton. Thus the Treasurer's position was in some ways a vulnerable one, and courtiers attacked him in a way they never would have challenged the Duke of Buckingham. As early as January 1630 it was reported that 'the Lord Treasurer Weston is he who hath the greatest vogue at court, but many great ones have clashed with him.' Later in the same year Wentworth learned from a resident of the capital that there had recently been a bitter squabble between Weston and Sir George Goring, an important member of the Queen's party.[30]

Weston and Henrietta Maria never had any affection for one another, since they saw themselves as competitors for influence with the King. Moreover, he obviously regarded her as a stupid and flighty woman, which she was, while she was annoyed by his refusal to assist her mother, Marie de Medici, now banished from the French court by Louis XIII and Richelieu. From time to time Henrietta Maria implored her husband to allow the Dowager Queen of France to visit England, but at the Treasurer's urging he always refused. Weston's objections were amply corroborated when, in 1638, the widow of Henry IV was finally allowed to enter the country. She arrived in London with a train of 600 attendants, settled down in St James's Palace for a long stay, and cost her son-in-law the enormous sum of £3000 a month.[31] The relationship between Weston and Henrietta Maria was of particular interest to Lord Clarendon, who maintained that the former was always 'solicitous to know what her Majesty said of him in private, and what resentments she had towards him.' Whenever he learned that she had been critical of his behaviour, he would 'fly to the King and make passionate complaints and representations.' Occasionally he bewailed his misfortunes to the Queen herself, which inevitably led to the discovery of the persons from whom he received his intelligence.[32]

Because the Queen's party included several avowed enemies of the Treasurer, including the Earl of Holland, Sir George Goring, and Henry Jermyn, there were periodic altercations at court that the weak-willed King was powerless to prevent. For a time Weston's antagonists were encouraged by M. de Castelnovo, the French Ambassador in London between 1630 and 1632. Castelnovo was a brash man who worked overtly for the Treasurer's overthrow. Shortly after his arrival he made contact with the Queen, who was easily persuaded to denounce his 'harmful influence' to her husband. But this crude attempt to undermine Weston's power came to nothing and indirectly served to weaken her position. The Treasurer was always suspicious of Castelnovo, and when he learned of his intrigues in 1632, he quickly secured his recall. The next French Ambassador, M. de Fontane, did not dare to oppose him so openly, for he could see 'that with him as an opponent it would be impossible ever to obtain anything.' Throughout his stay in England Fontane conducted himself discreetly and framed his courses according to 'reason rather than passion.' Consequently relations between Weston and this ambassador showed perceptible improvement within a brief time.[33]

To safeguard himself against such attacks, the Treasurer used every device at his disposal to ingratiate himself with his royal master. He insisted on the punctual supply of the King's sister and brother-in-law at their court-in-exile at The Hague, which relieved one of Charles's greatest worries. He also exploited his own appreciation and concern for the arts and thereby strengthened his position. In 1629 he commissioned a study of the Madonna and Child by Van Dyck, which was ultimately presented as a New Year's gift to the King. In addition Weston was careful to patronise Le Sueur, a favourite royal artist who received frequent payments from the crown. Whether the Treasurer was also a supporter of the poets and dramatists of the age is a more difficult question to answer. He had no time to participate in the masques that were such a prominent feature of court life, but both he and his son Jerome were known to Ben Jonson, who composed several works in their honour. In 1631 the poet addressed the following 'Epistle Mendicant' to Weston, whose financial assistance he was then seeking.

Poore wretched states, prest by extremities,
Are faine to seeke for succours, and supplies
of *Princes* aides, or good *men's Charities*.

Disease, the Enemie, and his Ingineers
Want, with the rest of his conceal'd compeeres,
Have cast a trench about mee, now five yeares.

And made those strong approaches, by *Falsebraies*,
Reduicts, *Half-moones*, *Horne-workes*, and such close wayes,
The *Muse* not peepes out, one of hundred dayes.

But lyes block'd up, and straightened, narrow'd in,
Fix'd to the bed, and boords, unlike to win
Health, or scarce breath, and she had never bin.

Unlesse some saving-*Honour* of the *crown*,
Dare thinke it, to relieve, no lesse renowne,
A *Bed-rid* Wit, then a *besieged* Towne.

In the next year Jonson composed the wedding ode for Jerome and Lady Frances Stuart, so it can be concluded that he received some assistance from the Treasurer.

Because of his efforts on behalf of the arts and his thorough knowledge of public finance, Weston never lost the King's confidence. Even Lord Clarendon conceded that 'no man better understood what method was necessary towards that husbandry [of the royal revenue] than he' and that aside from his opinions the King accepted 'no other advice in the large business of his revenue.'[34] If Charles took financial suggestions from no one except the Treasurer, he was always willing to listen to the views of others in regard to foreign affairs. Weston was indeed the King's chief foreign-policy adviser, mainly because every policy had to be weighed in terms of cost, but it would be wrong to assume that he enjoyed a free hand and made all the important decisions. Charles was still anxious to see his brother-in-law, the Elector Palatine, restored to his ancestral lands and titles, and once the financial situation began to improve he gave renewed thought to intervention in the war. This was encouraged by a number of courtiers, particularly the Marquess of Hamilton, who had little knowledge of, or concern for, the government's financial plight. Weston was horrified to learn that active support of Frederick V was again being contemplated, although he was in no position to declare so openly. 'No minister . . . could hope to keep his place for an hour who should venture to inform Charles that the recovery of the Palatinate was beyond his power to effect.'[35] Thus Weston had no choice but to humour the King, oppose his favourites, and trust that unexpected developments would block their plans in the end.

Fortunately for the Treasurer, rumours tailor-made to serve his purposes began to circulate in London concerning Hamilton's ultimate ambitions. While the marquess was away on a recruiting trip to Scotland, several of his closest associates, including Lords Ochiltree and Reay, proclaimed that he had no intention of leaving the British Isles at all. Rather they insisted that he planned to put himself at the head of his troops, seize control of the King's person, execute the Treasurer and other known partisans of Spain, and set himself up as an independent ruler of Scotland.[36] Whether there was any factual basis to this alleged conspiracy has never been determined. Probably there was not, for Lord Ochiltree was an inveterate schemer, having made similar charges in 1623 against Sir Gideon Murray, the Deputy Treasurer of Scotland. Furthermore Ochiltree had a long-standing grudge against the Hamiltons, who had helped to secure the arrest and execution of his relative Father John Ogilvie, a Jesuit priest, in 1615.[37]

At any rate the Treasurer decided to make whatever use he could of the rumours when they were called to his attention by Lord Ochiltree. Weston believed it might be possible to destroy the marquess's influence with the King and thereby prevent his troops from sailing forth to Germany. Shortly before Hamilton was scheduled to return from his final conscription trip to Scotland, the Treasurer secured an audience and reported everything he had heard to date. With great eloquence he attempted to convince Charles that his Scottish favourite, who was not only a Councillor in both kingdoms but also a gentleman of the Bedchamber and Master of the Horse, was on the verge of an attempted treason and that Charles must not 'permit the marquess to come near his Sacred Person, and in no kind to have the privilege to lie in his Majesty's Bed-Chamber, lest his Majesty's life were hazarded thereby.' Weston's testimony was corroborated by Lord Ochiltree, who was questioned by the Council on 20 and 21 June 1630, when he swore that the marquess was planning to use his troops to kidnap the entire royal family.[38]

Although other witnesses were willing to attest to the truth of the charges, the King refused to attach any importance to them. On Hamilton's return from Scotland, he greeted him with open arms and insisted that they spend a night together in the same bedchamber as a way of demonstrating the ridiculous nature of the accusations. Thus the marquess's influence remained unimpaired, and shortly afterwards he obtained permission to set sail for Germany. On 16 July 1631 a fleet of ships carrying Hamilton and his men cleared the entrance of Yarmouth harbour.[39]

Meanwhile steps had been taken to punish those responsible for the charges against Hamilton. Lord Ochiltree, a Scottish subject, was convicted of sedition in an Edinburgh court and sentenced to life imprisonment. He remained in confinement for twenty years, until finally released from his cell by Oliver Cromwell. Ochiltree's confederate, Lord Reay, sought to save himself by claiming that he had merely passed on information relayed to him by David Ramsay, a professional soldier who had served under both Hamilton and Christian IV of Denmark. Ramsay stoutly denied Lord Reay's allegations; and as there was no way to prove the truth of the matter, the two men demanded the right to settle their differences by a resort to combat. A Court of Chivalry was established under the joint presidency of Lord Arundel, Earl Marshal of the realm, and the Earl of Lindsey, who was appointed Lord Constable for the occasion. Before the combat could take place, the King intervened and directed the two firebrands to cool their heels in the Tower of London, from which they were not released until they had given securities against any future breach of the peace. While these events were occurring Charles addressed a letter to Hamilton in Germany in which he expressed his satisfaction that no plot had ever existed and pledged that the marquess would in no wise be dishonoured by the affair.[40]

The Treasurer alone escaped unscathed from the attempt to ruin Hamilton. His position at court was too well established and he had taken only a brief part in the proceedings. Furthermore he was already making arrangements for the marriage of his daughter Anne to Basil, Lord Feilding, the son and heir apparent of the Earl of Denbigh, who was by coincidence Hamilton's father-in-law. To those who were unaware that the marquess had been forced into his marriage by Buckingham and would rather fight in the continental wars than consummate it, it must have seemed that Weston had acted throughout on the basis of principle. His only desire had been to protect the safety and perhaps even the life of his King, and no action was ever contemplated against him. Although the Treasurer had failed to prevent Hamilton's departure for Germany, he managed to extract a promise from the King not to underwrite the mission indefinitely. Shortly before the marquess set sail, Charles granted him £26,015 for the maintenance of his troops, but it was clearly understood that he would have to rely on the King of Sweden or some other continental ruler for future support.[41]

Because Charles's outlook failed to 'base itself upon the realities of the world,' the Treasurer faced continued difficulties in successive years. This was particularly true during the latter half of 1632, when Spanish troops in the Low Countries were thrown back by the armies of the United Provinces. On 14 August Maestricht surrendered to the Dutch, and it briefly appeared that the entire

Spanish Netherlands might be overrun. In the interests of British security, Charles was determined to prevent the absorption of that strategic area by the Dutch republic or any other neighbouring country. During a conference at Putney Park in September 1632, it was decided to offer naval assistance to Spain and request Philip IV to make over a large part of Flanders to England, to be held under the suzerainty of the Spanish crown. But the authorities in Madrid were not pleased by these proposals, since they were unwilling to concede that their cause was hopeless. In November 1632 they returned a curt refusal to the suggestion that Dunkirk or some other fortified place in Flanders be entrusted to the King of England.[42]

Despite the weakness of the Spanish forces in the Low Countries, Charles was as anxious as ever to secure the restitution of the Palatinate and was convinced that Spanish assistance was essential for the achievement of that objective. Repeated overtures were therefore made to the authorities in Madrid, and in November 1633 the King instructed his three most trusted ministers, Portland, Cottington, and Windebank, to form a secret triumvirate to negotiate with the Spanish Agent in London, Juan de Necolalde, for a naval and military alliance.[43] More realistic than his master, Portland never believed that such negotiations would succeed, even though the English government allowed Spain to raise several companies of volunteers in the British Isles for service with the Cardinal-Infant in Flanders. England also permitted Spain to provision her ships at Kinsale and the other ports of southern Ireland and assisted with the transport of Spanish bullion through the pirate-infested waters of the Channel to the Low Countries.[44] Despite this valuable aid, the Spanish crown had no intention of cooperating in the restitution of the Palatinate, which the Treasurer instinctively realised. Thus the tortuous negotiations with Necolalde during the last year-and-a-half of his life had no chance of success and merely distracted Portland's attention from other, and more pressing, affairs.

11 The Embattled Minister

During the early years of Charles I's Personal Rule, Portland was the leading member of the Council Committee for Ireland, which also included Laud, Cottington, Sir Henry Vane, the two principal Secretaries, and several others. The Irish Committee met on Tuesday mornings, usually at Whitehall or in the Treasurer's apartments at Wallingford House. Portland's interest in Irish affairs had been evident since the last year of James I, when he helped with the drafting of an agreement between the crown and the City that led to the establishment of a new plantation in Ireland. Like most Englishmen of his age, the Treasurer was convinced that a larger English population was needed in Ireland: more English families would tighten the bonds between the two kingdoms and make it impossible for a foreign government to launch an attack on England from the smaller island to the west. During the years 1629–31 he actively encouraged the settlement of additional English families in Ireland, even if this meant seizing lands from the Earl of Ormonde and forcing his tenants to resettle among the rocky wastes of Connaught along the western shores.[1]

The Treasurer's authority over Irish affairs stemmed not only from his leadership of the Irish Committee but also from his dominant position on the Lords of the Admiralty, a body which normally met twice a week, often at Wallingford House, and with which the Irish government was in regular contact, owing to the problem of safeguarding the Irish coasts. He was also the senior member of a commission appointed in February 1632 to supervise the settlement of all land problems in Ireland.[2] Almost as important as the powers stemming from his official position was Portland's connection with Richard Boyle, the 'Great Earl of Cork' and perhaps the leading figure in Ireland during the early seventeenth century. An Englishman who had settled in southern Ireland at the time of the Armada, Cork was one of the wealthiest landowners in the entire British Isles, having developed an estate worth approximately £20,000 a year. His second wife, Katherine Fenton, was a cousin of the Treasurer's, being a descendant of Robert Weston, a younger brother of Richard Weston the Judge, Portland's grandfather. Through his relationship with Cork, the Treasurer was able to stay abreast of happenings in Ireland, and Cork was in a position to advance his own interests in England. Indeed the latter was not reluctant to exploit the connection whenever it migh prove beneficial, and he nourished it by sending his kinsman handsome New Year's gifts. In January 1629 the Treasurer was presented a 'great gilt cup' worth almost £25, and two years later he was paid £1000 for helping to speed the repayment of a loan of £25,000 advanced to the King in the spring of 1629.[3]

During the winter of 1630–1 Cork began to solicit his appointment as Lord Deputy of Ireland, an office that had been vacant since the recall of Lord Falkland in 1629. Cork wrote a series of discreet letters to the Treasurer and Sir William Beecher, the clerk of the Irish Committee; but he also covered his tracks by protesting to Secretary Dorchester that he was tired of the duties of public life and wished to retire. Eventually Cork realised that his nomination as Deputy was not even being considered, largely because of his failure to comply with instructions to export large quantities of cheap Irish grain to England. He then altered his course and pressed for the lesser office of Treasurer of Ireland. In this he had the warm support of his English kinsman, who informed him on 23 April 1631 that

> According to your desire I have moved his Majesty to confer upon you the place of Lord Treasurer of Ireland. And I find him graciously inclined to give ear to your suit . . . [and] if I may understand . . . what formalities are to be used in the passing of it, I will renew the motion, being always ready here to do you the offices of a friend when I meet with any fit occasion.[4]

In November 1631 Cork was sworn as Treasurer of Ireland, and shortly afterwards the post of Lord Deputy was filled. Early in 1632 Charles accepted the recommendation of Portland and the Irish Committee and conferred the office on Sir Thomas Wentworth.

Although the Treasurer had once been the Yorkshireman's strongest backer, he had recently turned away from him because of fears that his influence with the King was becoming too great. Wentworth was known to have great administrative abilities, and many observers believed he aspired to be appointed Lord Treasurer. Even his most sympathetic biographer maintains that it 'was clear enough that Wentworth's fingers itched to have control of the royal finances.' Largely because of his fears and suspicions, Portland decided to press for the Yorkshireman's nomination as Deputy, in which position he would be safely out of the country. A few of Wentworth's friends, including Edward Stanhope and Sir George Radcliffe, understood the reasons for his appointment and urged him not to accept the office. But the ambitious Wentworth was not the man to reject such an offer from the crown, though he was prepared to insist that certain conditions be met as the price of his acceptance.[5]

At a Council meeting on 19 February 1632, the relationship between the viceroy in Dublin and the Irish Committee in London was debated. After an extended discussion of the Deputy's responsibilities, the Council established procedures to be used by him in submitting reports to London. At the instance of Wentworth himself, all questions involving financial matters were to be referred directly to the Treasurer, 'without acquainting the rest of the Committee for Irish Affairs.' In order to simplify the handling of other problems, the Deputy's routine dispatches were to be read by only one of the principal Secretaries, in this case Sir John Coke. In an attempt to protect his flank on arriving in Dublin, Wentworth insisted that all offices in his gift 'be left entirely to his disposing' and that no new administrative positions be established without first asking his opinion. Once Wentworth had stated his views, the Council directed Lord Falkland, who was also present at the meeting, to submit a formal report concerning the government and revenue of Ireland, along with any personal observations he felt constrained to make, to the new Lord Deputy.[6]

Although Wentworth persuaded the Council to accept his demands at this juncture, he was not, at least until 1635, the all-powerful viceroy historians have pictured him to be. He could not appoint a Secretary of State or even swear in a new member of the Irish Privy Council without permission from London. Once he arrived in Dublin in July 1633, the Treasurer's influence confronted him at every turn. When Wentworth suggested the establishment of a tobacco monopoly, with the intention of making a large profit for himself, Portland objected to the project and had it shelved indefinitely. Worse, the Treasurer secured the adoption of measures, such as a ban on the export of Irish tallow to Scotland and continental countries, which Wentworth criticised as 'pressing hard' on the Irish economy. The Deputy also protested the arrangements made by Portland and the Lords of the Admiralty for the defence of the Irish coasts, complaining long and hard about them. He was even more incensed by the Treasurer's part in the periodic attempts of English officials to subvert his powers of appointment by disposing of offices and military commissions that were technically in his gift. In time Wentworth came to regard Portland as his greatest enemy. Shortly after the latter's death in 1635, he confided to a friend that he was at last free of 'the heartiest adversary I ever had.'[7]

If Wentworth had powerful enemies at court, who included the Earl of Holland and Sir Henry Vane as well as the Treasurer,[8] he had two devoted friends: Laud and Cottington. The co-operation between Laud and Wentworth had become a recognised factor in English politics by the winter of 1630–1, only a year after the latter's appointment to the Council. As Miss Wedgwood has noted, there was a temperamental similarity between the two men, an 'impatient desire for action, the need to be for ever up and doing . . . Laud had found in Wentworth the man whose zeal and energy would match in secular politics his own zeal and energy in the care of the Church.' Shortly before the new Deputy's departure, Laud sent him detailed instructions concerning improvements to be made in Ireland's religious life.[9]

Wentworth's relationship with the Chancellor was a more complex one. Cottington was a loyal associate of the Treasurer, now deeply suspicious of the Deputy, while he had no liking for the archbishop, to whom he made only occasional superficial gestures. There was nevertheless a genuine sympathy between Cottington and Wentworth, who once praised Sir Francis as a man 'ever so ready and affectionate to me.' For his part, the Chancellor was anxious to keep a foot in both camps by remaining on friendly terms with Wentworth and, if absolutely necessary, his political ally, Laud.[10]

No doubt Portland knew about Cottington's efforts to ingratiate himself with Wentworth and the archbishop, and was annoyed by them. Perhaps it was because of this that a tiff occurred between the two men early in 1634. On 12 January Laud reported to the Deputy that Cottington had recently spoken 'as bitterly against the Lord Treasurer as is possible.' The archbishop continued by confessing that

> This is a mystery that I understand not . . . Sure I am Lord Cottington is very often harshly used by the Lord Treasurer. The matter perhaps is not great in itself (as yet perhaps it is too), but I would fain know the riddle if I could, for never yet did I see the like of this.[11]

Several weeks later Sir Francis himself informed the Deputy of the strained relations between himself and Portland, which he attributed to the latter's irritability, a result of his chronically poor health. At the conclusion of his letter Cottington declared that the archbishop 'is now my very good friend. But why do I tell you of these foolish things?' That the Chancellor made a pretence of co-operating with Laud is clear enough, although the latter continued to be suspicious of his 'Spanish tricks.' Laud soon informed the Deputy that Cottington 'makes me believe he is my friend . . . [but] it seems he trusts me little, and prevail with him I cannot.'[12]

There was little hope of co-operation between Laud and Cottington so long as the enmity between Portland and the archbishop continued. Portland was not averse to an occasional show of support for Laud: at a Council meeting on 3 November 1633 he assisted the archbishop's efforts to impose stricter ceremonial requirements on the little church of St Gregory's, which was located in the shadows of St Paul's Cathedral.[13] But Laud had several reasons for disliking the Treasurer and refused to forget them. A thoroughly honest man himself, the archbishop always believed Portland to be more corrupt than he actually was. After the latter's death in 1635, he flatly asserted that the Treasurer had received a secret annual pension of £2000 from the Westminster soap syndicate, which was dominated by several of his Catholic friends.[14] Yet the archbishop never produced any evidence for this allegation, which has uncritically been accepted by most historians.

Laud was even angrier about the way the Treasurer used religion for secular purposes and primarily to safeguard his own personal position. In order to protect his family from the penalties of recusancy, Portland and his five sons attended occasional services of the established church, and at irregular intervals he even prevailed upon his wife to go, although she never took communion by Anglican rites. Lady Portland's Catholicism was known in all quarters of the capital, yet the Treasurer allowed her to keep a private chaplain, a Father Gott, who was commanded by the King in 1633 'to conform in his service to our book of Common Prayer.' With his mistress's approval, however, Gott ignored the Prayer Book, and was therefore 'opposed and persecuted by some pretended classes of ministers' in the neighbourhood of Putney Park.[15] Whether the Treasurer shared his wife's preference for Catholicism is unclear, but it is obvious that he made his £400 pledge for the repair of Old St Paul's for political reasons. The largest and most ostentatious amount promised at the time, there is no evidence that he ever paid it. Portland's outlook was basically a secular one, and he encouraged the King to increase the yield of clerical tenths, although church property was already taxed at considerably higher rates than lay property. This was deplored and resented by the archbishop, whose programme revolved around the need to strengthen the economic position of the church.

On a more personal level, Laud disliked the Treasurer because of his friendship with Bishop Williams. The archbishop was intent on destroying any political influence still exercised by the Welshman, whose lax attitudes were endangering his own campaign to revitalise the church. That Portland had long been a close friend of Williams angered the primate, who sneered in a coded letter to Wentworth how he 'did much favour the B. of Lincoln.' According to Hacket, Laud made periodic accusations against Williams before the Council, but Portland, assisted by the Earl of Pembroke, always managed to have them dismissed, thereby frustrating Laud's efforts to rid himself of his principal opponent within the church.[16]

On his part, the Treasurer had no fondness for Laud, 'a little, low red-faced man' whom many felt to be a dangerous troublemaker. The previous primate, George Abbot, once declared of him: '. . . such is his nature, that he will underwork any man in the world, so that he may gain by it.' Unhappily Portland was as disposed to intrigue as his adversary and tried to undermine the archbishop's power 'by all the arts and ways he could.' Indeed Laud noted in his diary in December 1633 that several times recently he had been compelled to inform the King 'of the falsehood and practices that were used against me, by L.T.'[17] Largely because of their mutual disdain for the archbishop, Portland and the Queen agreed shortly after their return from Edinburgh in July 1633 to sink their differences, at least for the moment, and close ranks against him. A reconciliation was arranged by the Treasurer's son-in-law, Lord Feilding, and his mother, Lady Denbigh; and on 2 August Sir George Goring informed a friend that Portland 'hath been two days past with the Queen my mistress upon new declarations of kindness' and that he had come away from these meetings 'with all satisfaction.' Despite Henrietta Maria's support, however, the Treasurer's efforts to accomplish Laud's downfall were of no avail, for, as Clarendon observed, 'by suggesting many particulars the King knew to be untrue, or believed to be no faults, he rather confirmed his Majesty's judgment of him and prejudiced his own reputation.'[18]

Because of the known animosity between them, few observers were surprised by Laud's attempt during the spring of 1634 to destroy the Treasurer's influence once and for all. Portland was ill (he had put himself under the care of Sir Theodore Mayerne and two other royal physicians in January) and was spending much of his time on his estate in Surrey. About the beginning of April his health took a turn for the worse, which prompted Cottington to inform the Deputy that 'my Lord Treasurer hath of late been very ill . . . and is a very infirm man, and cannot thus continue long.' So precarious was his condition that when the Earls of Morton and Danby were installed as Knights of the Garter, an order to which he belonged, he was compelled to remain away.[19] Laud was determined not to miss this opportunity to attack his great enemy and accomplish his overthrow; and because of a fortuitous turn of events, he now felt he had convincing proof of the Treasurer's dishonesty that he could lay before the King. He was probably unaware of Portland's order of 5 April 1634, instructing that he himself be paid £500 out of moneys soon to be paid into the Receipt.[20] But when the mismanagement of certain land sales was subsequently exposed, the archbishop was quick to bring charges of corruption against the Treasurer.

During the spring of 1634 Portland was unable to keep as close a watch as usual over the King's finances. Inevitably, perhaps, a large tract of royal forest land was sold at an unusually low price. Charles himself had ordered the sale for the construction of two new ships, the *James* and the *Unicorn*. When the terms of the contract were announced, Laud charged that the Treasurer had arranged for the tract to be sold at far below its real market value so he could eventually acquire it for himself in the name of a third party. With the assistance of Lord Keeper Coventry and the Earls of Manchester and Holland, the archbishop obtained a series of interviews with Charles and sought to convince him not only of Portland's dishonest methods but also that numerous administrative difficulties stemmed directly from his mismanagement. Wentworth had requested the Treasurer to make certain decisions of crucial importance for the maintenance of law and order in Ireland; but Portland had procrastinated, and the Deputy was now disclaiming responsibility for any disorders that might arise within his jurisdiction. Laud therefore demanded the appointment of a new Irish Committee and, in order to ensure the Treasurer's overthrow, he even suggested the summoning of a new parliament.[21]

There is no surviving evidence to substantiate Laud's allegations about the dishonest nature of the land sales. Yet Portland was unable to marshal an effective defence, which suggests that there may have been some truth to them. Sick and infirm, the Treasurer did not reappear at court until Sunday the 27th of April, when he simply threw himself on the King's mercy. Shortly afterwards he secured the good offices of the Duke of Lennox, whose sister Frances was the wife of his son Jerome. He also turned for assistance to Henrietta Maria and had himself appointed one of her Councillors, and at the same time he implored the Duchess of Buckingham, who had spent several years away from court, to return. Charles was deeply moved by the reappearance of his favourite's widow, who pleaded long and hard on the Treasurer's behalf. On 24 May the King permitted Portland to attend him at Greenwich and kiss the royal hand in the presence of the entire court.[22] The suggestion that a parliament be summoned was rejected out of hand, but Charles acceded to the demand for a new Irish Committee. Late in April he named Laud, Arundel, Cottington, Secretaries Coke and Windebank – and the Treasurer – to serve on it. That the new committee consisted of only these six men meant that it would inevitably remain under Portland's control.[23]

The Treasurer survived the archbishop's attack because of a combination of circumstances. First, he had rendered valuable service to the crown for a great many years, and, the celebrated Strafford case of 1641 notwithstanding, Charles had a tendency to stand loyally by his ministers, even when it would have been politically expedient to cast them aside. Second, the Treasurer was no more dishonest than the average civil servant of the early Stuart period; in fact he had made less money for himself than most previous holders of the white staff, of which the King was no doubt made aware. Third, Charles must have known that Laud's attack was prompted at least in part by a spiteful desire to rid himself of a powerful rival. The testimony of such influential persons as the Queen, the Duchess of Buckingham, the Duke of Lennox, the Earl of Denbigh, and Lord Feilding was doubtless designed to remind him of this. And fourth, the Treasurer was too involved in complex government matters, including the confidential negotiations with Necolalde and the preliminaries for the first writs of ship-money, to be summarily fired. Thus Laud's attack on Portland came at an awkward moment for Charles, who refused to give more than passing consideration to the charges.

The relations between Portland and the archbishop became more strained than ever after the spring of 1634, for the Treasurer was not the kind of man to forget such an attack on his character. According to Anthony Weldon, Portland bristled whenever he heard the archbishop's name mentioned and 'would often say to his friends in private, "That little priest would monopolise the King's ear, for he was ever whispering to the King." '[24] For his part, Laud was far from being through with the Treasurer. Within a few more months he was ready to launch a second, more dangerous attack upon him.

While the archbishop's first assault was proceeding, Wentworth was in the midst of a campaign to embarrass the Earl of Cork. The Deputy was demanding the removal of an elaborate marble tomb recently constructed in St Patrick's Cathedral in memory of Cork's second wife, Katherine Fenton, who had died in 1630. If Wentworth secured the dismantling of the monument, which had cost nearly £1000, he would succeed in humbling his chief Irish rival and making clear his domination of Irish politics. Cork naturally turned for assistance to Portland, who was at the moment in a poor position to render any. Yet the Treasurer was sympathetic to his kinsman's pleas since both Lady Cork and her grandfather, Robert Weston, Portland's great uncle, were buried in the tomb. During the first two weeks of April he argued against a plan proposed by Wentworth that a special commission be appointed to consider the matter of the tomb. This had been suggested to, and heartily approved by, Laud, whose insistence on the need for ceremonial and doctrinal purity meant that he was bound to oppose a monument that stood on the site formerly occupied by the high altar. Portland's resolve was of brief duration, and on 16 April Cottington informed the Deputy that

> My Lord of Cork has put much trouble into my Lord Treasurer's mind by means of his informations touching the Chancellor [Robert] Weston's bones over which he had built the tomb: thinking by that means to save the removing of the tomb, but he doth now believe it is a trick of Cork's cunning, and that the bones will have no dishonour done them by the remove.[25]

Cottington's views were corroborated by Cork's son Lord Dungarvan, who had been sent as a special emissary to England. Dungarvan reported that he had sought Portland's intercession concerning the monument but that this had hindered rather than helped his father's cause. Consequently Wentworth was able to proceed with the appointment of a special commission, which pondered the merits of the tomb at length and ultimately required Cork to dismantle it.[26]

During the campaign against Cork, Wentworth took steps to demonstrate his personal loyalty to Portland, whom he did not wish to alienate completely. He wrote a series of letters to his English friends protesting that he had absolutely no desire to be appointed Lord Treasurer. On 24 April he sent a message directly to Jerome Weston, in which he declared his sorrow on learning of Portland's illness. He hoped Jerome would assure the Treasurer of his sincere regard for him and that the younger Weston would soon be able to announce 'the happy tidings of my Lord's renewing in strength again.' After repeated professions of his loyalty and devotion, Wentworth closed by maintaining that the Treasurer's death would be 'the greatest loss to me in the whole world, next to that of my Master's favour and the life of my son.'[27]

Largely because of Wentworth's overtures, the relationship between the two men improved, and during the summer of 1634 they were on reasonably friendly terms. But their reconciliation, which was encouraged by Cottington, was of brief duration, for the Treasurer was annoyed that Wentworth would not break with the archbishop. Portland's attitude was inevitably reported in Dublin; and shortly after his death in March 1635, the Deputy informed a friend that 'I conceived my Lord Treasurer sometime before his death wished me no good, being grown extreme jealous of my often writing to my Lord of Canterbury.'[28]

Of greater concern to Portland than the Deputy's continued co-operation with Laud during the summer of 1634 was the challenge mounted by another adversary, the Earl of Holland. A flamboyant and volatile man, Holland had long been an avowed enemy of the Treasurer and his son Jerome, who, on his return from a continental mission in March 1633, had encountered a courier with letters from the earl and Henrietta Maria. Relying on his ambassadorial powers, the younger Weston stayed the courier and examined the letters, which had been sent abroad without a licence from either the Council or one of the principal Secretaries. It was his clear duty to confiscate them, and once back in England he handed them over to the King, who thanked him warmly. Although the letters were adjudged harmless, Holland became extremely angry and challenged Jerome to a duel, which caused Charles to place him under house arrest and suspend him from his position on the Council. Although the earl eventually recovered his freedom, the episode left a residue of tension and bitterness.[29]

Because they formed the core of the Queen's party, Holland and his friends were aghast in the summer of 1633 when Henrietta Maria began to consider the possibility of a rapprochement with Portland. On 9 August Henry Percy, a younger son of the Earl of Northumberland, confided to a friend that

> Holland and his train of women seem to be reconciled to the Treasurer: and make harangues to him, but secretly [they] practise to infuse such a gallantrie into the Queen that [she] might despise him.[30]

Determined to keep old quarrels alive, Holland soon found a way to make the Treasurer's affairs more difficult and worrisome than they would have been otherwise.

A Privy Councillor and an important royal favourite, Holland was Chief Justice in Eyre of all the forests and chases south of the river Trent, in which capacity he held a justice seat for the Forest of Dean in July 1634. At this court at Gloucester more than a dozen men were prosecuted, among them one of the Treasurer's secretaries, John Gibbons, who was partly responsible for transacting his master's personal affairs. Gibbons was found guilty of enclosing a tract of several acres and constructing a house upon it, for which he was required to pay the exceptionally heavy fine of £5130. The Treasurer's secretary was also punished on two other counts. For 'spoiling of coppices' he had to pay £500, and for cutting and selling a great many of the King's trees, he was ordered to pay an additional £6000, bringing the total of his fines to a whopping £11,630. Prosecuted at the same time as Gibbons was Sir Basil Brooke, a Roman Catholic and a close friend of the Treasurer's. Brooke and his partner, George Minne, were convicted of pilfering more than 172,000 cords of the King's lumber, for which they were sentenced to pay the enormous fine of £57,939 16s. 8d.[81]

Criticism of Portland now rose to a fever pitch. It was everywhere said that Gibbons, Brooke, and their confederates could not have encroached on the King's forest lands without the Treasurer's knowledge and connivance. Portland was sorely troubled by these charges, and he quickly discharged Gibbons from his service, driving the hapless secretary from his presence.[82] Public opinion was not so easily mollified, however, and proceedings against Gibbons and Brooke were introduced in the Star Chamber. An attempt was made to implicate other dependents of the Treasurer's, including his cousin Sir Richard Tichborne, another of his private secretaries William Lake, and a man who had long served as his general factotum, Sir James Bagg. While the net was thus being widened, Portland was all but isolated in the government, being defended only by the loyal Cottington.[83]

Because the King was willing for his courtiers to reap the profits of fines levied on encroachers, strong pressures developed for a wholesale revival of the forest laws. The Attorney-General, William Noy, argued strongly in favour of their strict enforcement, although he cautioned that the revenues should be reserved exclusively for the King's needs, a point conveniently ignored by Holland and his associates. Not only did the earl and his supporters hope to enrich themselves through the proceedings, but they wished to find new ways of embarrassing the Treasurer. Gardiner acknowledged long ago that 'the forest claims were owing to the motion' of Portland's enemies; and a recent authority suggests that they were deliberately used 'to make things awkward for Lord Treasurer Weston.'[34]

Similar justice seats were held for Havering Forest, the New Forest, and the Forest of Rockingham, and by 1637 several of the leading peers of England had been sentenced to pay exceptionally heavy fines. The Earl of Westmorland was required to pay £19,000, while the Earl of Salisbury was assessed £20,000, not because of any encroachments perpetrated by him but because his father had accepted the greater part of Rockingham Forest from a grateful Queen Elizabeth. Thus grants of land made in previous reigns could no longer be considered safe possessions, free from resumptive attempts by the favourites of the present occupant of the throne. The revival and reimposition of the forest laws did incalculable damage to Charles's reputation. Devised as a way of striking at Portland, the campaign caused deep resentment among those confronted by staggering fines (even if they were later remitted) as well as nagging doubts concerning the King's respect for the property rights of his subjects. Clarendon noted that the forest laws 'lighted most upon persons of quality and honour, who thought themselves above ordinary oppressions, and [were] therefore like to remember it with more sharpness.' Yet less than £20,000 was realised by the King's coffers, the lion's share of the profits being skimmed off by voracious courtiers.[35] All things considered, it was a tragedy that Charles failed to show greater firmness and did not stop the factions within his government from conspiring against one another, at the ultimate expense of the crown.

Although Holland failed to turn up additional evidence to incriminate the Treasurer, the damage already done to his reputation was impossible to repair. Most politically-informed residents of the capital were convinced that Gibbons had been sacrificed to save the career of his employer. Once again the archbishop had an opportunity to launch an attack on Portland, whose authority with the King might at last be destroyed for good. He conferred with two important but dissatisfied figures, John Harrison and Sir Thomas Roe, who were able to provide him with telling criticisms of the Treasurer's financial and foreign policies. He then secured an audience with Charles and made renewed accusations against his enemy, which amounted to an indictment not only of his personal conduct but of his entire administration during the past six years.[36]

With the archbishop's new allegations against him and the heavy cloud still hanging over his head from the Gibbons affair, Portland was ordered by the King to submit a record of all his receipts since becoming Treasurer in July 1628. Public opinion virtually compelled Charles to take cognisance of the accusations, although he was as unwilling as ever to act upon them. Portland presented the list of his gains and receipts to the King at Hampton Court on 21 October. Aware of the fate that had befallen Middlesex, the Treasurer had been extraordinarily careful to cover his tracks; and he first reminded Charles that

> When your most excellent Majesty was pleased to confer upon your most humble servant the place of Treasurer of England . . . you were pleased to give him leave to acquire some means to himself by such suits, and businesses which passed through his hands, which without your Majesty's knowledge he would not have done: and hath from time to time acquainted your Majesty therewith; but doth now, for your Majesty's better satisfaction, make remembrances of such monies as he hath had, to be subject to your Majesty's view.[37]

Portland then proceeded to list sixteen different items that had produced £44,000 for him during the past six years. From the King himself he had received total grants of £10,000; and just before the settlement of large royal debts owed to Philip Burlamachi, he had been offered another £10,000. Portland had duly informed Charles of this offer, and with royal approval had accepted £9000. The Treasurer acknowledged the receipt of £6000 from Sir Cornelius Vermuyden 'for my part of adventure in the lead-mines,' and of £4000 from the farmers of the impositions on sea-coals. He had also received payments totalling £4000 from Sir Allen Apsley, one of the Surveyors of Marine Victuals; and Sir Arthur Ingram had given him £2000 for helping to secure changes in Ingram's patent as Secretary of the Council of the North. The remaining £9000 had come to him by way of six smaller payments; a New Year's gift of £1000 from his Irish kinsman, the Earl of Cork; a similar gift of £1000 from the Duchess of Buckingham, whose interests he had overseen during recent years; and payments of

£1000 each from two office-seekers who desired his assistance: James Maxwell, now Clerk of the Court of Wards, and Sir Thomas Fanshawe, recently named Clerk of the Crown in the King's Bench.[38]

Once he received Portland's list, the King gave only perfunctory attention to it. To demonstrate his continued confidence in his minister, he scribbled at the bottom of the paper:

> I have taken all these several particulars into my consideration, and do acknowledge your clear and true dealing with me in the matters and sums above-mentioned, and in acquainting me with them from time to time; and, weighing with myself the good service you have done me in the Treasurership, and the great charge you have and must be at in sustaining that place, I do approve and allow of all monies by you to your own use received, amounting to £44,500 [*sic*] sterling.[39]

The question that inevitably arises is whether Portland's list was a complete one. That the Treasurer was honest with Charles about his most important gains seems indisputable, since it would be easy for the latter to check his figures if he chose to do so. But it is also clear that there were other receipts not mentioned in the Treasurer's report. Archbishop Laud always insisted that he received substantial kickbacks from the Westminster soap syndicate, but there is no reference to them on the list accepted by the King. Nor was any allusion made to the farmers of the great customs, from whom Portland often received New Year's gifts amounting to £1000 or more, and larger payments whenever new leases were negotiated. Possible bribes from foreign envoys were passed over in silence; and it seems unlikely that he received gratuities from only two aspiring office-seekers. All things considered, the Treasurer must have omitted a number of items from the list presented to Charles, and his yearly profits were undoubtedly greater than the average of £7500 he calculated for himself. A guess that they were in the neighbourhood of £11,000 or £12,000 does not seem unreasonable. But it is highly unlikely that he made the average 'of nearly £16,000 a year' that J. P. Cooper suggests.[40]

Archbishop Laud, who was conscientious almost to a fault, was willing to permit an honest Treasurer rewards of no more than £7000 a year from office. Portland did not of course conform to the archbishop's pattern: he seems to have made about 50% more each year than Laud considered tolerable. It was partly because of this that the archbishop made such determined efforts to overthrow him. But this does not mean that the Treasurer should be regarded as a hopelessly corrupt man. All his recent predecessors in the post, Salisbury, Suffolk, Middlesex, and Marlborough, had made as much or more; and the King was doubtless aware of the approximate value of his yearly receipts, which he was willing to accept without demur. Portland's illustrious contemporary, the future Earl of Strafford, was currently making more for himself in the less important position of Lord Deputy of Ireland. It has been estimated that during the 1630s Wentworth had official receipts of at least £17,000 a year, an excessive income that Laud never bothered to question. Even a courtier like the Earl of Holland, whose only administrative duty was to preside over occasional sessions of the forest courts, had a yearly income of between £10,000 and £12,000 from royal grants, about the same that Portland was making for himself in the great and demanding office of Lord Treasurer.[41]

That Portland has been castigated by so many historians as a hopelessly corrupt man is due in part to a case in the Star Chamber eight months after his death. In November 1635 Sir Anthony Pell, the Keeper of the King's Hawks, lodged a formal complaint against Sir James Bagg, who had frequently served as a middleman between the Treasurer and suitors for his favour. Pell claimed that during the winter of 1634–5 he had paid £2500 to Bagg for his assistance in securing a warrant from Portland for the release of £6000 from the Exchequer, a sum owed him by the crown for a great many years. Because no warrant had been procured by the time the Treasurer died in March 1635, Pell decided to sue for the recovery of the £2500 given to Bagg, whose degree of honesty can be inferred from his reputation as 'the bottomless Bagg.' Pell charged that no money had been paid over to Portland as he had intended and that his memory was now being defiled.

When the case was considered in the Star Chamber, the defendant insisted that he had handed over all sums received to Portland and could not assume any further responsibility. Once the merits of the case had been debated at length, nine Councillors, led by the archbishop, voted that Bagg should be punished as a broker of bribery, regardless of whether the money in question had been paid over to the Treasurer. But nine others, on the urging of Cottington, voted that Pell was entitled to no sympathy whatever, for in approaching Bagg he no doubt realised that he was taking his chances and would receive no rebate should the attempt fail. When it became clear that the Councillors were evenly divided on the matter, the Lord Keeper exercised his casting vote in favour of the plaintiff who, it now appeared, would recover his £2500. However, the King had followed the deliberations closely; and at the urging of his wife, who had sympathised with Bagg throughout, he refused to take any steps to punish the latter. In the end the case did great harm not only to the Treasurer's memory but also to the moral position of the central government. As Professor Trevor-Roper has observed, it publicly confirmed the existence of wholesale corruption among the King's ministers, many of whom supported Bagg by arguing that 'political society was necessarily built upon a foundation of jobbing and corruption.'[42]

Athough Bagg continued to protest that he had turned over the entire £2500 to Portland, other facts suggest that he had done nothing of the kind. Only a year earlier Pell had introduced another bill in the Star Chamber against Bagg, Gibbons, Lake, and several other dependents of the Treasurer, against whom the campaign to punish all encroachers on the royal forests was being directed.[43] Thus Bagg must have been amazed when the naïve Pell approached him shortly afterwards with a plea for help in convincing Portland to release the £6000 owed him by the crown. Bagg could not refrain from taking advantage of the situation and pocketing whatever his onetime accuser could be talked into supplying. Of course there is only circumstantial evidence to prove that this is what happened. It is entirely possible that Portland and Bagg were in collusion and were jointly milking Pell for whatever they could get out of him. But the fact that the Treasurer was in financial difficulties and had less than £100 in ready money in his house at the time he died suggests that he received only a small part of the £2500 Pell paid over to Bragg, if even a penny of that amount.[44]

Regardless of whether Portland was an honest or a corrupt man (and there was a thinner line between honesty and corruption in the seventeenth century than there is today), the King refused to listen to Laud's allegations against him. Nevertheless the Treasurer's influence showed a perceptible decline during the autumn of 1634. Shunned by old friends and acquaintances, he was increasingly isolated at court, which he now frequented as little as possible. On Wednesdays and Fridays he travelled by coach to Whitehall for meetings of the Privy Council; but immediately afterwards he returned to his estate in Surrey, where he hoped that solitude and freedom from government cares would help his poor body to mend. Inevitably his grip on power began to weaken, and he was unable to direct the work of the Council and the various committees and commissions to which he belonged as he had done in the past. Away in Ireland the Deputy was finding ways to circumvent the control of the Irish Committee, which the Treasurer had long dominated. Indeed Wentworth was sending only occasional dispatches to the Irish Committee, reserving most of his reports for the Lords of the Admiralty, a body over which Portland's influence remained fairly strong, however.[45]

While Wentworth was seeking to escape the Treasurer's control, Portland was doing everything he could to undermine the cooperation between him and the archbishop. On occasion he resorted to malicious tactics and encouraged rumours of hypocritical back-stabbing between the two men. This was easily seen for what it was, and in October 1634 Laud facetiously chastised the Deputy:

> The Lord Treasurer says that the Archbishop of Canterbury and the Lord Deputy of Ireland are very great; and the Lord Deputy poisons me by letters, and then the Archbishop doth him all the ill offices that may be [done] to the King. If ever I hear this again, I will call you blab and never write more.[46]

Meanwhile Portland was ignoring his enemies' proposals and recommendations, which caused him to seem more dilatory than ever. Despite their impatience at the way he was neglecting 'the King's affairs,' they responded jokingly by dubbing him 'Lady Mora,' or 'Madame Delay.' In a more serious vein, the Treasurer began to raise embarrassing questions concerning Wentworth's use of the cash balances resulting from his collection of crown rents in northern England. On information supplied by Sir Arthur Ingram, the disgruntled Secretary to the Council of the North, he demanded the deposit of large sums into the Exchequer long before Wentworth planned for his agents to pay them in. When Portland took this tack, one of Wentworth's most lucrative financial schemes was endangered.[47]

In April 1635, shortly after Portland's death, Wentworth complained to the newly appointed commissioners of the Treasury that he had frequently been required to pay in his receipts before they were due. This had prevented him from using the cash balances for his own speculative purposes and 'did indeed take away the chief profit of my grant.' In the future he insisted on being allowed the full benefits of his patent, 'which requires me to pay in no rents but once a year and that at Midsummer only.'[48] Wentworth also communicated his views directly to the archbishop, who served as chief commissioner of the Treasury until a successor to Portland could be found. Laud was less sympathetic than the Deputy had hoped, however, and wrote drily in reply:

> Your letters to the commissioners of the Treasury were read and referred to Sir William Russell, for that part of them which concerns the payment of the navy. For the rest, some conceive you desire to keep the King's money too long in your hands. But so soon as Sir William's answer is given, you will receive ours by Mr. Secretary.[49]

Although the archbishop never sanctioned Wentworth's use of the cash balances, his accession to power meant that the Deputy was in a stronger position, with firmer support and virtually no opposition from the capital. This was of course apparent to Laud, who could see that the millstone around Wentworth's neck had suddenly been lifted. Only a few weeks after Portland died, the archbishop confided to his friend that 'the Lord Treasurer was a heavy block in your way. But I wonder not at it. For the same block lay in my way too, when I could have wished it otherwise.'[50]

12 Death Claims the Treasurer

Portland's last year of life was, almost without exception, an unhappy period. His hold on the King's affection remained strong, but his popularity with his fellow countrymen had collapsed altogether, he was being attacked and buffeted by his political enemies, and his namesake Richard had just died, insane, at Coventry. His own health was precarious owing to periodic kidney-stone attacks, although it was from intestinal cancer that he died. Unable to digest solid foods, he resorted to a liquid diet, pouring 'in all kinds of drinks, and that in a great quantity, which makes him sick, and forceth him to much vomiting.' Because his father and grandfather had both died from 'imposthumes in their heads,' he was particularly concerned about his frequent headaches, fearing they might develop into such 'imposthumes.'[1]

During the summer of 1634 he was urged by the Attorney-General to take the waters at Tunbridge Wells, in Kent. Noy was also a desperately sick man, being even then on the verge of death. Yet he had found a measure of relief at the Kentish spa, from whence he returned to London 'with some appetite restored, and [some] obstructions opened.' Portland decided to follow Noy's advice, and on 3 July he informed a friend that he planned to spend a few days at Tunbridge Wells, 'whither I intend to go as soon [as] their Majesties shall be on their progress, which will be about a fortnight hence.' He remained at the spa almost a month and was visited there by his old friend and associate Cottington.[2]

While the Treasurer was away from London, criticism of a business venture involving several of his Catholic friends, the Westminster soap syndicate, became more intense than ever. Organised during the winter of 1631–2, the soap syndicate was dominated by Thomas Russell, Sir Basil Brooke, and a distant cousin of the Treasurer's, the Sir Richard Weston who lived at Sutton Place, near Guildford, Surrey. They and their associates claimed that they had perfected a process for making soap of a higher quality than that currently available out of barilla and such vegetable matter as kelp fern and bean and pease straw. In May 1632 they struck a bargain with the crown, promising to market at least 5000 tons of soap each year and to pay a royalty of £4 on each ton sold. They also pledged to offer their product at the relatively low price of 3d. per pound, or £25 a ton, which would enable them to make a profit of £15,000 a year after paying the royalties of £20,000 reserved for the government. Technically the Westminster Soapers, as they were popularly known, were to enjoy a monopoly only over the soap manufactured by their own methods, but by the agreement of May 1632 they were authorised to test all soap made in the traditional way and to prohibit the sale of brands they themselves judged to be of an inferior quality.[3]

Portland had ambivalent feelings about the scheme. He was clearly sceptical of its chances, for at one point he confessed his fears that it would 'prove like other projects, glorious in show, difficult to effect, and of little profit in the end.' Yet his friends were the instigators of the plan, and they apparently offered financial inducements to him and his associate, Arundel. Furthermore the Attorney-General was a strong supporter of the scheme and recommended it to the King. So crucial was Noy's role that Clarendon maintained '. . . he moulded, framed, and pursued the odious and crying project of soap.' For various reasons, therefore, the Treasurer forgot his initial objections and gave his support to the plan, which was tragic for both his own reputation and the welfare of the English consumer.[4]

Just as Portland suspected, the soap project never enjoyed any success. Technical and organisational skill were sorely lacking, and the soap marketed by the company was of such low quality that it was shunned by the ordinary consumer. To guarantee a few sales the Westminster Soapers had to resort to disreputable tactics that outraged the mainstream of English opinion. Serious protests were voiced long before the monopoly was in a position to produce a substantial sum for the Exchequer. In 1633 the company paid royalties of only £251 to the crown, although it wisely provided a loan of almost £11,000 at the same time. The outlook for the company during the following year was just as bleak, and in September 1634 its charter was revoked on the grounds that it had failed to fulfil the conditions of its contract with the crown.[5]

Although the Westminster Soapers lost their monopoly within

three years of being incorporated, they had managed to disrupt the entire soap industry by that time. Late in June 1632 a royal proclamation announced the appointment of a company searcher with power to forbid the sale of any soap that did not meet the standards that he himself established. This meant that the independent soap-boilers were now at the mercy of the company and that the soap trade would enter a period of declining standards and rising prices. Bitter complaints were immediately voiced by the independent soap-boilers, who charged that the product being marketed by the monopoly was of an inferior quality, since it damaged linen and burned the hands of washerwomen who used it. Furthermore it was alleged that the company's regulatory activities had caused rival brands to be excluded from the retail trade, with the result that a black market was developing on which the independent brands were selling for as much as triple their former price. Because the monopoly was believed to be dominated by Catholics, its product was widely denounced as 'Popish soap,' and in a series of demonstrations that occurred in London and the home counties, the slogan 'No Popery!' was used as a rallying cry.[6]

Public opinion was uniformly against the Westminster Soapers, and nothing the government could do would persuade the consumer to buy their product. This did not prevent a rival syndicate from being formed by two independent soap-boilers, Thomas Overman and Edmund Whitwell. Overman and Whitwell were among those imprisoned in 1633 for refusing to submit to the test of the company searcher. Shortly after their release from the Fleet, they proposed that the soap monopoly be transferred to them, in return for which they would pay the crown £8 for each of ton of soap sold, or twice what the Westminster Soapers had promised. Because of the extravagance of their proposal, they were at first unable to interest the government in their scheme, even after the Treasurer's friends lost their charter in September 1634. As long as Portland lived, he opposed the establishment of another monopolistic corporation, which he felt would be as unsuccessful as the first. It was only after his death in March 1635 that steps were taken to legalise a second monopoly, with results as unfortunate as he had foreseen.[7]

While the soap project was proving a dismal failure, another scheme in which the Treasurer had an interest was doing little better. This was the Society of the Fishery of Great Britain and Ireland, or, more simply, the fishing association, which was legally established in June 1632. The purpose of the fishing association, which was organised along the lines of a craft guild, was to raise funds for the development of the British fishing industry, which had faced increasingly stiff competition from the Dutch during recent years. A central agency in London, consisting of a governor and an advisory court of twelve men, was to raise the capital needed for the undertaking and to co-ordinate the affairs of a number of local subsidiary companies, each of which would mobilise the capital of its own neighbourhood and channel it into the fishing industry. In the words of the ablest student of the subject, 'the idea was bold and striking, a fit product of the mercantilest mind.' Yet the scheme ultimately failed because the central agency was unable to evoke a response from local investors, 'whose capital was to be the life-blood of the whole undertaking.'[8]

The chief sponsors of the scheme were Portland and Secretary Coke, both associated with the navy for many years. The Treasurer and the Secretary agreed that a national fishing association would serve not only to create new jobs and stimulate the country's economy but also to encourage the growth of English naval power. A paper dating from the time the association was founded described the fishing industry as England's 'training academy for mariners and naval captains.' It also held that 'in trade and fishing we have given so much way to the Low Countrymen of late years, that we have more cause to be jealous of them, than of the Spanish or the French.'[9] Thus there were more convincing reasons for the association's establishment than for the creation of the soap monopoly. It was conceived in the national interest and was not designed simply to make a few men rich, although it was of course hoped that a large profit would in time result. Moreover, it was unlikely that it would interfere with the activities of men already engaged in the business for themselves, as was the danger with the soap monopoly. Unhappily the fishing association proved no more successful than its kindred undertaking, since the founding members underestimated the strength of the inevitable Dutch opposition and were never able to secure adequate capitalisation for their activities.

Portland served as governor of the association from its establishment in 1632 until poor health forced him to resign in 1635.

Initially he subscribed £1000 to the venture, while the other charter members provided lesser amounts. Sir John Wintour and the Earl of Rutland advanced £500 each, the Duchess of Buckingham, £300, the Earl of Castlehaven, Lord Savage, and several others, £200 each, and the remaining subscribers either £100 or £50 each. Altogether the eighty founding members provided a total of £11,750, which was a far cry from the £167,000 that Portland and Secretary Coke believed would be needed.[10]

A report compiled by the Secretary in 1632 or 1633 estimated that the association would eventually require a fleet of 200 fishing boats, or busses, each of which should be of approximately 70 tons, with a 45-foot keel and a storage capacity of 412 barrels. Such busses normally cost £500 apiece, so to procure 200 of them would entail an outlay of £100,000. Coke realised that it would be some years before a fleet of that size would be available and recommended that the association be content to send out ten or twelve busses during the summer of 1633.[11] The Secretary's proposal was accepted, and in June 1633 the association launched its first year of operations.

Great things were expected of the original busses sent forth, with several investors anticipating a profit of £8000 or more. Such optimism was completely unfounded, for a variety of reasons. Not only were the busses poorly supplied with casks, hoops, and salt, but almost nothing was known about the technique of curing fish: six years later it was ruefully acknowledged that this technique had just been mastered. Although the first busses sent out were instructed to operate in the waters surrounding the Isle of Lewis off the northwestern coast of Scotland, where fish were known to be plentiful, they brought back a disappointingly small catch at the end of the season. Even worse, four of the busses were captured by Dutch men-of-war or Dunkirk privateers before the end of the year. As a consequence the association suffered a net loss of £4261 during its first year of operations.[12]

The association was even less successful in 1634, owing to unseemly quarrels between its agents and fishermen. Arrangements were made for a catch of 18,000 barrels, but only about 5000 were actually taken. The majority of these were exported to Dunkirk and Danzig, where they arrived just before the end of the season, when prices on the European market had fallen to their lowest point. Consequently the association suffered a loss of

£8164 during its second year of operations, or almost twice what it had lost during the first year. Because of these staggering reverses, Portland and his associates decided that any new subscriptions advanced should be exempted from liability for the previous deficits incurred by the society.[13]

When poor health compelled the Treasurer to resign as governor in 1635, his place was taken by his old friend Arundel, who was even less capable of providing the leadership necessary for the association to prosper. Steady losses were incurred during the next three seasons, and by the end of 1637 the society's indebtedness had increased to slightly more than £21,000. Within three more years the association was completely bankrupt, as was a smaller rival association led by the Earl of Pembroke.[14]

Appreciations of Portland's contributions as Treasurer have always been influenced by his acceptance of the soap monopoly organised by his friends and his leadership of the fishing association established through his own efforts. That both projects ended in failure has caused most historians to overlook the important and largely successful work he accomplished before 1632 and to underestimate his whole career and positive achievements. A number of recent writers, including Barry Supple, Charles Wilson, and H. R. Trevor-Roper, have disregarded him altogether, believing that nothing of a constructive nature was accomplished during his term of office.[15] It was a tragedy for both his later reputation and the welfare of his fellow countrymen that he gave his support to the soap monopoly, in which he never believed, and put himself at the head of the fishing association, which, although patriotically conceived, was almost bound to fail. Had it not been for this he might now be regarded as highly as Salisbury and Middlesex, the most notable of England's Lord Treasurers during the early seventeenth century. Certainly he never sponsored reforms comparable to the ones they sought to implement; but his day-to-day management of the King's finances was so successful that Laud was dismayed by the findings of a later inquiry undertaken to show negligence or a lack of probity on his and Cottington's part.[16] Furthermore the massive savings that resulted from his insistence on England's withdrawal from the continental wars was at least as important as anything accomplished by his two better known predecessors, who, as Professor Hurstfield has reminded us, were both in a sense failures, for they sacrificed their careers fighting ɔr unrealisable goals.[17] In regard to Portland's achievement, he ttempted less than either Salisbury or Middlesex but paradoxically ccomplished more.

The affairs of the soap monopoly and the fishing association ıust have weighed on Portland's mind during the winter of 634–5. Yet because of a third project in which he was interested, e had cause for some cheerfulness. This was the government's ecision to revive the old tax known as ship-money as a way of ıising funds for the navy. The Treasurer's involvement with naval ffairs was of long duration, and between 1628 and 1635 he ınctioned almost as a later-day First Lord of the Admiralty. How ɔ increase the country's naval strength was never far from his ıind, and proposals for putting the navy's finances on a more table footing were periodically reviewed by him. Indeed David loyd maintained that 'the paying of the navy' was one of his chief oncerns as Treasurer.[18]

On 21st January 1634 the Lords of the Admiralty met at Whiteall to consider how a new source of revenue, a permanent tax or nposition, might be developed for the maintenance of the fleet. ortland and his six associates, Cottington, Vane, the Earls of indsey and Dorset, and the two principal Secretaries, discussed ıe matter at length and emphasised the need to strengthen the avy, owing to 'the many depredations, violence, and hostile acts ɔmmitted daily on the Narrow Seas, and even within his Majesty's orts' by Dunkirk privateers and Dutch men-of-war. A state of uneclared naval war had developed during the past year, and actions ıuch 'to the dishonour of his Majesty's sovereignty in those ːas . . . and the infinite disturbance and prejudice of trade' were ːgularly occurring. After an extended discussion, the board reuested Attorney-General Noy and the Chief Judge of the dmiralty, Sir Henry Martin, to consider the problem and sugest a possible solution.[19]

An immediate consequence of the Lords' meeting was the publiation of Selden's *Mare Clausum*, which vigorously asserted Engınd's claims to sovereignty in the Narrow Seas but had circulated nly in manuscript since its composition fifteen years earlier. Of reater practical importance was the inspiration given to the ttorney-General, whose brain was already busy with ideas as to ɔw the government's revenues might be increased. A year earlier ımes Howell had reported that Noy 'hath lately found out among the old records of the Tower some precedents for raising a tax called Ship-money in all the port-towns when the kingdom is in danger.'[20]

During the spring of 1634 there were prolonged discussions on the possibilities of ship-money among the seven Lords of the Admiralty, the Attorney-General, and the leading customs farmers. Several of these men were already thinking in terms of converting the imposition from a regional into a national tax. Noy, for example, was convinced the 'cause' under consideration should be adopted on a nationwide basis. If only the government would decree that 'all are to join in this work' and impose the tax on the entire population, some twenty additional ships could be supplied during the first year and fourteen more during the second.[21]

Portland was among those who believed that ship-money should be a permanent annual tax, imposed on the inland as well as the maritime counties. During the summer of 1634 Abraham Dawes, who, on orders from the Treasurer, had just drawn up a new book of rates whereby duties on imported goods were steeply increased, informed a friend that Portland was becoming more enthusiastic with each passing day and soon expected to present the King 'with the greatest and most valuable service that ever one Treasurer had done . . . which was a revenue brought to the crown for over and above £300,000 per annum by his especial skill and means, which was by the ship-money and the imposts raised and received by his new book of rates.'[22] Yet Portland was also aware that there was likely to be opposition to the scheme, despite the precedents for the tax that had been collected from the records by the Attorney-General. During the Elizabethan and early Stuart periods the tax had been levied on a frequent, albeit irregular, basis. It had been assessed in 1587, 1588, 1596, 1617, 1618, 1626, and 1628. In the last of those years the government had attempted to collect ship-money from taxpayers throughout England and had issued writs for a total of £173,411. This had caused such a storm of protest that the government had withdrawn the writs almost as soon as they were issued.[23] It was probably for this reason that Portland insisted on the need for strict secrecy during the spring of 1634, when the reimposition of the tax was being considered. He held that any arguments against its legality should be answered well in advance and that the King's legal advisers and the most mportant judges should be consulted. The views of the Council hould also be given some consideration.

The most important preliminary steps had been taken by the eginning of June 1634, when Portland received a confidential etter from Secretary Windebank, who informed him that

> I came late from Greenwich the last night, where I attended his Majesty, and acquainted him with your Lordship's opinion concerning the forbearing to communicate the great business to the whole Board, until the manner of ordering it (whereupon the good or ill success entirely depends) were thoroughly debated and fully settled. His Majesty will by no means be removed from his former resolution of publishing it to the whole Council on Sunday next, telling me that to consult it first were an unnecessary delay, where law and precedents are so clear, as well for the manner and the thing itself . . . if you please to debate it farther with the King, you may go so much the sooner this day to Greenwich, where your Lordship will find him at very good leisure.[24]

ecause of the pressure being exerted by the Lord Keeper and the ord Privy Seal, both of whom were enthusiastic for the tax, ortland knew it would be impossible to convince the King to vithhold his announcement of the project for a few more weeks.)n Sunday the 8th of June, therefore, Secretary Coke delivered a arefully framed address in which he informed the Council of the ourse now to be followed.[25]

During the summer of 1634 additional steps were taken to preare for the first writs of ship-money, which were not issued ntil 20 October. Possibly at Portland's suggestion, it was decided hat the matter was of such great importance that it should be nanaged by the Council itself, which could easily receive the eports of all receipts and disbursements. The revenues themselves, vhich were to be used entirely for purposes associated with the avy, were to by-pass the Exchequer and go directly to the 'reasurer of the Navy, Sir William Russell.[26] The chief officers of he corporate towns along the coast were to assess the tax on he owners of all landed property within their bailiwicks, while the heriffs would be responsible for the assessment in any other, unncorporated towns. It was agreed that the inhabitants of the naritime counties should be exempted from the first writs, since the public response could be determined by taxing only the port and coastal towns at first. If feeling was restrained and relativel quiet, ship-money could then be extended the following year t the maritime counties and perhaps even to the inland regions wit a good chance of not repeating the fiasco of 1628.[27]

By the first writs of ship-money, the most important ports an coastal towns were instructed to provide ships of a specified siz and tonnage and to send them to Portsmouth by 1 March 1635 when they should be ready to set sail. London, for example, wa directed to provide six ships, one of 900 tons, four of 500 tons and one of 150 tons, which were to be manned by crews totallin at least 1300 men.[28] Shortly after the writs were issued, it wa announced that any town of which ships had been demande could compound with the government and provide money instead should that prove more convenient. Rather than make six ship available, London might contribute £20,688 to the King's coffers and the other ports and coastal towns, in return for payments o slightly more than £83,500, would be excused from the obligatio to provide ships.[29]

At the outset it appeared as if the reimposition of ship-mone was going to be accepted without demur. Yet during the autum of 1634 a groundswell of criticism developed against the Treasure who was generally considered the chief proponent of the tax, sinc Noy had died the previous August. Strenuous objections wer voiced by the City on 2 December, which prompted the Counci to summon and rudely order the Lord Mayor to direct his fello citizens to be more co-operative.[30]

At a Council meeting attended by Portland on 1 February 1635 it was decided that the ship-money fleet should be kept entirel separate from the royal navy and that the former should be admin istered by the King and Council rather than the Lords of th Admiralty.[31] Such a course might allay the doubts of those wh had questioned the government's explanation for building a mor powerful fleet, namely that the rapid increase of privateering in th Channel required a resort to emergency measures. It may als have been agreed on 1 February to extend ship-money to th counties, inland as well as maritime, during the coming year. Re gardless when that decision was made, it was not announced unti 17 June, when the Lord Keeper addressed the judges shortly befor their departure from Westminster for the summer assizes.[32] Th second ship-money writs were issued on 4 August 1635, when towns and counties throughout England were called upon to raise £208,900 for the government. The public reaction was more critical than during the previous year, and by March 1636 only £156,000 had been collected, leaving arrears of almost £53,000. Yet on the writs of 1635 all but £188 1s. 11d. was ultimately received.[33]

Although Portland and Noy were both dead by mid-March 1635, the tax continued to be assessed on an annual basis for the remainder of the 1630s, since the entire Council supported it. By the writs issued between 1636 and 1640, a total of £872,650 was demanded of the English people, or the equivalent of more than a dozen parliamentary subsidies.[34] Unhappily for the government popular opposition mounted alarmingly during these years, especially after the celebrated trial in 1637 of John Hampden, who challenged the tax on constitutional grounds. By 1638 local officials were finding it increasingly difficult to raise the sums demanded by the crown, and their collections were falling off dramatically. There was virtually the same degree of opposition from the coastal towns and counties as from the inland regions. Of greater significance, almost all the criticisms of ship-money were based on practical rather than constitutional considerations, the Hampden case notwithstanding.[35] This suggests that the government made a fundamental mistake in attempting to convert the tax into an annual one at the very time it was taking steps to impose it on the inland counties for the first time. In previous years ship-money had been an occasional tax, imposed at irregular intervals on the coastal regions only. Thus it appears that the King and his ministers might have succeeded in establishing ship-money as an annual imposition on the coastal towns and counties alone, or in extending it to the inland regions on a sporadic, irregular basis. But to attempt both courses simultaneously was more than the government could reasonably expect to accomplish and deprived its efforts of lasting success. Since Portland and Noy helped to initiate the course followed after their deaths, they must be held partly responsible for a policy that heightened discontent throughout England and contributed to the bitter conflict of the next decade.

A century ago Gardiner noted the close connection between ship-money and the diplomatic objectives of the English government. It was his view that the reimposition of the tax was designed 'to carry out the foreign policy to which he [the Treasurer] gave his approval . . .' But almost immediately Gardiner conceded that it was the King rather than Portland who was guiding the course of English policy at this juncture: 'The deliberate preparation for an aggressive war against the Dutch bears the stamp of his master's mind, and it may well be that he [the Treasurer] lived in the hope that this warlike project would come to nothing, as so many warlike projects of Charles's had come to nothing before.'[36]

Victorian historians like Gardiner were united in their criticism of England's foreign policy during the 1630s, since it was conceived in secret and offered little hope of achieving the restoration of the Palatinate. Furthermore it did nothing to assist the beleaguered Protestants of northwestern Europe. Whether such an interpretation should continue to hold sway is open to question. That Portland concentrated on solving the financial problems of his own government, instead of pouring out blood and treasure for Calvinists and Huguenots, is hardly reason for complaint. Moreover, it cannot be doubted that he and his master had as clear an understanding of the European situation as the bulk of English opinion. The Treasurer was well aware of the increasing strength of France and the declining power of Spain, and he never questioned the assumption that future threats to England's security would come from Paris rather than Madrid. By the early 1630s the greater part of the Palatinate was in the hands of Maximilian of Bavaria, who was now an ally of Louis XIII, since he had renounced his allegiance to the Emperor. Thus the English government might be able to promote its two primary objectives, the safeguarding of British security and the restoration of the Palatinate, by co-operating with the Habsburgs against the Bourbons. Whether this view is accepted or not, it must still be acknowledged that Portland's policy of non-intervention was necessary if the powers of the English crown were to be maintained against the rising claims of parliament.

In regard to the plan for an Anglo-Spanish attack on the Dutch republic, which Gardiner naturally deplored, it is essential to remember three things. First, the scheme seems to have originated with the King rather than with Portland, as Gardiner himself conceded; second, the Treasurer never took it very seriously and generally attempted to restrain his master's aggressive inclinations; and third, the plan was prompted by the peculiar rivalry that persisted between London and The Hague during the greater part of the seventeenth century. On the one hand England and the United Provinces sympathised with one another because they were both overwhelmingly Protestant and had been allied together in the sixteenth-century struggle against Spain and the Counter-Reformation. On the other hand they disliked one another because of the economic and colonial rivalries that were becoming more important every year. Only by keeping in mind this peculiar love-hate relationship can the historian make any sense of the complicated diplomacy of the third quarter of the seventeenth century, when the English and Dutch governments waged three fierce wars against one another but occasionally stood shoulder to shoulder against Louis XIV and French expansionism. Thus to judge Portland and his master too severely for contemplating an attack on the Dutch is to ignore the fact that their views were shared by many other Englishmen of the age. Neither should it be forgotten that the complex relationship between England and the United Provinces was not surmounted until Dutch William was raised to the English throne in 1689 and a revolution in foreign policy was accomplished under his *aegis*.

While the preparations for the first ship-money writs were being made, the English government was engaged in secret negotiations with Necolalde, the Spanish Agent in London, the purpose of which was to promote Anglo-Spanish co-operation against the Dutch. These talks began in November 1633, when the King directed Portland, Cottington, and Windebank to form a special triumvirate to confer with Necolalde.[37] The negotiations had little chance of success, however, for Olivares and Philip IV had no desire for an alliance with England, nor were they willing to co-operate in the restoration of the Palatinate. The King never seems to have grasped this, although Portland clearly did. He recognised that Necolalde's obstructiveness was an accurate reflection of the atttitude in Madrid and that the talks, which took much of his time and sorely tried his patience, were likely to accomplish nothing.[38]

Because Charles allowed Spain to raise several regiments of volunteers in the British Isles and assisted with the transport of Spanish bullion through the Channel, he felt justified in requesting a measure of financial aid from the Spanish government. He proposed that Philip IV provide England with a loan of 700,000 crowns, which would be applied towards the preliminary expenses of the ship-money fleet. To be used for the defence of Spanish as well as English shipping, the ship-money fleet would thus be supported in part by the Spanish government, and would at first consist of twenty ships or more, each of at least 400 tons.[39]

During the early summer of 1634 the Spanish authorities gave periodic encouragement to Charles and his advisers, in order to keep the ship-money-fleet scheme from being abandoned but without committing themselves to a definite promise of support. Early in August the English Agent in Madrid, Sir Arthur Hopton, attempted to convince the Treasurer that Olivares and Philip IV were genuinely interested in pursuing the negotiations and that the devious courses followed by Necolalde were of his own making and should not be regarded as a true reflection of the official attitude in Madrid. Throughout this period the Spanish authorities assured Hopton and a fellow Agent in Spain, John Taylor, who was also in communication with Portland, that they were on the verge of replacing Necolalde with another emissary, someone who would be more willing to engage in serious discussions with the English triumvirs. In this way they came as close as they possibly could to a disavowal of Necolalde's courses without really committing themselves to a change of policy. By the middle of August, however, the Treasurer and his associates had penetrated this ruse, and during one of the periodic conferences at Putney Park they absolutely required Necolalde to agree to a loan of 200,000 crowns to the English government.[40]

Once the first ship-money writs were issued, Philip IV and Olivares found reasons to avoid completing the promised loan. With more ingenuousness than insight, Gardiner argued that the Spanish authorities were dismayed by the phrasing of the writs, which asserted that the ship-money fleet was intended solely for the protection of English shipping and would be directed against all countries that interfered with England's maritime trade, even Spain should that prove necessary. Thus it was Gardiner's view that English duplicity caused Portland and his colleagues to lose the financial assistance promised so grudgingly by Necolalde.[41] Although the ship-money writs were drafted in language to recommend them to the English people, it is nevertheless clear that the Spanish authorities had no intention of honouring the pledge wrung from them and were determined to find a pretext to avoid sending the loan. By April 1635 even Hopton in Madrid was beginning to see this.[42]

By then the Treasurer, who had never taken Spanish professions very seriously, was in his grave. He died after a debilitating illness in March 1635, although he retained his influence over the course of English diplomacy until the very end. Because his two closest associates remained in office and continued to enjoy the King's special confidence, his demise did not cause any reorientation of the country's foreign policy. Archbishop Laud, with whom Charles seldom discussed diplomatic matters, became chairman of the Council Committee for Foreign Affairs, and Secretary Coke began to play a more active role than during the past few years. But Cottington and Windebank continued the basic policy initiated by the Treasurer, holding England to a neutral course while negotiating for an unobtainable alliance with Spain in order to placate the King. Whether a more ambitious policy, one in conjunction with the French or Swedish government, was either possible or desirable during the 1630s is a doubtful matter. Because of the crown's straitened finances, Portland was convinced that such a policy was neither possible nor desirable, and no Englishman of the period was in a better position to know.

While involved in the tenuous relations with Necolalde during the winter of 1634–5, Portland was facing difficulties with two of his closest associates, Arundel and Cottington. Arundel was now anxious to cultivate closer relations with Wentworth, and during the autumn of 1634 he made a lengthy visit to Dublin, where he was sworn of the Irish Privy Council and received valuable assistance in the handling of his private affairs. When the earl returned to England, there was a tension between him and the Treasurer that had never existed before. At a Council meeting in January 1635, Arundel made belated criticisms of the soap monopoly, which he denounced for raising consumer prices without producing any added revenue for the Exchequer. Portland listened indignantly and then retorted that if the earl opposed 'things that are for the King's profit,' his own pension might have to go unpaid in the future. The proud head of the Howard connection took the Treasurer's rejoinder seriously, and the two men had a bitter falling-out.[43]

Cottington was also attempting to bolster his relations with the Deputy, who was delighted by the periodic overtures made to him.

The correspondence between the two men was unusually warm during the winter of 1634–5, and Cottington frequently performed useful services for Wentworth at court. The Treasurer was bound to have sensed this, but there was little he could do.

During the last few months of his life, the only figures with whom Portland's relations were completely untroubled were Secretary Coke, who continued to assist him with the administration of the navy,[44] and Lord Feilding, the husband of his daughter Anne. In September 1634 Feilding was appointed Ambassador to Venice at the handsome daily fee of £6. Lord and Lady Feilding set out on their journey to northern Italy during the following month. They did not reach their destination until early in February, after which the Treasurer's daughter became desperately ill. Her condition grew steadily worse, and on 10 March she died.[45]

By the time Feilding wrote with the news, Portland himself was dead. By the beginning of March 1635 it was apparent his end was fast approaching. Haggard and emaciated, he was now so weak he could hardly walk. A malignant growth beneath his chin made his throat so sore that it was all he could do to swallow. On 8 March the Treasurer sent for Cottington and informed him the doctors had given up all hope for his recovery. He thanked the Chancellor for his many years of faithful service and declared that his most pressing task now was to make his peace with God. On the following day Cottington returned to the sickbed with the new Attorney-General, Sir John Bankes, who assisted with the preparation of his will. That afternoon the King made the exceptionally kind gesture of visiting his dying minister. Yet Charles stayed for only a few minutes because he could not endure the sound of Portland's laboured breathing. Just as he was leaving the Treasurer pressed for his son Jerome's appointment as Master of the Wards and recommended his cousin Tichborne for his 'honesty and abilities.'[46]

Portland's death occurred at about three o'clock on Friday morning the 13th of March. During his last few hours he was attended only by known Catholics and was given extreme unction. This was probably at his wife's instigation, but the capital was nevertheless filled with rumours that on his deathbed he at last became a convert to Rome. The day after he died an autopsy was performed. His heart was found to be sound, though surrounded by a heavy layer of fat. His liver, lungs, and spleen were also judged healthy for a man of fifty-eight. But his kidneys were clogged with stones, and his lower abdominal tract was found to be 'very foul, being corroded with some malignant humours.'[47]

At Charles's command the court passed Palm Sunday, the 22nd of March, in official mourning for the Treasurer. Two days later he was quietly buried in the Guardian Angel's Chapel at Winchester Cathedral, where an elaborate monument was subsequently erected in his memory. Until recently it was believed that this monument was the work of Le Sueur. Art historians now hold that it should be attributed to Francesco Fanelli, whose work was of a somewhat higher quality.[48] Only a month before he died, Portland was granted Winchester Castle and all its tenements by the King. This generous gift, intended as a final reward for his many years of able service, would descend in the future to his heirs male. Consequently he declared it his wish to be buried at Winchester, 'because, he said, his son would make his seat there.'[49]

In the will prepared for him on 9 March, Portland bequeathed to his son Jerome the bulk of his landed property, reputedly worth £6000 a year. To his wife Frances, who lived on until 1645, he left his estate in Surrey and an income of £1500 a year; to his second surviving son Thomas, the manors of Skreens and Tye Hall in Essex, valued at £925 a year. For his two youngest sons, Nicholas and Benjamin, he provided annuities of £300 each; and for two of his six daughters, Elizabeth, Lady Netterville, and Mary, who was destined never to marry, he left sums of £1000 and £4000, respectively.[50]

Despite the efforts he had made to increase the wealth of his family, Portland left an estate burdened with heavy debts. Although the King is said to have given him £12,000 since Christmas, he owed nearly £13,000 to moneylenders in the City. This caused the new Lord Portland to sell £1200 worth of plate within two weeks to meet the most pressing demands of the hordes of creditors now descending upon him.[51] In all, the Treasurer's obligations amounted to approximately £21,000, or roughly 30% more than his annual income between 1628 and 1635. Most of his debts stemmed from the construction of his mansion in Surrey, but he had always tended to live beyond his means. As Clarendon noted, he died 'after six or eight years spent in outward opulency . . . without any sense of delight in so great prosperity, with the agony it was no greater.'[52]

Portland's heavy obligations necessitated an immediate series of land sales, which led to the break-up of the estate acquired so patiently by him, his father, and his grandfather. During the few remaining years before the Civil War, Jerome and his brothers disposed of numerous manors and other properties. By 1643 they had reduced the size of the family holdings by more than 50% and had severed nearly all their connections with Essex. Within a brief period, moreover, the second Earl of Portland had surrendered Winchester Castle and its tenements, which he could ill afford to keep, to the crown, in return for which he received a grant of 2000 acres of fenland in Cambridgeshire and the Isle of Ely. Undoubtedly the sale most regretted by the family was that of Putney Park, which was alienated to Sir Thomas Dawes in 1640 for only £11,300. It was probably the sale of this property, the most obvious symbol of the Westons' new-found status, that caused Clarendon to observe how the Treasurer's descendants 'outlived the fortune he left behind him.'[53]

Portland's failure to provide adequately for his heirs must be weighed against his enviable record of government service. In 1635 there was no reason for anyone to suspect that his political and economic programme would ultimately fail. Parliament had not met in six years; the agitated mood of 1628–9 had declined and all but disappeared; and the chief opposition spokesmen, Sir Edward Coke and Sir John Eliot, were both in their graves. It is true that the debts of the crown were still dangerously high, estimated at more than £1,160,000 in July 1635. They would have been higher still had Portland not kept the King from following an expensive foreign policy and had he and Marlborough not raised more than £2,402,000 in special revenues between 1624 and 1635. During his own term as Treasurer Portland had managed to increase the ordinary revenues of the crown from £570,000 in 1628 to approximately £620,000 by the time he died. He had also reduced pensions and annuities from £125,000 in 1630 to £80,000 in 1635, thereby providing the King with a net increase of £95,000 annually. If in the future ship-money could be converted into a permanent annual tax while it was being imposed on the inland counties, the crown would have revenues sufficient for its peacetime needs, particularly if the receipts from the customs duties grew at the anticipated rate.

When Portland died in 1635 the Hampden case contesting the

legality of ship-money was two years in the future and the first of the Scottish Wars, four years. Thus he can hardly have visualised the bloody conflict that broke out in the summer of 1642. Had the ship of state been kept on the same steady course he followed between 1628 and 1635, there is no reason to believe that the complicated events of the 1640s would have taken the form they did. Without the domination of his two successors, whose absolutist policies revived the old tensions and animosities, the Civil War might have been avoided. This is not to say that the constitution inherited by the early Stuarts would have remained unaltered. Because of the changing nature and developing forces of English society, royal power was almost bound to decline as parliament increased its role in the government of the kingdom. But how this happened might have been altogether different. A continuation of Portland's programme would have meant that the King made political concessions on a gradual basis, with the effect that a new constitutional balance slowly emerged between crown and parliament. The policies actually sponsored by Laud and Wentworth after 1635 convinced Charles that he need make no concessions at all. As a result he and the monarchy crashed down together during the 1640s, after a long and largely futile conflict.

Notes

ABBREVIATIONS USED IN THE NOTES

B.M	British Museum
Cabala, 2nd ed.	*Cabala, Sive Scrinia Sacra: Mysteries of State and Government, in Letters of Illustrious Persons, and Great Ministers of State, as well Foreign as Domestick, in the Reigns of King Henry the Eighth, Queen Elizabeth, King James, and King Charles*, 2nd ed. (London, 1691)
Cal. S.P. Dom.	*Calendar of State Papers, Domestic Series, of the Reigns of James I and Charles I, preserved in the State Paper Department of Her Majesty's Public Record Office*, 27 vols, ed. M. A. E. Green, John Bruce, and others (London, 1857–97)
Cal. S.P. Ireland	*Calendar of State Papers, Relating to Ireland, of the Reign of Charles I, preserved in the Public Record Office*, 4 vols, ed. R. P. Mahaffy (London, 1900–3)
Cal. S.P. Ven.	*Calendar of State Papers and Manuscripts, Relating to English Affairs, Existing in the Archives and Collections of Venice, and in other Libraries of Northern Italy*, 37 vols, ed. A. B. Hinds (London, 1864–1939)
Chester Waters, *The Chesters of Chicheley*	Robert E. Chester Waters, *Genealogical Memoirs of the Extinct Family of Chester of Chichley*, 2 vols (London, 1878)
Clarendon State Papers	*State Papers collected by Edward Earl of Clarendon, commencing from the Year 1621*, 3 vols, ed. R. Scrope and T. Monkhouse (Oxford, 1767–86)
Clarendon, *The History of the Rebellion*	Edward Hyde, Earl of Clarendon, *The History of the Rebellion and Civil Wars in England begun in the Year 1641*, 6 vols, ed. W. D. Macray (Oxford, 1888)
E.H.R.	*English Historical Review*
E.R.O.	Essex Record Office, Chelmsford

Hardwicke State Papers	*Miscellaneous State Papers. From 1501–1726*, 2 vols, ed. Philipe Yorke, Earl of Hardwicke (London, 1778)
H.M.C.	Historical Manuscripts Commission
Lloyd, *The States-men and Favourites of England*	David Lloyd, *The States-men and Favourites of England Since the Reformation. Their Prudence and Policies, Successes and Miscarriages, Advancements and Falls* (London, 1665)
P.C.	Privy Council
P.R.O.	Public Record Office, London
Rushworth, *Historical Collections*	John Rushworth, comp., *Historical Collections, of Private Passages of State, Weighty Matters in Law, Remarkable Proceedings in Five Parliaments*, 6 vols (London, 1659)
Rymer, *Foedera*	Thomas Rymer, comp., *Foedera, conventiones literae, et cujuscunque generis acta publica, inter reges Angliae*, 17 vols (London, 1704–17)
Scott, *English, Scottish and Irish Joint-Stock Companies*	W. R. Scott, *The Constitution and Finance of English, Scottish and Irish Joint-Stock Companies to 1720*, rev. ed., 3 vols (New York, 1951)
S.C.L.	Sheffield Central Library
S.P.	State Papers
T.R.H.S.	*Transactions of the Royal Historical Society*
V.C.H.	*Victoria History of the Counties of England*, ed. H. A. Doubleday, William Page, R. B. Pugh, and others (London, 1900–?)

CHAPTER 1

1 For an explanation of how Weston may have come to Gondomar's attention, see M. V. C. Alexander, 'A Biography of Sir Richard Weston, First Earl of Portland (1577–1635), until his Appointment as Lord Treasurer in July 1628' (Unpublished Ph.D. dissertation, University of North Carolina, 1969) pp. 99–101.

2 *Ibid.*, pp. 5–15. See also B.M., Add. MS. 18667, fol. 16, and Add. MS. 31890; Chester Waters, *The Chesters of Chichley*, I, 93; Morant, *The History and Antiquities of Essex*, II, 70–1, 171; Wright, *The History and Topography of Essex*, I, 179; *V.C.H. Staffordshire*, IV, 170–3; Owen Manning and John Bray, *The History and Antiquities of the County of Surrey*, 3 vols (London, 1804–14) I, 133–4. For an analysis of the estate bequeathed to Sir Richard in 1603, see Chapter 3 below.

3 Clarendon, *The History of the Rebellion*, I, 59; Lloyd, *The States-men and Favourites of England*, pp. 684–5.

4 *The Book of Matriculations and Degrees: A Catalogue of those who have been Matriculated or been admitted to any Degree in the University of Cambridge from 1544–1659*, ed. John Venn and J. A. Venn

(Cambridge U.P., 1913) p. 717; *Middle Temple Records. Minutes of Parliament,* 4 vols, ed. C. H. Hopwood (London, 1904) I, 344.

5 *Ibid.*, pp. 354, 361, 367, 407; Clarendon, *The History of the Rebellion,* I, 59.

6 *Ibid.*, pp. 59–60; Lloyd, *The States-men and Favourites of England,* p. 684. For the European tour taken by Sir Richard's sons Jerome and Thomas during the early 1630s, see P.R.O., S.P. 80/7, fols 50, 62, 172.

7 P.R.O., S.P. 38/7, fols 78, 263; *Members of Parliament,* I, 446; *D.N.B.*, XX, 1275.

8 For evidence of Weston's work as a justice of the peace in Essex, see E.R.O., Q/SR 177/96; Q/SR 184/45, 47; Q/SR 204/117; Q/SR 210/104–5.

9 Clarendon, *The History of the Rebellion,* I, 60.

10 For the bitter quarrel in 1609 between Salisbury and 'Sir Richard Weston', who was probably a member of the branch of the family whose seat was at Sutton Place near Guildford, Surrey, see *Cal. S.P. Dom., 1603–1610,* pp. 503, 551, 553; *D.N.B.*, XX, 1275. This was doubtless the same man who performed miscellaneous duties for Salisbury between 1604 and 1609 and was appointed a keeper of the King's deer in 1604.

11 For evidence of Weston's role in the parliament of 1614, see *Commons' Journals,* I, 456–7, 462–5, 488–9, 502–5.

12 A. F. Upton, *Sir Arthur Ingram, c 1565–1642; a Study of the Origins of an English Landed Family* (Oxford U.P., 1961) pp. 69, 80.

13 P.R.O., Index 6805 (unfoliated; grants dated Jul 1616 and Feb 1618). See also S.P. 14/141, fol. 227.

14 F. C. Dietz, *English Public Finance, 1558–1641* (New York, 1932) p. 165.

15 Menna Prestwich, *Cranfield, Politics and Profits under the Early Stuarts* (Clarendon Press, 1966) p. 206; R. H. Tawney, *Business and Politics: Lionel Cranfield as Merchant and Minister* (Cambridge U.P., 1958) p. 155.

16 Michael Oppenheim, *A History of the Administration of the Royal Navy and of Merchant Shipping in Relation to the Navy, from MDIX to MDCLX,* rev. ed. (Hamden, Conn., 1961) pp. 196, 202.

17 For the composition of the naval commission, see P.R.O., S.P. 14/105, fol. 94; *Acts of the Privy Council,* XXXVI, 174.

18 *Ibid.*, p. 263; Godfrey Goodman, *The Court of King James the First,* 2 vols, ed. J. S. Brewer (London, 1839) II, 165; Prestwich, *Cranfield,* pp. 212–15, 227; Tawney, *Business and Politics,* pp. 160–1.

19 Cranfield to Buckingham, 17 Nov 1618, in *The Fortescue Papers,* ed. S. R. Gardiner (London: Camden Society, 1871) p. 61.

20 Oppenheim, *A History of the Administration of the Royal Navy,* pp. 199–215. Cf. the comments of one of the naval commissioners, in H.M.C., *The Manuscripts of the Earl Cowper, K.G., preserved at Melbourne Hall, Derbyshire,* 3 vols, Twelfth Report, Appendix, Part I (London, 1888–9) I, 285.

21 For the material related in this paragraph, see *Acts of the Privy Council,* XXXVI, 264; XXXVII, 127; Rymer, *Foedera,* XVII, 171–4; H.M.C.,

The Manuscripts of His Grace the Duke of Rutland, G.C.B., Preserved at Belvoir Castle. Twelfth Report, Appendix, Part IV (London, 1888) I, 457–8; *The Letters of John Chamberlain,* 2 vols, ed. N. E. McClure (Philadelphia, 1939) II, 187, 203, 243, 255.

22 *Ibid.*, pp. 133, 148, 204, 281. See also *The Memoirs of Sir Benjamin Rudyerd,* ed. J. A. Manning (London, 1841) pp. 30–1.

23 P.R.O., S.P. 38/11 (unfoliated); Index 6806 (also unfoliated; grant dated 1 Jun 1620; Dietz, *English Public Finance,* p. 378; Prestwich, *Cranfield,* pp. 270–1, 278.

24 P.R.O., S.P. 14/116, fol. 13; *Cal. S.P. Ven., 1619–1621,* pp. 296–7, 309–10; L. P. Smith, *The Life and Letters of Sir Henry Wotton* (Clarendon Press, 1907) II, 168–77; Gardiner, *The History of England,* III, 363.

25 P.R.O., S.P. 81/7, fols 83–90; B.M., Add. MS. 35832, fols 19–22.

26 *Ibid.*, fol. 11; Gardiner, *The History of England,* III, 364, 387.

27 *Cal. S. P. Ven., 1619–1621,* p. 437.

28 See Weston's letter to Conway of 10 Aug 1621, in B.M., Add. MS. 35832, fol. 77. Weston observed that as 'for Doctor Winston, he went as my friend . . . and therefore is only to be paid by me'. See also P.R.O., S.P. 14/116, fol. 13.

29 H.M.C., *The Manuscripts of the Right Honourable The Earl De La Warr (Baron Buckhurst) at Knole Park, Co. Kent,* Fourth Report, Appendix, Part I (London, 1874) p. 281. For the financial records of the embassy of 1620–1, see P.R.O., S.P. 39/12, fol. 35; S.P. 81/20, fol. 296; E 403/2604, fol. 32; E 403/2667, Part III, fol. 18; E 405/215, fols 139, 161, 168; E 405/224 (unfoliated).

30 P.R.O., S.P. 77/14, fol. 163.

31 *Ibid.*, fols 163, 172. See also Weston's letter to Buckingham of 22 Jul 1620, in B.M., Harleian MS. 1581, fol. 194.

32 P.R.O., S.P. 81/17, fol. 190.

33 *Ibid.*, fols 302, 304.

34 *Ibid.*, fol. 333. See also Gardiner, *The History of England,* III, 368.

35 *Ibid.*, pp. 368–9; P.R.O., S.P. 81/18, fol. 189; S.P. 81/19, fol. 77.

36 P.R.O., S.P. 81/18, fol. 18; S.P. 81/19, fol. 73. B.M., Add. MS. 5950, fols 44–6.

37 *Ibid.*, fols 188–9; P.R.O., S.P. 81/19, fols 35, 73, 77. See also Carola Oman, *Elizabeth of Bohemia,* rev. ed. (London, 1964) pp. 220–1.

38 P.R.O., S.P. 81/19, fol. 162.

39 *Ibid.*

40 P.R.O., S.P. 81/18, fol. 52; S.P. 81/19, fol. 121; S.P. 84/97, fol. 88; Oman, *Elizabeth of Bohemia,* pp. 228–9.

41 B.M., Harleian MS. 1581, fol. 281; *Original Letters, illustrative of English History,* 3 vols, ed. Henry Ellis (London, 1824) III, 111–13; *The Autobiography and Correspondence of Sir Simonds D'Ewes,* 2 vols, ed. J. O. Halliwell-Phillips (London, 1845) I, 162; Bohdan Chudoba, *Spain and the Empire, 1519–1643* (University of Chicago Press, 1952) p. 248.

42 Arthur Wilson, *The History of Great Britain, being the Life and Reign of King James* (London, 1653) p. 142.

43 P.R.O., S.P. 81/19, fol. 234.

44 P.R.O., S.P. 81/20, fols 229, 296; E 403/2740, fol. 100.
45 Clarendon, *The History of the Rebellion*, I, 60. Cf. *The Letters of John Chamberlain*, II, 350.

CHAPTER 2

1 B.M., Add. MS. 36445, fol. 148. For a detailed account of the first session of the parliament of 1621, see Robert Zaller, *The Parliament of 1621* (University of California Press, 1971) pp. 30–138.
2 For the charges against Southampton, see *Proceedings and Debates of the House of Commons, in 1620 and 1621*, 2 vols (Oxford, 1766) II, Appendix, 367–70. (This source hereafter cited as *Proceedings and Debates.*) See also R. E. Ruigh, *The Parliament of 1624* (Harvard U.P., 1971) pp. 122–6.
3 P.R.O., S.P. 14/121, fol. 104; *The Letters of John Chamberlain*, II, 384.
4 *Commons Debates, 1621*, 7 vols, ed. Wallace Notestein, F. H. Relf, and Hartley Simpson (Yale U.P., 1935) VII, 425; Prestwich, *Cranfield*, p. 278.
5 *The Letters of John Chamberlain*, II, 392.
6 P.R.O., S.P. 14/122, fol. 152; *Acts of the Privy Council*, XXXVII, 46–110 *passim*.
7 P.R.O., S.P. 14/122, fol. 152; S.P. 14/123, fols 15, 63; E 403/2517, fols 56–7. See also *Letters and Memorials of State*, 2 vols, ed. Arthur Collins (London, 1746) II, 352.
8 *Members of Parliament*, I, 453. Cranfield had been made a baron in July 1621. He was granted the Earldom of Middlesex in September 1622. See P.R.O., S.P. 14/141, fols 351, 359.
9 M. F. S. Hervey, *The Life, Correspondence, and Collections of Thomas Howard, Earl of Arundel and Surrey*, ed. G. C. Williamson (Cambridge U.P., 1921) p. 262. (This source hereafter cited as Hervey, *Life of the Earl of Arundel.*) See also Ruigh, *The Parliament of 1624*, p. 260n.
10 *Commons Debates, 1621*, II, 518–19; V, 237, 415; VI, 236, 482; Goodman, *The Court of King James I*, II, 210.
11 Philip III had recently died and was succeeded on the Spanish throne by Philip IV, who ruled until 1665.
12 *Commons Debates, 1621*, III, 464; *Proceedings and Debates*, II, 208–9.
13 *Ibid.*, pp. 226, 241, 243–5.
14 Rushworth, *Historical Collections*, I, 40–3.
15 *Commons Debates, 1621*, V, 229. Cf. *Proceedings and Debates*, II, 270.
16 *Ibid.*, p. 271.
17 Rushworth, *Historical Collections*, I, 43–4; Zaller, *The Parliament of 1621*, p. 156.
18 Rushworth, *Historical Collections*, I, 45–6.
19 *Commons' Journals*, I, 657, 663; *Proceedings and Debates*, II, 299–300, 317–27; *Cal. S.P. Ven., 1621–1623*, p. 184n.
20 *Commons' Journals*, I, 663; *Commons Debates, 1621*, VI, 236; *Proceedings and Debates*, II, 328; Zaller, *The Parliament of 1621*, pp. 165–7.
21 *Commons Debates, 1621*, II, 522.

22 *Ibid.*, pp. 522–3, and vi, 238. For another account of Weston's speech on 15 Dec, see *Proceedings and Debates*, ii, 331–2.

23 In 1626, for example, when the radicals in the Commons were attempting to impeach Buckingham, Weston defended the favourite's foreign policy and charged that many members seemed more inclined to provoke dissatisfaction at home than to grant the funds needed for effective action abroad. See D. H. Willson, *The Privy Councillors in the House of Commons, 1604–1629* (University of Minnesota Press, 1940) p. 266.

24 P.R.O., S.P. 14/124, fol. 45; *Commons Debates, 1621*, ii, 525; John Forster, *Sir John Eliot: a Biography, 1590–1632*, 2 vols (London, 1865) i, 106.

25 Rushworth, *Historical Collections*, i, 53. For an analysis of the Protestation, and a comparison between it and the Apology and Satisfaction of 1604, see Zaller, *The Parliament of 1621*, pp. 177–83.

26 Lloyd, *The States-men and Favourites of England*, p. 684.

27 James I to Ferdinand II, 12 Nov 1621, in *Cabala*, 2nd ed., p. 240.

28 Rushworth, *Historical Collections*, i, 56.

29 See the letter of Ferdinand II to Philip IV of 11 May 1622 (n.s.), in *Cal. S.P. Ven., 1621–1623*, p. 351.

30 *Cabala*, 2nd ed., p. 225.

31 P.R.O., S.P. 77/15, fol. 98; E 403/2562, fol. 56; B.M., Add. MS. 35845, fol. 157; *Acts of the Privy Council*, xxxviii, 169–70; *The Letters of John Chamberlain*, ii, 428–9, 434. Weston's stay in Brussels cost the crown £5195, apart from the expenses of Dickinson. See P.R.O., E 403/2667, Part ii, fol. 54; E 403/2742, fol. 211.

32 B.M., Add. MS. 35845, fols 157–8; P.R.O., S.P. 77/15, fol. 122.

33 P.R.O., S.P. 84/106, fol. 198. For other letters exchanged by the two men, see S.P. 84/107, fols 110, 198, 203, 222; and S.P. 77/15, fol. 127.

34 B.M., Add. MS. 35845, fol. 168.

35 P.R.O., S.P. 77/15, fol. 198.

36 *Cabala*, 2nd ed., p. 468.

37 P.R.O., S.P. 77/15, fol. 292.

38 Copies of Weston's report are available in the British Museum (Add. MS. 35845, fols 157–70) and in the P.R.O. (S.P. 77/15, fols 296–306).

39 Clarendon, *The History of the Rebellion*, i, 60; Lloyd, *The States-men and Favourites of England*, p. 684; *Cal. S.P. Ven., 1621–1623*, p. 481; John Hacket, *Scrinia Reserata: a Memorial offer'd to the Great Deservings of J. Williams, Lord Keeper of the Great Seal, and Archbishop of York* (London, 1693) Part i, p. 180; H.M.C., *The Manuscripts of George Wingfield Digby, Esq., of Sherborne Castle, Co. Dorset*, Eighth Report, Appendix, Part i (London, 1881) p. 215; T. A. Birch, *The Court and Times of James the First*, 2 vols, ed. R. F. Williams (London, 1848) ii, 335–6.

40 *The Letters of John Chamberlain*, ii, 446–7

41 According to Lord Clarendon (*The History of the Rebellion*, i, 80) Conway served as principal Secretary 'for many years with very notable insufficiency', a judgement that has been upheld by Mrs

Higham, who maintains that Conway's opinions 'varied with alarming rapidity according to the changing whims of Buckingham, to whom he was entirely subservient'. See Mrs C. S. S. Higham (F. M. G. Evans), *The Principal Secretary of State; a Survey of the Office from 1558–1680* (London, 1923) p. 79. For evidence that James and Buckingham wanted a 'martial Secretary' at this juncture, see *Cabala*, 2nd ed., I, 198–9.

CHAPTER 3

1 Clarendon, *The History of the Rebellion*, I, 60–1.
2 Birch, *The Court and Times of James I*, II, 306.
3 H.M.C., *The Manuscripts of His Grace the Duke of Portland, preserved at Welbeck Abbey*, 10 vols, Thirteenth Report, Appendix, Part I (London, 1891–1931) I, 1–2; Chester Waters, *The Chesters of Chicheley*, I, 98; M. J. Havran, *The Catholics in Caroline England* (Oxford U.P., 1962) p. 135.
4 Clarendon, *The History of the Rebellion*, I, 63.
5 Garrard to Wentworth, 17 Mar 1635, in *The Earl of Strafford's Letters and Dispatches*, 2 vols, ed. William Knowler (London, 1739) I, 389.
6 P.R.O., S.P. 16/229, fol. 121; *Commons' Journals*, I, 703; Pory to Mead, 28 Nov 1628, in T. A. Birch, *The Court and Times of Charles the First*, 2 vols, ed. R. F. Williams (London, 1848) I, 440.
7 Chester Waters, *The Chesters of Chicheley*, I, 96, 99.
8 *The Letters of Sir Peter Paul Rubens*, ed. R. S. Magurn (Harvard U.P., 1955) p. 339.
9 *Admissions to Trinity College, Cambridge*, 2 vols, ed. W. W. Rouse Ball and J. A. Venn (London, 1911–13) II, 271; *Middle Temple Records*, II, 615, 625.
10 E.R.O., D/DSx/354; Birch, *The Court and Times of James I*, II, 306.
11 Venn, *The Book of Matriculations and Degrees*, p. 717; Ball, *Admissions to Trinity College, Cambridge*, II, 304; *Middle Temple Records*, II, 705.
12 For the information in this and the succeeding paragraph, see Chester Waters, *The Chesters of Chicheley*, I, 99–105; *The Tixall Letters*, 2 vols, ed. Arthur Clifford (London, 1815) I, 116 ff.; and J. Venn and J. A. Venn, *Alumni Cantabrigienses: a Bibliographical List of all Known Students, Graduates and Holders of Office at the University of Cambridge, from the Earliest Times to 1900*, 10 vols (Cambridge U.P., 1922–54) IV, 373–4.
13 P.R.O., S.P. 14/141, fol. 227; S.P. 38/11 (unfoliated); Index 6805 (unfoliated); Index 6806 (unfoliated); *Commons Debates, 1621*, VII, 425. See also Hubert Hall, *The Antiquities and Curiosities of the Exchequer* (London, 1891) pp. 87–8; Francis Peck, *Desiderata Curiosa; or, a Collection of Scarce and Curious Pieces relating chiefly to Matters of English History*, 2 vols in 1 (London, 1779) II, 2. For an analysis of the value of various administrative positions during the 1620s and 1630s, see G. E. Aylmer, *The King's Servants: The Civil Service of Charles I, 1625–1640* (Columbia U.P., 1961) pp. 203–15. Unhappily Professor Aylmer gives scant attention to the office of Chancellor and Under-

treasurer of the Exchequer, which seems to have been worth between a third and a fourth of the Lord Treasurership, the annual value of which was at least £7000 and perhaps a good deal more.

14 P.R.O., Index 6806 (unfoliated); Index 6807 (also unfoliated).

15 *V.C.H. Bedfordshire*, III, 275–7.

16 For the history of Neyland, see B.M., Add. MS. 18479, fols 31–2; and Augustine Page, *A Supplement to the Suffolk Traveller; or Topographical and Genealogical Collections concerning the County*, 2 vols (London, 1844) II, 958. For evidence that Skreens was worth £600 a year during the early Stuart period, see *Strafford's Letters and Dispatches*, I, 389.

17 *Ibid.*; Morant, *The History and Antiquities of Essex*, II, 71, 73, 215, 238; Wright, *The History and Topography of Essex*, I, 181, 427–8, 448–9.

18 B.M., Harleian MS. 608, fols 75–6; Morant, *The History and Antiquities of Essex*, I, 136, and II, 70, 423, 457, 490; Wright, *The History and Topography of Essex*, I, 178–81; and II, 213; *V.C.H. Essex*, IV, 199–200; Chester Waters, *The Chesters of Chicheley*, I, 95; John Norden, 'Speculi Britanniae; an historical and chorographical description of the County of Essex', ed. Henry Ellis (London: Camden Society, 1840) p. 33. When Weston died in March 1635, it was reported that his estates were worth £6000 a year. On this point, see *Strafford's Letters and Dispatches*, I, 389. While serving as Lord Treasurer, he managed to make sizable additions to his estate but certainly did not suceed in doubling its annual value. Thus it would appear, and it should be emphasised that the evidence is very spotty, that he probably inherited lands worth at least £3500 a year and perhaps even more.

19 For Weston's land transactions before 1625, see *V.C.H. Hampshire and the Isle of Wight*, II, 476–7, 513; *V.C.H. Surrey*, II, 78.

20 E.R.O., D/DSx/447.

21 *V.C.H. Essex*, IV, 199–201. According to Morant, Weston lost Long Barnes in 1605 on a writ of entry. See *The History and Antiquities of Essex*, I, 136.

22 P.R.O., Index and Calendar to the Patent Rolls, XIII, 204; Morant, *The History and Antiquities of Essex*, II, 215; Wright, *The History and Topography of Essex*, I, 427–8; *V.C.H. Essex*, IV, 200–1.

23 Clarendon, *The History of the Rebellion*, I, 60. It should be noted, however, that Sir Richard's landed income during the 1620s was at least £1100 less than what he had inherited in 1603, owing to the land sales just discussed and the voluntary settlement made for his son Richard's benefit in May 1621.

24 *Cal. S.P. Colonial, 1617–1621*, pp. 81, 99; *Cal. S.P. Colonial, 1622–1624*, p. 137; *Cal. S.P. Colonial, 1625–1629*, pp. 600–1; Upton, *Sir Arthur Ingram*, p. 79; K. N. Chaudhuri, *The English East India Company; the Study of an Early Joint-Stock Company, 1600–1640*, rev. ed. (New York, 1965) p. 22.

25 Prestwich, *Cranfield*, p. 458.

26 Clarendon, *The History of the Rebellion*, I, 61, 64.

27 Weston to Boyle, 28 Jun 1603, in *The Lismore Papers (Family Muni-*

ments preserved in Lismore Castle) 10 vols, ed. A. B. Grosart (London, 1886–8) 2nd series, I, 79–80.

28 *The Workes of Benjamin Jonson* (London, 1640) pp. 244–5.
29 Smith, *The Life and Letters of Sir Henry Wotton*, II, 335.
30 Clarendon, *The History of the Rebellion*, I, 60.
31 *Members of Parliament*, I *passim*.
32 J. E. Neale, *The Elizabethan House of Commons* (Yale U.P., 1950) Chapters 7–8.
33 For evidence of the friendship between Weston and Conway, see B.M., Add. MS. 35832, fol. 77; P.R.O., S.P. 14/149, fols 60, 73.
34 *Cabala*, 2nd ed., pp. 276–7.
35 *Ibid.* In 1627, while Buckingham was absent with an army on the Isle of Ré, Weston complained that the Exchequer was empty and briefly attempted to withhold funds from him. This will be discussed in Chapter 7 below.
36 Weston to Buckingham, 17 Jul 1623, in B.M., Harleian MS. 1581, fol. 202. There is no evidence of Weston's alleged disloyalty to Buckingham in 1623. Lord Clarendon was convinced, however, that Middlesex was attempting to withhold funds from the favourite, who had accompanied Prince Charles on his journey to Madrid. Perhaps the duke suspected that Weston was involved in this business and was giving it his support. See *The History of the Rebellion*, I, 27–8. Cf. Goodman, *The Court of King James I*, II, 267–72, 289.
37 Weston to Conway, 19 Oct 1623, in P.R.O., S.P. 14/153, fol. 76.
38 Clarendon, *The History of the Rebellion*, I, 59, 61.

CHAPTER 4

1 Clarendon, *The History of the Rebellion*, I, 60; Lloyd, *The States-men and Favourites of England*, pp. 684–5.
2 Clarendon, *The History of the Rebellion*, I, 60.
3 Tawney, *Business and Politics*, pp. 221, 288.
4 S. B. Baxter, *The Development of the Treasury, 1660–1702* (Harvard U.P., 1957) p. 262.
5 Henry Roseveare, *The Treasury. The Evolution of a British Institution* (Columbia U.P., 1969) p. 16; Baxter, *The Development of the Treasury*, p. 219.
6 During the early seventeenth century the royal revenues were increasing at a more rapid rate than is generally realised. They stood at about £305,000 a year in 1603, at £485,000 annually in 1621, and at approximately £618,000 per year during the period 1630–5. Yet the amount of money passing through the hands of the four tellers of the lower Exchequer remained almost constant, especially during the 1620s and 1630s. For evidence of this, see P.R.O., E 403/2802–10 (Order Books, Auditors) and E 405/223–5, 270–3, and 282–4 (Certificate Books, Auditors, and Declaration Books, Pells). See also B.M., Add. MS. 41578, fols 1–122 (the records for 1621–2 of Sir William Heyricke, one of the tellers of the lower Exchequer).

7 For an indication of the way two seventeenth-century magnates profited from their use of unpaid cash balances, see Upton, *Sir Arthur Ingram*, pp. 180–2; C. V. Wedgwood, *Thomas Wentworth, First Earl of Strafford. A Revaluation* (London, 1961) pp. 197–8; J. P. Cooper, 'The Fortune of Thomas Wentworth, Earl of Strafford', in *Economic History Review*, 2nd series, XI, No. 2 (1958) 233–4, 245.

8 Aylmer, *The King's Servants*, pp. 195–6, 450. For the defalcation of revenues received from the crown lands, see Dietz, 'The Receipts and Issues of the Exchequer during the Reigns of James I and Charles I', p. 127.

9 Thomas Fanshawe, *The Practice of the Exchequer Court* (London, 1658) pp. 20–1; M. S. Giuseppi, *Guide to the Contents of the Public Record Office*, 2nd ed., 2 vols (London, 1963) I, 74; Baxter, *The Development of the Treasury*, pp. 34–5, 111–12.

10 Christopher Vernon, *Considerations for Regulating the Exchequer* (London, 1642) pp. 35–6, 39; Fanshawe, *The Practice of the Exchequer Court*, pp. 85–6, 101–2; Giuseppi, *Guide to the Contents of the P.R.O.*, I, 69–70.

11 Prestwich, *Cranfield*, pp. 383, 596, 602.

12 P.R.O., E 403/2455, fols 87–8, 156–8.

13 P.R.O., E 403/2457, fols 95–6; E 403/2458, fols 76–7.

14 P.R.O., E 126/2, fols 232–4, 247, 263, 278; Fanshawe, *The Practice of the Exchequer Court*, pp. 19–20.

15 P.R.O., S.P. 14/149, fol. 38; *Foedera*, XVII, 457–8; *Acts of the Privy Council*, XXXVIII, 59, 68, 134–5, 372.

16 *Ibid.*, pp. 329–33, 364, 406–7, 480–1; *Foedera*, XVII, 367–8; *Cal. S.P. Dom., 1619–1623*, pp. 343, 458, 515; *Cal. S.P. Dom., 1623–1625*, p. 54; H.M.C., *The Manuscripts of the Corporation of Reading*, Eleventh Report, Appendix, Part VII (London, 1888) p. 222; Prestwich, *Cranfield*, p. 345.

17 See Philip IV's undated letter to Olivares in *Cabala*, pp. 314–15. For Olivares's reply, *ibid.*, pp. 315–16.

18 P.R.O., S.P. 14/214, fol. 1; *Foedera*, XVII, 477.

19 *Ibid.*, p. 478; *The Letters of John Chamberlain*, II, 438, 527–8, 541.

20 P.R.O., E 403/2562, fol. 83; E 403/2670, fol. 163. E 403/2742, fol. 289; E 403/2743, fol. 135; E 403/2981, fol. 38.

21 *Cal. S.P. Dom., 1623–1625*, p. 27; J. G. Nichols, *The Progresses, Processions, and Magnificent Festivities of King James the First*, 4 vols (London, 1828), IV, 882–4.

22 Wilson, *The History of Great Britain*, p. 240.

23 *Hardwicke State Papers*, I, 479; *Cal. S.P. Dom., 1623–1625*, p. 69.

24 P.R.O., S.P. 39/17, fol. 35; Birch, *The Court and Times of James I*, II, 420.

25 In January 1624 the Venetian Ambassador in London informed his government that he had recently had a long talk with Buckingham, who had declared that 'without going to Spain one would never believe her weakness.' See *Cal. S.P. Ven., 1623–1625*, p. 191.

26 *Foedera*, XVII, 571. For a good account of the diplomatic manœuvring during the autumn of 1623, see Ruigh, *The Parliament of 1624*, pp. 16–40.

27 Clarendon, *The History of the Rebellion*, I, 13.

28 *The Works of the Most Reverend Father in God, William Laud, D.D.*, 7 vols, ed. William Scott and James Bliss (Oxford, 1847–60) III, 144–5.

29 Tawney, *Business and Politics*, p. 227.

30 *The Letters of John Chamberlain*, II, 541–2.

31 D. H. Willson, *The Privy Councillors in the House of Commons, 1604–1629* (University of Minnesota Press, 1940) pp. 162–3.

32 *The Letters of John Chamberlain*, II, 538, 543.

33 *Members of Parliament*, I, 456; Ruigh, *The Parliament of 1624*, pp. 48, 57–8.

34 W. M. Mitchell, *The Rise of the Revolutionary Party in the English House of Commons, 1603–1629* (Columbia U.P., 1957) pp. 93–4; Ruigh, *The Parliament of 1624*, pp. 1, 43.

35 P.R.O., S.P. 84/116, fol. 175.

36 P.R.O., S.P. 14/159, fols 72–7; *The Lismore Papers*, 2nd series, III, 100; *Foedera*, XVII, 561–78; Ruigh, *The Parliament of 1624*, pp. 162–6.

37 P.R.O., S.P. 84/116, fol. 175.

38 P.R.O., S.P. 14/160, fol. 33.

39 P.R.O., S.P. 14/159, fol. 86; *Commons' Journals*, I, 720.

40 P.R.O., S.P. 14/160, fol. 33; Ruigh, *The Parliament of 1624*, pp. 177–80.

41 *Commons' Journals*, I, 724.

42 P.R.O., S.P. 14/160, fol. 33.

43 *Ibid.*, fol. 62; B.M., Add. MS. 10119, fol. 3; *Commons' Journals*, I, 682; *The Memoirs of Sir Benjamin Rudyerd*, pp. 78–82; Prestwich, *Cranfield*, p. 439. Perhaps it should be noted that in this speech Weston calculated the King's debts at £666,666, a figure recently accepted by Conrad Russell. See *The Origins of the English Civil War* (London: Macmillan, 1973) p. 102. However, this rather suspicious looking figure is unquestionably too low. Professor Russell himself points out that the debt stood at £900,000 in 1618 and that Middlesex's efforts between 1617 and 1624 merely 'came near to putting the king's revenue and expenditure in balance . . .' *Ibid.*, pp. 98, 101. Furthermore, in their speeches of 11 March, both Middlesex and Weston maintained that James's debts had risen by £300,000 since 1619, even though war had not been declared. Thus the crown's indebtedness could not have been as low as £666,666, and was probably somewhere between £1,000,000 and £1,200,000. Doubtless it should be remembered that throughout the 1620s the government was reluctant to reveal the true picture of the royal finances to parliament, for fear that the members would draw back in indignation and amazement.

44 Prestwich, *Cranfield*, p. 440.

45 Ruigh, *The Parliament of 1624*, p. 219; Willson, *The Privy Councillors*, pp. 280–1.

46 *Ibid.*, p. 281.

47 *Debates in the House of Commons in 1625* [*sic*], ed. S. R. Gardiner

(London: Camden Society, 1873) pp. iii-iv. It should be noted that the subsidy bill was not formally introduced until 24 April and was not passed on third reading until 14 May. The first subsidy, tenth, and fifteenth were to be collected and paid at the Receipt by July 1624, the second levies by December 1624, and the third by May 1625. These grants produced a revenue of £278,118, or far less than had been intended by parliament. See Dietz, *English Public Finance*, p. 393.

48 *The Works of Archbishop Laud*, III, 149; Rushworth, *Historical Collections*, I, 138–40.

49 *Cabala*, p. 275; *Hardwicke State Papers*, I, 453. For the intrigues against Buckingham at this juncture, see Ruigh, *The Parliament of 1624*, pp. 257–302.

50 *Ibid.*, p. 249; *Clarendon State Papers*, I, 21–4; Nichols, *The Progresses of James I*, IV, 971; Sir John Finett, *Finetti Philoxenis: Some Choice Observations of Sir John Finett, Knight* (London, 1656) p. 139.

51 Arthur Brett and his sister Anne were cousins of the duke's wife, Lady Katherine Manners; it was at the duke's urging that Middlesex married Anne Brett after the death of his first wife, Elizabeth Shepherd.

52 P.R.O., E 403/2517, fol. 105; S.P. 39/14, fol. 17.

53 P.R.O., S.P. 14/170, fol. 44; *The Letters of John Chamberlain*, II, 553; *Cal. S.P. Ven., 1623–1625*, p. 268.

54 P.R.O., S.P. 14/170, fol. 44; E 406/47, fol. 28.

55 Clarendon, *The History of the Rebellion*, I, 28.

56 Hacket, *Scrinia Reserata*, Part I, pp. 189–90.

57 Prestwich, *Cranfield*, p. 485.

58 *Ibid.*, pp. 434–5, 439; Goodman, *The Court of King James I*, I, 325; Ruigh, *The Parliament of 1624*, pp. 316–25; Aylmer, *The King's Servants*, pp. 311–12, 354.

59 Prestwich, *Cranfield*, pp. 435, 439; Tawney, *Business and Politics*, pp. 242–3, 259, 271. Mrs Prestwich maintains that, aside from Sir Richard, only the Earl of Arundel stood by the Treasurer; but Professor Tawney states that Lord Brooke, Weston's predecessor at the Exchequer, and Sir Arthur Ingram were both loyal to him. According to Professor Ruigh, 'Longtime friends and associates, Sir Arthur Ingram and Sir Richard Weston, tried to remove the onus of bribery from his name. Usually the Treasurer's friends were most obvious by their silence.' See *The Parliament of 1624*, p. 329. For a more hostile view of Weston at this time, see Willson, *The Privy Councillors*, pp. 250–1.

60 Carleton to Carleton, 15 Apr 1624, in *Cal. S.P. Dom., 1623–1625*, p. 215.

61 Prestwich, *Cranfield*, pp. 439, 455.

62 *The Letters of John Chamberlain*, II, 559; Ruigh, *The Parliament of 1624*, pp. 337–8.

63 Prestwich, *Cranfield*, p. 453.

64 *The Letters of John Chamberlain*, II, 560.

65 P.R.O., S.P. 14/165, fol. 48; S.P. 38/12 (unfoliated); E 403/2455, fols. 156–8.

66 Williams to Buckingham, 24 May 1624, in *Cabala*, pp. 276–7.

67 P.R.O., S.P. 14/165, fol. 4.

68 *Ibid.*, fol. 48; H.M.C., *The Manuscripts of His Grace the Duke of Portland*, I, 1–2; *Hardwicke State Papers*, I, 455–6; Ruigh, *The Parliament of 1624*, p. 261.

69 Doubtless the King was sincere when he instructed the members to meet again on 2 November. It was chiefly because of repeated outbreaks of plague that he later postponed the autumn session, first until 16 February 1625 and then until the 15th of March following. Yet because of his rapidly failing health, parliament did not meet as scheduled on 15 March. See *Foedera*, XVII, 625, 648.

70 Weston to Buckingham, 29 May 1624, in B.M., Harleian MS. 1581, fol. 206.

CHAPTER 5

1 B.M., Harleian MS. 1581, fol. 206.

2 P.R.O., S.P. 31/3, fol. 59; *Cal. S.P. Ven., 1623–1625*, p. 335; Tawney, *Business and Politics*, pp. 268, 271.

3 P.R.O., S.P. 14/170, fol. 36.

4 *Ibid.*, fol. 45.

5 *Ibid.*, fol. 82; S.P. 14/171, fol. 78; B.M., Harleian MS. 1581, fol. 208.

6 P.R.O., S.P. 14/174, fols 41, 76; H.M.C., *The Manuscripts of the Right Honourable The Earl De La Warr*, pp. 278, 288.

7 *Ibid.*; P.R.O., S.P. 39/20, fol. 50; Prestwich, *Cranfield*, pp. 475, 477.

8 P.R.O., E 403/2562, fol. 76; S.P. 39/15, fols 31, 77.

9 P.R.O., T 56/16, fols 40, 46; *Cal. S.P. Ven., 1619–1623*, p. 512.

10 For the material related in this paragraph, see B.M., Harleian MS. 3796, fol. 36; Dietz, *English Public Finance*, pp. 298–9; Dietz, 'The Receipts and Issues of the Exchequer during the Reigns of James I and Charles I', in *Smith College Studies in History*, XIII, No. 4 (1928) 127; S. J. Madge, *The Domesday of Crown Lands* (London, 1938) p. 60 ff.; Aylmer, *The King's Servants*, p. 65; Prestwich, *Cranfield*, pp. 373–4.

11 Dietz, *English Public Finance*, p. 271 note.

12 P.R.O., E 403/2458, fols 117–20.

13 Robert Ashton, *The Crown and the Money Market, 1603–1640* (Clarendon Press, 1960) p. 162; Scott, *English, Scottish and Irish Joint-Stock Companies*, I, 190.

14 *Cabala*, 2nd ed., p. 369.

15 *The Letters and the Life of Francis Bacon*, VII, 517–18, 521.

16 P.R.O., S.P. 14/167, fol. 62.

17 P.R.O., E 403/2567, fol. 35; see also S.P. 39/21, fol. 9.

18 P.R.O., E 403/2606, fol. 50.

19 P.R.O., S.P. 14/175, fol. 34; T 56/16, fols 44, 47.

20 P.R.O., S.P. 14/151, fol. 48; S.P. 14/214, fol. 74; S.P. 39/15, fol. 47; E 404/233, fol. 243; E 406/45, fols 88–9. See also *Cal. S.P. Dom., 1623–1625*, pp. 389, 395–6.

21 Hatfield House, Salisbury MS. 206, fol. 79.

22 P.R.O., S.P. 14/167, fols 35, 37; S.P. 14/168, fol. 65; S.P. 14/171, fol.

14; S.P. 14/172, fol. 47; S.P. 14/214, fol. 142; *Foedera*, XVII, 636–7; Ruigh, *The Parliament of 1624*, pp. 364–5.

23 P.R.O., S.P. 14/152, fol. 63; S.P. 14/175, fol. 73; E 403/2505, fols 25–9.

24 B.M., Stowe MS. 326, fol. 58; Dietz, *English Public Finance*, p. 334.

25 P.R.O., S.P. 14/171, fol. 66.

26 John Stow, *A Survey of the Cities of London and Westminster*, 2 vols, ed. John Strype (London, 1720) I, Book II, 111. See also P.R.O., T 56/16, fol. 47; and H. B. Wheatley, *London Past and Present*, 3 vols (London, 1891) I, 278–9, and III, 441–3.

27 P.R.O., S.P. 14/168, fol. 65.

28 P.R.O., S.P. 14/173, fols 86, 105; S.P. 14/214, fols 158, 161.

29 P.R.O., S.P. 14/173, fols 48, 86; see also S.P. 14/174, fol. 76.

30 P.R.O., S.P. 14/173, fol. 116; E 403/2455, fol. 179; *The Letters of John Chamberlain*, II, 583, 585.

31 Aylmer, *The King's Servants*, pp. 39, 61. For similar estimates of Ley, see Clarendon, *The History of the Rebellion*, I, 59; Lloyd, *The Statesmen and Favourites of England*, I, 59; Gardiner, *The History of England*, V, 310; Tawney, *Business and Politics*, p. 267.

32 Prestwich, *Cranfield*, p. 215.

33 P.R.O., S.P. 46/70, fols 207, 209, 211, 213, 226, 231; T 56/16, fols 48–9, 50–1, 58–9.

34 Pye to Coke, 20 Nov 1625, in H.M.C., *The Manuscripts of the Earl Cowper*, I, 229.

35 P.R.O., S.P. 14/181, fol. 20.

36 P.R.O., E 403/2981, fols 69, 84–5; E 403/2604, fols 331, 333. For the discharge of the £50,000 to Buckingham, which had been effected by 18 March 1625, see E 403/2667, fols 76–7. In all fairness it should be noted that the greater part of the money paid over to him was used for the support of a planned naval expedition. See S.P. 14/185, fol. 41.

37 P.R.O., S.P. 14/185, fol. 39; S.P. 39/17, fols 19–20; E 403/2667, fol. 77; E 403/2604, fol. 343; B.M., Add. MS. 35832, fol. 175.

38 *The Letters of John Chamberlain*, II, 608; *Original Letters, illustrative of English History*, 1st series, III, 182–3; Wilson, *The History of Great Britain*, p. 790; D. H. Willson, *King James VI and I* (London, 1963) pp. 446–7.

39 B.M., Add. MS. 34217, fol. 50; *Acts of the Privy Council*, XL, 2–5.

40 *Ibid*., p. 14; P.R.O., S.P. 14/185, fol. 41.

41 Clarendon, *The History of the Rebellion*, I, 131; H.M.C., *The Manuscripts of Henry Duncan Skrine, Esq., Salvetti Correspondence*, Eleventh Report, Appendix, Part I (London, 1887) pp. 6–7; *Cal. S.P. Ven., 1625–1626*, p. 21.

42 Ashton, *The Crown and the Money Market*, pp. 61, 122–9, 149. See also Valerie Pearl, *London and the Outbreak of the Puritan Revolution* (Oxford U.P., 1961) p. 72, and esp. note 9.

43 *The Works of Archbishop Laud*, III, 147.

44 *The Letters of John Chamberlain*, II, 615.

45 H.M.C., *The Manuscripts of Henry Duncan Skrine*, p. 3.
46 P.R.O., E 403/2753, fol. 56; *The Letters of John Chamberlain*, II, 609, 616, 619; H.M.C., *The Manuscripts of J. Eliot Hodgkin*, p. 293; Willson, *King James VI and I*, p. 447.
47 For copies of the Anglo-French marriage treaty, see B.M., Egerton MS. 2554, fols 27–33, and Add. MS. 34217, fols 27–34. For a sound treatment of the main diplomatic developments during the summer and autumn of 1624, see C. V. Wedgwood, *The Thirty Years War* (Garden City, N.Y., 1961), Chapter 4.
48 *Cabala*, 2nd ed., pp. 13–14; *Finetti Philoxenis*, p. 139.
49 Dietz, *English Public Finance*, pp. 216–17; Dietz, 'The Receipts and Issues of the Exchequer during the Reigns of James I and Charles I', p. 131.
50 Hacket, *Scrinia Reserata*, Part II, p. 4.
51 *Members of Parliament*, I, 463; *The Letters of John Chamberlain*, II, 614–17; Willson, *The Privy Councillors*, pp. 66, 81, 100.
52 *Lords' Journals*, III, 432.

CHAPTER 6

1 Willson, *The Privy Councillors*, p. 66 ff.
2 H.M.C., *The Manuscripts of the Earl Cowper*, pp. 187, 192; S. R. Gardiner, ed., *Documents Illustrating the Impeachment of the Duke of Buckingham in 1626* (London: Camden Society, 1889) pp. ix–x, 264–5; Donald Nicholas, *Mr. Secretary Nicholas (1593–1669): His Life and Letters* (London, 1955) pp. 42, 44.
3 *Commons' Journal*, I, 801; *Debates in the House of Commons in 1625*, pp. 17, 28; *The Manuscripts of the House of Lords, XI (New Series. Addenda, 1514–1714)*, ed. M. F. Bond (London, 1962) pp. 181–6, 195. See also Sir John Eliot, *An Apology for Socrates and Negotium Posterorum*, 2 vols, ed. A. B. Grosart (London, 1881) I, 70–3. (This source hereafter cited as Eliot, *Negotium Posterorum*.)
4 For the debates on 30 June, see *Debates in the House of Commons in 1625*, pp. 30–3. For an account of Rudyerd's speech, see Eliot, *Negotium Posterorum*, I, 66–8. For the receipts of the grant of 1625, which was not passed on third reading until 8 July, see Dietz, *English Public Finance*, pp. 226–7, 393.
5 *Acts of the Privy Council*, XL, 40.
6 Dietz, *English Public Finance*, pp. 226, 334.
7 *Debates in the House of Commons in 1625*, pp. 43, 47.
8 Eliot, *Negotium Posterorum*, I, 110–13; Willson, *The Privy Councillors*, p. 177.
9 *Ibid.*; *Debates in the House of Commons in 1625*, pp. 56–9.
10 *Ibid.*, p. 68; *Lords' Journals*, III, 464.
11 *Ibid.*, pp. 470–1; *Debates in the House of Commons in 1625*, pp, 73, 76–7.
12 *Ibid.*, pp. 78–9; *Commons' Journals*, I, 810.
13 *Debates in the House of Commons in 1625*, pp. 81–2.
14 *Ibid.*, pp. 83–4. Cf. Eliot, *Negotium Posterorum*, I, 36–9.

15 *Ibid.*, pp. 39–50; *Commons' Journals*, I, 810–11; *Debates in the House of Commons in 1625*, pp. 87–9.
16 *Ibid.*, pp. 95–105; *Lords' Journals*, III, 479–85. For a copy of the duke's speech on 8 August, see *Clarendon State Papers*, I, 26–7.
17 Rushworth, *Historical Collections*, I, 184–5.
18 *Debates in the House of Commons in 1625*, pp. 106–7; Eliot, *Negotium Posterorum*, II, 79–80; *Commons' Journals*, I, 813.
19 *Ibid.*, pp. 813–14; Eliot, *Negotium Posterorum*, II, 91–2.
20 *Commons' Journals*, I, 814; *Debates in the House of Commons in 1625*, p. 110.
21 *Ibid.*, p. 122; White Kennet, *A Complete History of England, with the Lives of all the Kings and Queens thereof*, 3 vols (London, 1706) III, 11.
22 *Cal. S.P. Ven., 1625–1626*, p. 168.
23 S.C.L., Strafford MS. xx, fol. 243.
24 Higham, *The Principal Secretary of State*, p. 86.
25 As the duke's chaplain, Laud was in a good position to intrigue against Bishop Williams. According to Buckingham's mother, Laud 'was the man that did underwork him [Williams] with her son, and would underwork any man in the world, that himself would rise.' See Hacket, *Scrinia Reserata*, Part II, pp. 19, 27.
26 Clarendon, *The History of the Rebellion*, I, 57–8; *The Letters of John Chamberlain*, II, 599–608; Goodman, *The Court of King James I*, I, 376–7.
27 For the diplomacy of 1625, see Dumont, *Corps universel diplomatique*, V, Part II, 475–85.
28 Gardiner, *The History of England*, VI, 14–23, 37; Oppenheim, *A History of the Administration of the Royal Navy*, p. 220; Nicholas, *Mr. Secretary Nicholas*, p. 48; Peck, *Desiderata Curiosa*, II, 15–16.
29 *Cal. S.P. Dom., 1625–1626*, p. 323; Oppenheim, *A History of the Administration of the Royal Navy*, p. 225.
30 *Letters and Memorials of State*, ed. Collins, II, 363.
31 H.M.C., *The Manuscripts of Rye and Hereford Corporations*, pp. 175, 444; H.M.C., *The Manuscripts of the Earl Cowper*, p. 213; *Hardwicke State Papers*, II, 10–11.
32 H.M.C., *The Manuscripts of Henry Duncan Skrine*, p. 43; Dietz, *English Public Finance*, p. 228.
33 *Acts of the Privy Council*, XL, 271, 276, 289–99, 326–7.
34 *The Diary of Walter Yonge*, ed. George Roberts (London: Camden Society, 1856) pp. 2–3.
35 For Eliot's attitude towards the duke in 1626, see *Negotium Posterorum*, I, 76, where the Cornishman laments the hundreds of men killed and the 'millions of treasure that was spent, without success, in profit or honour to the kingdom'. See also Harold Hulme, *The Life of Sir John Eliot* (New York University Press, 1957) pp. 86, 245; J. N. Ball, 'The Parliamentary Career of Sir John Eliot, 1624–1629' (unpublished Cambridge University Ph.D. dissertation, 1953) pp. 18–19, 21–2, 70, 116, 142–3, 199.

36 *Members of Parliament*, I, 455, 461, 467–8, 479; Willson, *The Privy Councillors*, pp. 78, 80.
37 *Ibid.*, pp. 66–7.
38 *Commons' Journals*, I, 824; Willson, *The Privy Councillors*, p. 273.
39 For the material related in this paragraph, see Rushworth, *Historical Collections*, I, 217; Birch, *The Court and Times of Charles I*, I, 87–9; Eliot, *Negotium Posterorum*, II, 64–75; *Cal. S.P. Ven., 1625–1626*, p. 366.
40 *Commons' Journals*, I, 834; Rushworth, *Historical Collections*, I, 219; Paul de Rapin-Thoyras, *The History of England, as well ecclesiastical as civil*, 2nd ed., 2 vols (London, 1733), II, 245; Gardiner, *The History of England*, VI, 73–4.
41 B.M., Sloane MS. 1710, fol. 283; W. A. J. Archbold, 'A Diary of the Parliament of 1626', in *E.H.R.*, XVII (1902), 732–3; Paul de Rapin-Thoyras, *Acta Regia: Being the Account which Mr. Rapid de Thoyras Publish'd of the History of England*, ed. Stephen Whatley (London, 1732) p. 560; Willson, *The Privy Councillors*, p. 285.
42 *Commons' Journals*, I, 817; John Campbell, *The Lives of the Chief Justices of England*, 3rd ed., 4 vols (London, 1874) I, 380.
43 *Commons' Journals*, I, 817; H. R. Trevor-Roper, *Archbishop Laud, 1573–1645*, rev. ed. (London, 1962) pp. 74–5.
44 *Cabala*, 2nd ed., p. 188; John Campbell, *The Lives of the Lord Chancellors and Keepers of the Great Seal of England*, 7 vols (London, 1845–7) II, 520.
45 *Ibid.*; *Acts of the Privy Council*, XL, 373, 420; *The Letters of John Chamberlain*, II, 631; Hervey, *The Life of the Earl of Arundel*, pp. 240–51.
46 Birch, *The Court and Times of Charles I*, I, 82. See also Hulme, *The Life of Sir John Eliot*, pp. 105–6; Ball, 'The Parliamentary Career of Sir John Eliot', p. 131.
47 *Ibid.*, pp. 167, 171, 175, 215; Gardiner, *The History of England*, VI, 76–7; Kennet, *A Complete History of England*, III, 18.
48 H.M.C., *The Manuscripts of His Grace the Duke of Northumberland at Alnwick Castle*, Third Report, Appendix (London, 1872) p. 67; Bulstrode Whitelocke, *Memorials of the English Affairs from the Beginning of the Reign of Charles the First to the Happy Restoration of King Charles the Second*, 4 vols (Oxford, 1843) I, 3.
49 *Commons' Journals*, I, 837; Willson, *The Privy Councillors*, pp. 307–8.
50 *Camden Miscellany*, 3rd series, LXXXIII (London, 1953) 39–40.
51 *Ibid.*, p. 40.
52 *Commons' Journals*, I, 840–2; Dietz, *English Public Finance*, p. 285.
53 Gardiner, *The History of England*, VI, 80–1.
54 *Ibid.*, V, 434.
55 *Commons' Journals*, I, 843.
56 Rushworth, *Historical Collections*, I, 228; Gardiner, *The History of England*, VI, 82–3.
57 *Commons' Journals*, I, 844; Birch, *The Court and Times of Charles I*, I, 192.
58 *Commons' Journals*, I, 844.

59 B.M., Add. MS. 34324, fol. 246.

60 For the material related in this paragraph, see *Commons' Journals*, I, 846–7, 853, 856; H.M.C., *The Manuscripts of the Earl of Lonsdale*, Thirteenth Report, Appendix, Part VII (London, 1893) pp. 14, 24; 'The Diary of Sir Richard Grosvenor, M.P', pp. 21, 24, 45. (The original of this diary has been deposited in the Library of Trinity College, Dublin, while a typescript of it is available in the Yale University Library. I wish to thank the trustees of Trinity College for allowing me to examine a microfilm of the typescript at Yale.)

61 H.M.C., *The Manuscripts of the Earl of Lonsdale*, pp. 2–3, 11–12; 'The Diary of Sir Richard Grosvenor', pp. 13, 50; Eliot, *Negotium Posterorum*, II, 80–4.

62 Willson, *The Privy Councillors*, p. 259.

63 Hulme, *The Life of Sir John Eliot*, p. 146.

64 'The Diary of Sir Richard Grosvenor', pp. 62–3, 67.

65 *Ibid.*, p. 129; Birch, *The Court and Times of Charles I*, I, 105.

66 *Commons' Journals*, I, 860; H.M.C., *The Manuscripts of the Earl of Lonsdale*, p. 10; Rushworth, *Historical Collections*, I, 360; 'The Diary of Sir Richard Grosvenor', pp. 98, 100; Hulme, *The Life of Sir John Eliot*, pp. 140–2.

67 'The Diary of Sir Richard Grosvenor', p. 160.

68 Rushworth, *Historical Collections*, I, 410–15.

69 Clarendon, *The History of the Rebellion*, I, 38.

CHAPTER 7

1 *Strafford's Letters and Dispatches*, I, 34–6; C. V. Wedgwood, *Thomas Wentworth, First Earl of Strafford 1593–1641: A Revaluation* (London, 1964) p. 56.

2 *Strafford's Letters and Dispatches*, I, 42; *Letters and Memorials of State*, ed. Collins, II, 370; Prestwich, *Cranfield*, pp. 490–1, 494–5.

3 *Foedera*, 2nd ed., VIII, Part II, 99; *Cal. S.P. Dom., 1627–1628*, p. 361; G. E. Aylmer, 'Attempts at Administrative Reform, 1625–1640', in *E.H.R.*, LXXII (1957) 250–1.

4 *Foedera*, 2nd ed., VIII, Part II, 92–4.

5 *Acts of the Privy Council*, XXXIX, 325.

6 P.R.O., S.P. 16/39, fol. 56; S.P. 16/66, fol. 57; S.P. 16/73, fol. 81; S.P. 16/75, fol. 29; S.P. 16/77, fol. 24; S.P. 16/164, fol. 44; S.P. 63/244, fol. 541. *Acts of the Privy Council*, XLI, 41; XLII, 47–8; XLIII, 109–10; *Cal. S.P. Ireland, 1625–1632*, pp. 121–2.

7 *Letters and Memorials of State*, ed. Collins, II, 368–9; *Acts of the Privy Council*, XLII, 60.

8 *Ibid.*, pp. 58–9.

9 *Ibid.*, p. 339.

10 P.R.O., S.P. 16/82, fol. 48; *Acts of the Privy Council*, XLI, 390.

11 *Foedera*, 2nd ed., VIII, Part II, 71–2, 149–50; H.M.C., *The Manuscripts of Henry Duncan Skrine*, pp. 108–9.

12 *Foedera*, 2nd ed., VIII, Part II, 77; Whitelocke, *Memorials of the English Affairs*, I, 7; *Acts of the Privy Council*, XLI, 63.
13 P.R.O., E 403/2605, fols. 266–7.
14 *Acts of the Privy Council*, XLI, 47, 55–6.
15 P.R.O., S.P. 16/33, fol. 107; *Acts of the Privy Council*, XLI, 108–9, 137, 140–1, 148–51.
16 P.R.O., S.P. 16/35, fol. 85; *Foedera*, 2nd ed., VIII, Part II, 89–90.
17 P.R.O., E 405/216, fols 32–51.
18 P.R.O., Index 6807 (unfoliated).
19 *Ibid.*; S.P. 16/58, fol. 52; S.P. 39/13, fol. 50.
20 *Acts of the Privy Council*, XLIII, 207–8; H.M.C., *The Manuscripts of Henry Duncan Skrine*, p. 77; Ashton, *The Crown and the Money Market*, pp. 130–1.
21 For materials relating to the agreement between the crown and the City, see P.R.O., S.P. 16/186, fol. 58; T 56/16, fols 64–6; *Acts of the Privy Council*, XLIII, 163, 225–6, 231–2, 455–65, 500; Ashton, *The Crown and the Money Market*, pp. 132, 140–4.
22 *Ibid.*, p. 64; Birch, *The Court and Times of Charles I*, I, 304; Scott, *English, Scottish and Irish Joint-Stock Companies*, II, 112.
23 H.M.C., *The Manuscripts of Henry Duncan Skrine*, pp. 80–1; *Acts of the Privy Council*, XLI, 111–12, 167; Birch, *The Court and Times of Charles I*, I, 292; *Cal. S.P. Dom., 1625–1626*, p. 489; *Cal. S.P. Dom., 1627–1628*, p. 41.
24 H.M.C., *The Manuscripts of the Earl Cowper*, I, 296; Campbell, *The Lives of the Chief Justices*, 3rd ed., I, 443–5; *The Diary of John Rous*, p. 7.
25 T. D. Whitaker, *The Life and Original Correspondence of Sir George Radcliffe* (London, 1810) pp. 142–5.
26 *Acts of the Privy Council*, XLII, 395–6, 449.
27 F. H. Relf, 'The Petition of Right', in *University of Minnesota Studies in the Social Sciences* (1917) pp. 1–4; Gardiner, *The History of England*, VI, 216–17.
28 Scott, *English, Scottish and Irish Joint-Stock Companies*, I, 190.
29 Dietz, *English Public Finance*, p. 239.
30 Professor Dietz contends that Weston shouldered most of the administrative burdens at this time. Concerning the Treasurer's role, he maintains that Marlborough 'had little contribution to make to the efficiency of the treasury'. *Ibid.*
31 *Cal. S.P. Dom., 1627–1628*, pp. viii–ix.
32 *Ibid.*, pp. ix–x.
33 *Letters of the Kings of England*, 2 vols, ed. J. O. Halliwell-Phillips (London, 1848) II, 272.
34 *Cal. S.P. Dom., 1627–1628*, p. xvii. See also *Acts of the Privy Council*, XLII, 498; XLIII, 2, 79–80, 106.
35 P.R.O., S.P. 16/80, fol. 60.
36 Dietz, *English Public Finance*, pp. 243–4.
37 *A Collection of Scarce and Valuable Tracts*, 2nd ed., 5 vols, ed. Sir Walter Scott (London, 1810) IV, 100–2. See also William Cobbett,

The Parliamentary History of England, 36 vols (London, 1806–1820) I, 213–17.

38 *Cal. S.P. Ven., 1626–1628*, p. 605.

39 Mitchell, *The Rise of the Revolutionary Party*, pp. 115–16.

40 H.M.C., *The Manuscripts of the Earl Cowper*, p. 343; Willson, *The Privy Councillors*, p. 62.

41 Stone, *The Crisis of the Aristocracy*, p. 105.

42 *Strafford's Letters and Dispatches*, I, 44.

43 *Lords' Journals*, III, 445.

44 *Ibid.*, pp. 743, 778–9, 794, 806, 825, 836, 855.

45 Gardiner, *The History of England*, VI, 226, 230–1, 235–7. For a discussion of opposition tactics during the spring of 1628, see Lindsay Boynton, 'Martial Law and the Petition of Right', in *E.H.R.*, LXXIX (1964), 272–8.

46 *Commons' Journals*, I, 878–9.

47 *The Memoirs of Sir Benjamin Rudyerd*, pp. 119–25; Rushworth, *Historical Collections*, I, 531.

48 *Lords' Journals*, III, 715.

49 *Ibid.*, pp. 766–9, 785, 788, 794, 803, 806, 813–20, 822, 824.

50 *Lords' Debates, 1621–1628*, ed. F. H. Relf (London: Camden Society, 1929) p. 29; *D.N.B.*, xx, 1276.

51 Hervey, *The Life of the Earl of Arundel*, p. 261; *Lords' Journals*, III, 801; Hacket, *Scrinia Reserata*, Part II, p. 77.

52 *Lords' Journals*, III, 824; M. A. Judson, *The Crisis of the Constitution, 1603–1645* (Rutgers U.P. Press, 1949) p. 266.

53 *Lords' Journals*, III, 772. Cf. *The Memoirs of Sir Benjamin Rudyerd*, p. 125.

54 *Commons' Journals*, I, 897, 905; Cobbett, *The Parliamentary History of England*, II, 324–343.

55 *Ibid.*, p. 377; Rushworth, *Historical Collections*, I, 598; Relf, 'The Petition of Right', p. 50.

56 Rushworth, *Historical Collections*, I, 598–601.

57 *Lords' Journals*, III, 844.

58 *Commons' Journals*, I, 912.

59 *Ibid.*, p. 911; Hulme, *The Life of Sir John Eliot*, p. 260; Ball, 'The Parliamentary Career of Sir John Eliot', pp. 283, 290.

60 P.R.O., S.P. 16/108, fol. 67.

61 *Ibid.*

62 *Lords' Journals*, III, 857–9.

63 Gardiner, *The History of England*, VI, 323–4.

64 *Lords' Journals*, III, 879; Rushworth, *Historical Collections*, I, 643.

65 *Ibid.*, p. 644; *Commons' Journals*, I, 919–20.

CHAPTER 8

1 H.M.C., *The Manuscripts of the Earl Cowper*, pp. 343, 366.

2 P.R.O., S.P. 16/108, fol. 29.

3 Dietz, *English Public Finance*, pp. 245–6. The grant of 1628 ultimately produced £275,000, or £25,000 less than what had been expected.
4 P.R.O., S.P. 16/105, fol. 80; S.P. 16/107, fol. 58; S.P. 39/26, fol. 59; *Acts of the Privy Council*, XLIII, 486–7.
5 Hamon L'Estrange, *The Reign of King Charles* (London, 1655) p. 89. Cf. Clarendon's remark that Marlborough 'was removed under pretence of his age and disability for the work, which had been a better reason against his promotion so few years before that his infirmities were very little increased . . .' See *The History of the Rebellion*, I, 59.
6 P.R.O., E 403/2606, fol. 98.
7 P.R.O., S.P. 16/110, fol. 31; S.P. 39/26, fol. 13; Rushworth, *Historical Collections*, I, 646; Birch, *The Court and Times of Charles I*, I, 382; *Cal. S.P. Dom., 1628–1629*, pp. 47, 189.
8 Clarendon, *The History of the Rebellion*, I, 59, 61; Lloyd, *The Statesmen and Favourites of England*, p. 553.
9 Dietz, *English Public Finance*, p. 272; Aylmer, *The King's Servants*, p. 203.
10 *Clarendon State Papers*, I, 158. The attacks on Weston in 1634, and the question of whether he was corrupt or not, will be considered in Chapter 11 below.
11 P.R.O., S.P. 16/112, fol. 75.
12 P.R.O., S.P. 16/113, fol. 14; Dietz, *English Public Finance*, p. 250.
13 Clarendon, *The History of the Rebellion*, I, 59; See also p. 61.
14 Laud was translated from Bath and Wells to London in July 1628. For an account of his activities during the remainder of the year, see Trevor-Roper, *Archbishop Laud*, rev. ed., pp. 87–92.
15 P.R.O., S.P. 16/121, fol. 38; *Cal. S.P. Ven., 1628–1629*, p. 432.
16 B.M., Stowe MS. 326, fol. 59.
17 *Cal. S.P. Dom., 1628–1629*, p. 269.
18 P.R.O., S.P. 16/117, fols 39–40; S.P. 16/120, fol. 27; S.P. 16/121, fols 71, 74; Oppenheim, *A History of the Administration of the Royal Navy*, pp. 279, 282–3; Nicholas, *Mr. Secretary Nicholas*, pp. 68–9.
19 Birch, *The Court and Times of Charles I*, I, 390–1, 399–400; Forster, *Sir John Eliot*, II, 366.
20 Birch, *The Court and Times of Charles I*, I, 390–1, 419.
21 *Ibid.*, pp. 290, 438, 441–2, 448–50; *The Diary of John Rous*, p. 33.
22 Birch, *The Court and Times of Charles I*, I, 403, 423; Gardiner, *The History of England*, VII, 31.
23 *Ibid.*, VI, 364–9; *Original Letters, illustrative of English History*, 1st series, III, 262.
24 For a printed copy of the Treaty of Susa, see Dumont, *Corps universel diplomatique*, V, Part II, 580–1. For other materials relating to the treaty, see P.R.O., S.P. 92/15, fols 13, 81–3; B.M., Add. MS. 24311, fols 281–6; Gardiner, *The History of England*, VII, 100–1.
25 P.R.O., S.P. 16/116, fol. 97; S.P. 16/119, fol. 28.
26 *Foedera*, 2nd ed., VIII, Part II, 270.
27 *Ibid.*, p. 284.

28 Gardiner, *The History of England*, x, 223.
29 Birch, *The Court and Times of Charles I*, I, 434, 437; Forster, *Sir John Eliot*, II, 406; Dietz, *English Public Finance*, p. 375.
30 P.R.O., S.P. 16/119, fol. 44; Rushworth, *Historical Collections*, I, 680.
31 *Ibid*., pp. 652–4, 681.
32 Birch, *The Court and Times of Charles I*, I, 432; *Acts of the Privy Council*, XLIV, 171; Gardiner, *The History of England*, VII, 3–5.
33 Rushworth, *Historical Collections*, I, 654.
34 P.R.O., E 126/3, fols 262–3; E 128/66 (unfoliated); Birch, *The Court and Times of Charles I*, I, 438–9.
35 P.R.O., S.P. 92/14, fols 145–6.
36 Rushworth, *Historical Collections*, I, 654; Birch, *The Court and Times of Charles I*, I, 439, 451–2, and II, 2, 5; Warwick, *Memoires of the Reign of Charles I*, 2nd ed., pp. 47–8; Gardiner, *The History of England*, VII, 23–4; Dietz, *English Public Finance*, pp. 252–3.
37 S.C.L., Strafford MS. XII a, fol. 38; *Strafford's Letters and Dispatches*, I, 47; Wedgwood, *Thomas Wentworth*, rev. ed., pp. 72–3; Smith, *The Life and Letters of Sir Henry Wotton*, II, 314.
38 Hacket, *Scrinia Reserata*, Part II, pp. 82–3.
39 For a detailed analysis of the administrative changes that took place in December 1628, see Aylmer, *The King's Servants*, pp. 88–9, 104–5, 110, 113.
40 P.R.O., S.P. 92/15, fol. 83.
41 Gardiner, *The History of England*, VII, 31; 'A True Relation of Every Days Proceedings in Parliament Since the Beginning thereof Being the 20th of January 1628 [*sic*]', in *Commons' Debates, 1629*, ed. Wallace Notestein and F. H. Relf (University of Minnesota Press, 1921) p. 5.
42 *Ibid*., pp. 5–8; Gardiner, *The History of England*, VII, 32–3.
43 *Ibid*., pp. 33–4; 'A True Relation', p. 11.
44 'The Notes of Sir Edward Nicholas for the Session of the Commons in 1629', in *Commons Debates, 1629*, p. 108.
45 *Ibid*., pp. 109–10; 'A True Relation', pp. 12–13; H.M.C., *Report on the Manuscripts of the Duke of Buccleuch and Queensberry*, III, 331–2; Gardiner, *The History of England*, VII, 34–5.
46 *Ibid*., pp. 49–51; 'A True Relation', pp. 77–8; 'The Notes of Sir Edward Nicholas', p. 146; Rushworth, *Historical Collections*, I, 478–9; J. G. Nichols, ed., 'The Discovery of the Jesuits' College at Clerkenwell in March 1627–8', in *The Camden Miscellany*, II, No. 55, pp. 9, 12–13 and *passim*.
47 Ball, 'The Parliamentary Career of Sir John Eliot', pp. 22, 311–12, 315.
48 'The Notes of Sir Edward Nicholas', p. 136.
49 *Ibid*., p. 142; 'A True Relation', pp. 60–2; Rushworth, *Historical Collections*, I, 666.
50 Ball, 'The Parliamentary Career of Sir John Eliot', pp. 300–1, 318–21.
51 'A True Relation', p. 101; Hacket, *Scrinia Reserata*, Part II, p. 83; *Cal. S.P. Ven., 1628–1629*, pp. 579–80; Gardiner, *The History of England*, VII, 64–7; Willson, *The Privy Councillors*, p. 199; Hulme, *The Life of Sir John Eliot*, p. 308.

52 'A True Relation', pp. 103–4.

53 'March 2nd Account', in *Commons Debates, 1629*, pp. 253–8; 'A True Relation', pp. 102–3. There is an almost identical account of Eliot's speech in Add. MS. 33468, fols 20–1. See also Eliot, *Negotium Posterorum*, II, 143–4; Rushworth, *Historical Collections*, I, 669–670.

54 'March 2nd Account', p. 262.

55 'A True Relation', p. 105.

56 'March 2nd Account', pp. 262–3; Birch, *The Court and Times of Charles I*, II, 12.

57 'March 2nd Account', pp. 266–7; 'A True Relation', p. 102; Gardiner, *The History of England*, VII, 74–6.

58 'A True Relation', p. 106; 'March 2nd Account', pp. 266–7.

59 Hacket, *Scrinia Reserata*, Part II, p. 83; Warwick, *Memoires of the Reign of Charles I*, 2nd ed., p. 47.

60 Clarendon, *The History of the Rebellion*, I, 41; Lloyd, *The States-men and Favourites of England*, p. 686; *Cal. S.P. Ven., 1628–1629*, pp. 580–1. See also Whitelocke, *Memorials of the English Affairs*, I, 35.

61 *Cal. S.P. Ven., 1629–1632*, pp. 177, 227.

62 Of obvious importance in this regard is J. H. Hexter's appraisal of Pym as the architect of parliament's victory over the King, since it was Pym who established the committee system in the lower House which enabled Cromwell and the other generals to maintain sufficient forces in the field to do the job. See *The Reign of King Pym* (Harvard U.P., 1941).

63 D. D. Brunton and D. H. Pennington, *Members of the Long Parliament* (Harvard U.P., 1954) pp. 15–16.

64 See for example the suggestions made by H. F. Kearney in *Scholars and Gentlemen. Universities and Society in Pre-industrial Britain, 1500–1700* (London, 1970) p. 170.

CHAPTER 9

1 P.R.O., S.P. 46/78, fol. 118.

2 Rushworth, *Historical Collections*, I, Appendix, 10–11; Hulme, *The Life of Sir John Eliot*, pp. 308, 316; Edmund Lodge, *The Life of Sir Julius Caesar* (London, 1810) p. 34; Gardiner, *The History of England*, VII, 360.

3 P.R.O., S.P. 16/146, fols 21–2; S.P. 16/147, fol. 19; S.P. 16/155, fol. 55; Dietz, *English Public Finance*, pp. 256, 263.

4 P.R.O., E 128/71 (unfoliated).

5 P.R.O., E 128/81 (unfoliated).

6 P.R.O., E 126/3, fols 310–11; E 128/67 (unfoliated); E 128/72 (unfoliated); S.P. 16/205, fol. 40; Rushworth, *Historical Collections*, I, 680–1; Birch, *The Court and Times of Charles I*, II, 40–1, 53, 88.

7 For evidence of Weston's work in the Exchequer Chamber, see P.R.O., E 126/3, fols 311, 325, 361; E 126/4, fols 20, 35; E 128/69 (unfoliated).

8 P.R.O., E 128/73 (unfoliated).

9 P.R.O., Index 6808 (unfoliated); *Acts of the Privy Council*, XLVI, 216–17;

Rushworth, *Historical Collections*, II, *passim*; *Cal. S.P. Ven., 1629–1632*, p. 148.

10 *Acts of the Privy Council*, XLV, 105–7; *Cal. S.P. Dom., 1629–1631*, p. 373; E. R. Turner, 'The Origin of the Cabinet Council', in *E.H.R.*, XXIX (1913) 187.

11 P.R.O., P.C. 2/44, fols 1–2.

12 *Ibid.*; *Acts of the Privy Council*, XLV, 276–7; XLVI, 4.

13 H.M.C., *The Manuscripts of the Coke Family, of Melbourne Hall, County Derby*, Twelfth Report, Appendix, Part I (London, 1888) p. 476.

14 Birch, *The Court and Times of Charles I*, II, 20, 23–5; *Cal. S.P. Ven., 1629–1632*, p. 204.

15 *The Letters of Sir Peter Paul Rubens*, pp. 283–6; *Original Unpublished Papers illustrative of the Life of Sir Peter Paul Rubens*, ed. W. N. Sainsbury (London, 1859) pp. 129–30.

16 *The Letters of Sir Peter Paul Rubens*, pp. 299–300.

17 *Ibid.*, p. 300.

18 H.M.C., *The Manuscripts of the Earl Cowper*, p. 387; *Cal. S.P. Ven., 1629–1632*, p. 93.

19 *The Letters of Sir Peter Paul Rubens*, p. 301.

20 *Ibid.*, pp. 304, 308.

21 *Ibid.*, p. 316.

22 *Ibid.*, pp. 324–6.

23 *Cal. S.P. Ven., 1629–1632*, pp. 168, 178.

24 *Ibid.*, pp. 204, 239.

25 *Ibid.*, pp. 218–19.

26 P.R.O., S.P. 94/34, fol. 137; Birch, *The Court and Times of Charles I*, II, 67; *Cal. S.P. Ven., 1629–1632*, p. 275.

27 P.R.O., S.P. 78/84, fols 128, 140; *Acts of the Privy Council*, XLV, 34–5, 194–5, 327; XLVI, II, 32; Dumont, *Corps universel diplomatique*, V, Part II, 581–2; Gardiner, *The History of England*, VII, 104–5; Havran, *The Catholics in Caroline England*, pp. 53–4.

28 B.M., Egerton MS. 2554, fols 19–20; P.R.O., S.P. 94/35, fols 5–10, 39–41, 81–5.

29 *Cal. S.P. Ven., 1629–1632*, p. 311; Gardiner, *The History of England*, VII, 172, 175–6. For a copy of the treaty, see B.M., Egerton MS. 2554, fols 16–24. There is another copy in Add. MS. 19877, fols 45–52.

30 *Cal. S.P. Ven., 1629–1632*, p. 510.

31 B.M., Harleian MS. 3796, fol. 27.

32 Lawrence Stone, *Family and Fortune* (Clarendon Press, 1973) p. xvi.

33 H. R. Trevor-Roper, *The Crisis of the Seventeenth Century* (New York, 1968) pp. 87, 89.

34 H.M.C., *The Manuscripts of the Earl Cowper*, pp. 291–3.

35 P.R.O., S.P. 39/29, fol. 82; S.P. 39/30, fol. 30; E 403/2606, fol. 209; E 403/2750, fol. 367; E 403/2751, fol. 138; E 403/2752, fol. 34.

36 B.M., Egerton MS. 2597, fol. 169; P.R.O., E 403/2753, Part II, fol. 60; E 404/234 (unfoliated); E 405/284, fols 37–8; Clarendon, *The History of the Rebellion*, I, 104; H. W. Chapman, *The Tragedy of Charles II in the Years 1630–1660* (London, 1965) pp. 27, 39.

37 Some years earlier the English government had settled pensions of £1000 and £500 a month on the Queen of Bohemia and the Elector Palatine, respectively. Smaller sums were provided for their children, and from time to time generous grants were made to their servants. While Weston held the white staff, he was careful to see that funds for the royal exiles at The Hague were dispatched punctually.

38 Dietz, *English Public Finance*, pp. 260–1.

39 For the material related in this paragraph, see Stone, *The Crisis of the Aristocracy*, p. 422; and A. S. Foord, 'The Waning of the Influence of the Crown', in *Essays in Eighteenth-Century History*, ed. Rosalind Mitchison (London, 1966) p. 177. It should be noted that Charles I had almost 500 more household servants during the 1630s than George I employed ninety years later. See J. H. Plumb, *The Growth of Political Stability in England, 1675–1725* (London, 1967) p. 108.

40 P.R.O., S.P. 16/98, fol. 74; S.P. 16/169, fol. 48; S.P. 16/258, fol. 46, S.C.L., Strafford MS. I, fol. 59; Kennet, *A Complete History of England*, II, 62–4; Wright, *The History and Topography of Essex*, I, 152; Gardiner, *The History of England*, VII, 240, and VIII, 81; Dietz, *English Public Finance*, pp. 268, 303–4, 436.

41 Clarendon, *The History of the Rebellion*, I, 63. For the actual yields of the recusancy fines, see Dietz, *English Public Finance*, p. 268.

42 P.R.O., S.P. 16/159, fols. 22, 32; *Cal. S.P. Dom., 1629–1631*, pp. 175–6; *Acts of the Privy Council*, XLV, 277.

43 P.R.O., S.P. 14/172, fol. 19; S.P. 16/155, fol. 49; E 407/35, fols 52–3, 89–93, 200 *passim*; Dietz, *English Public Finance*, pp. 262–3.

44 B.M., Harleian MS. 3796, fols 35–6; P.R.O., E 403/3040, fol. 28; Scott, *English, Scottish and Irish Joint-Stock Companies*, I, 215; Dietz, *English Public Finance*, p. 263.

45 P.R.O., E 403/2591, fols 4, 12–13.

46 Clarendon, *The History of the Rebellion*, I, 84.

47 P.R.O., S.P. 39/28, fol. 30; S.P. 39/29, fol. 24; S.P. 39/30, fol. 69; Scott, *English, Scottish and Irish Joint-Stock Companies*, I, 199–200.

48 Charles Wilson, *England's Apprenticeship 1603–1763* (New York, 1965) pp. 52–3, 77–80, 85–6; B. E. Supple, *Commercial Crisis and Change in England 1600–1642* (Cambridge U.P., 1964) pp. 101–5, 110–12, 116, 119–20.

49 B.M., Stowe MS. 326, fols 59–60, 89; Ashton, *The Crown and the Money Market*, pp. 98–9; Dietz, *English Public Finance*, pp. 335–6.

50 In his admirable monograph, *The Crown and the Money Market* (pp. 99–102) Robert Ashton has, I feel, exaggerated the significance of John Harrison's proposals in 1627 and 1628 that the crown should resume direct management of all the customs duties. In a short memoir written during the late 1630s, Harrison himself acknowledged that there was no chance his proposals would be adopted so long as Weston remained in office. For Harrison's comments, see B.M., Stowe MS. 326, fols 59–60.

CHAPTER 10

1 P.R.O., Index and Calendar to the Patent Rolls, XVIII, 193; *Acts of the Privy Council*, XLVII, 407; G. E. Cokayne, *The Complete Peerage*, 2nd ed., 13 vols, ed. Vicary Gibbs (London, 1910–59) X, 584; Morant, *The History and Antiquities of Essex*, II, 71; *V.C.H. Hampshire*, V, 156, 224.

2 P.R.O., S.P. 39/30, fol. 79; Index and Calendar to the Patent Rolls, XVIII, fols 193–4; S.P. 16/150, fol. 63; Index 6808 (unfoliated); Index 6809 (also unfoliated).

3 Clarendon, *The History of the Rebellion*, I, 63.

4 *Clarendon State Papers*, I, 158–9; P.R.O., S.P. 38/15 (unfoliated; docquett dated 14 Dec 1632). It should be noted that Clarendon also charged that the King gave his Treasurer 'a whole forest, Chute forest in Hampshire, and much other land belonging to the Crown'; but there is no evidence for this contention either. For Chute forest, which lay partly in Hampshire and partly in Wiltshire, see *V.C.H. Wiltshire*, IV, 427.

5 P.R.O., Index 6809 (unfoliated; grants dated Sep 1632 and Jul 1633); *Strafford's Letters and Dispatches*, I, 468; Morant, *The History and Antiquities of Essex*, II, 108–9, 490; Wright, *The History and Topography of Essex*, I, 218, II, 297; Chester Waters, *The Chesters of Chicheley*, I, 102; *V.C.H. Cambridgeshire and the Isle of Ely*, IV, 127–8.

6 P.R.O., Index 6808 (unfoliated).

7 Samuel Lewis, *A Topographical Dictionary of England*, 7th ed., 4 vols (London, 1849) III, 690; E. W. Brayley, *A Topographical History of Surrey*, 4 vols, ed. Edward Walford (London, n.p.d.) III, 198–9.

8 *The Letters of Sir Peter Paul Rubens*, p. 314.

9 P.R.O., S.P. 16/153, fol. 69; S.P. 16/158, fol. 48; Whinney and Millar, *English Art 1625–1714*, p. 52; Manning and Bray, *The History and Antiquities of the County of Surrey*, III, 290; *D.N.B.*, VII, 1106–8.

10 P.R.O., S.P. 16/158, fols 48, 54; Whinney and Millar, *English Art 1625–1714*, p. 52.

11 For the material related in this paragraph, see Chester Waters, *The Chesters of Chicheley*, I, 103–4; J. G. Mann, 'The Charles I Statue at Charing Cross', in *Country Life*, 16 May 1947, pp. 908–9; Wheatley, *London Past and Present*, I, 115–16.

12 P.R.O., S.P. 80/7, fols 50, 62, 172; Index 6808 (unfoliated); Birch, *The Court and Times of Charles I*, II, 97.

13 P.R.O., S.P. 16/218, fol. 27; *Epistolae Ho-elianae*, p. 282; *Cal. S.P. Ven., 1629–1632*, p. 637; *D.N.B.*, XX, 1274.

14 *Cal. S.P. Ven., 1629–1632*, p. 623.

15 Hervey, *The Life of the Earl of Arundel*, pp. 323–4, 336, 340; Chester Waters, *The Chesters of Chicheley*, I, 106n.

16 P.R.O., S.P. 38/15 (unfoliated); Index 6809 (also unfoliated).

17 E.R.O., D/DSx/342; Chester Waters, *The Chesters of Chicheley*, I, 100–5; *The Tixall Letters*, II, 124; Nichols, *The Progress of James I*, IV, 844n.

18 *Strafford's Letters and Dispatches*, I, 243; *The Tixall Letters*, I, 55–8.

19 P.R.O., E 407/35, fols 75–6.

20 Clarendon, *The History of the Rebellion*, I, 61, 64, 67.

21 P.R.O., S.P. 16/121, fols 46, 60; S.P. 16/123, fol. 3; H.M.C., *Report on the Manuscripts of the Earl of Denbigh*, Part V, p. 8.

22 P.R.O., S.P. 39/29, fol. 37; S.C.L., Strafford MS. XII b, fol. 86; *Acts of the Privy Council*, XLV, 174; Birch, *The Court and Times of Charles I*, II, 25; Warwick, *Memoires of the Reign of Charles I*, 2nd ed., pp. 47–8; Gardiner, *The History of England*, VII, 220–1.

23 *Clarendon State Papers*, I, 159; Clarendon, *The History of the Rebellion*, I, 62.

24 *The Letters of Sir Peter Paul Rubens*, p. 308.

25 P.R.O., S.P. 16/196, fol. 96; S.P. 16/239, fol. 37; Hervey, *The Life of the Earl of Arundel*, pp. 340–1.

26 *Strafford's Letters and Dispatches*, I, 214.

27 Gardiner, *The History of England*, VII, 134. See also p. 377.

28 S.C.L., Strafford's MS. VIII, fol. 92.

29 Clarendon, *The History of the Rebellion*, I, 65; Lodge, *The Life of Sir Julius Caesar*, pp. 58–9; Aylmer, *The King's Servants*, p. 71.

30 S.C.L., Strafford MS. XII c (unfoliated); *Epistolae Ho-elianae*, p. 281.

31 Mrs. C. S. S. Higham (F. M. G. Evans), *Charles I. A Study* (London, 1932) p. 110.

32 Clarendon, *The History of the Rebellion*, I, 64.

33 *Cal. S.P. Ven., 1629–1632*, pp. 331, 450, 464.

34 Clarendon, *The History of the Rebellion*, I, 62.

35 Gardiner, *The History of England*, VI, 362.

36 Gilbert Burnet, *The Memoires of the Lives and Actions of James and William, Dukes of Hamilton and Castleherald* (London, 1677) pp. 10–12; Gardiner, *The History of England*, VII, 182.

37 Hacket, *Scrinia Reserata*, Part II, p. 91; Cobbett, *A Complete Collection of State Trials*, II, 883–90.

38 Rushworth, *Historical Collections*, II, 62; Burnet, *Memoires of the Dukes of Hamilton*, p. 4; H.M.C., *Report on the Manuscripts of the Earl of Mar and Kellie, preserved at Alloa House* (London, 1904) pp. 185–6.

39 Burnet, *Memoires of the Dukes of Hamilton*, p. 16; H.M.C., *Report on the Laing Manuscripts preserved in the University of Edinburgh*, I, 187–8; Gardiner, *The History of England*, VII, 182–3.

40 For the proceedings in the Court of Chivalry between Reay and Ramsay, see Rushworth, *Historical Collections*, II, 62, 106, 112, 142–3; Cobbett, *A Complete Collection of State Trials*, III, 483–520. For Charles's letter to Hamilton see *Letters of the Kings of England*, ed. Halliwell, II, 284–5.

41 H.M.C., *Supplementary Report on the Manuscripts of His Grace the Duke of Hamilton*, p. 16; Gardiner, *The History of England*, VII, 178; Dietz, *English Public Finance*, p. 260n.

42 Gardiner, *The History of England*, VII, 211–14.

43 *Clarendon State Papers*, I, 76.

44 *Ibid.*, p. 104; B.M., Egerton MS. 1820, fols 288–92, 321–3; S.C.L., Strafford MS. IV, fols 17–18; V, fols 188, 219; IX, fol. 16.

CHAPTER 11

1 B.M., Add. MS. 19832, fol. 31; S.C.L., Strafford MS. III, fols 117, 120; *Acts of the Privy Council*, XXXIX, 325; XLV, 276; *The Lismore Papers*, 2nd series, III, 162–7; H. F. Kearney, *Strafford in Ireland, 1633–1641* (Manchester U.P., 1961) pp. 13–14; Dorothea Townshend, *The Life and Letters of the Great Earl of Cork* (London, 1904) pp. 195–6.

2 P.R.O., S.P. 63/247, fol. 150; S.P. 63/249, fols 63–4; S.P. 63/254, fols 15, 53, 65, 143.

3 For the relationship between Portland and the Earl of Cork, see *The Lismore Papers*, 1st series, II, 293, 307, 311, 314, 319, 336–7; William Prynne, *Canterburies Doome* (London, 1646) p. 83; Kearney, *Strafford In Ireland*, pp. 10, 13; Townshend, *The Life and Letters of the Great Earl of Cork*, pp. 171–2.

4 *The Lismore Papers*, 2nd series, III, 177.

5 S.C.L., Strafford MS. XII d, fol. 272; XL, fols 48–9; *Strafford's Letters and Dispatches*, I, 51, 79–80; Wedgwood, *Thomas Wentworth*, rev. ed., p. 122.

6 P.R.O., P.C. 2/41, fols 395–9; B.M., Add. MS. 29975, fols 113–15; S.C.L., Strafford MS. I, fols 21–2, 25; *Strafford's Letters and Dispatches*, I, 66–7.

7 For the material related in this paragraph, see S.C.L., Strafford MS. III, fols 9, 14, 28, 71–2, 101, 118, 122–3, 140–75; IV, fols 26, 41–5, 55, 88–9, 113–14; V, fols 124–6; VI, fols 169, 178; VIII, fols 39–40, 76, 221; XIII a, fol. 64. See also Kearney, *Strafford in Ireland*, pp. 182–3.

8 Clarendon, *The History of the Rebellion*, I, 197.

9 S.C.L., Strafford MS. XX b (unfoliated); Wedgwood, *Thomas Wentworth*, p. 91.

10 *Ibid.*, p. 206; S.C.L., Strafford MS. III, fol. 7; *Strafford's Letters and Dispatches*, I, 75, 140–1, 144–5, 227; *The Works of Archbishop Laud*, VII, 79. Laud became Archbishop of Canterbury during the autumn of 1633, after the death of George Abbot.

11 *The Works of Archbishop Laud*, VII, 109.

12 S.C.L., Strafford MS. VI, fol. 92. *Strafford's Letters and Dispatches*, I, 214.

13 P.R.O., P.C. 2/43, fol. 304; Gardiner, *The History of England*, VII, 310–11.

14 S.C.L., Strafford MS. VI, fol. 192.

15 P.R.O., S.P. 16/233, fol. 4.

16 S.C.L., Strafford MS. VI, fol. 191; Hacket, *Scrinia Reserata*, Part II, p. 113.

17 *Stuart Tracts 1603–1693*, ed. Sir Charles Firth (Westminster, 1903) p. 323; *The Works of Archbishop Laud*, III, 220; VII, 40.

18 S.C.L., Strafford MS. XIII a, fol. 20; Clarendon, *The History of the Rebellion*, I, 130.

19 S.C.L., Strafford MS., III, fol. 81; *Strafford's Letters and Dispatches*, I, 177, 242–3.

20 P.R.O., E 404/234 (unfoliated).
21 *Cal. S.P. Ven., 1632–1636*, pp. 220, 225–6; Gardiner, *The History of England*, VII, 355–6.
22 *Strafford's Letters and Dispatches*, I, 177, 242–3; *Cal. S.P. Ven., 1632–1636*, pp. 220, 223, 233; Cokayne, *The Complete Peerage*, X, 584.
23 P.R.O., P.C. 2/44, fol. 2; S.C.L., Strafford MS. VI, fol. 50.
24 Anthony Weldon, 'The Court of King Charles', in *The Secret History of James the First*, 2 vols, ed. Sir Walter Scott (London, 1811) II, 50.
25 S.C.L., Strafford MS. III, fol. 81. See also VI, fols 32, 36–7, 55, 82.
26 *Ibid.*, fols 51–2, 59, 202; B.M., Add. MS. 19832, fol. 40; *The Lismore Papers*, 1st series, IV, 39; 2nd series, III, 197; Townshend, *The Life and Letters of the Great Earl of Cork*, p. 214.
27 S.C.L., Strafford MS. III, fol. 83; VIII, fols 106–7, 222, 234–8.
28 *Ibid.*, fol. 221.
29 For the altercation between Lord Holland and Jerome Weston, see P.R.O., S.P. 16/236, fols 43, 47, 49, 52, 55, 59–60; P.C. 2/42, fols 565–70; Smith, *The Life and Letters of Sir Henry Wotton*, II, 338–41; H.M.C., *The Manuscripts of S. H. Le Fleming, Esq., of Rydall Hall*, Twelfth Report, Appendix, Part IV (London, 1890) pp. 16–17; Clarendon, *The History of the Rebellion*, I, 197.
30 S.C.L., Strafford MS. XIII a, fol. 24.
31 B.M., Lansdowne MS. 151, fol. 87; Harleian MS. 3796, fol. 22; *Cal. S.P. Ven., 1632–1636*, p. 264; Gardiner, *The History of England*, VII, 362; Harold Hulme, 'Charles I and the Constitution', in *Conflict in Stuart England: Essays in Honor of Wallace Notestein*, ed. W. A. Aiken and B. D. Henning (New York U.P., 1960) pp. 108–9.
32 *Cal. S.P. Ven., 1632–1636*, pp. 293, 295.
33 S.C.L., Strafford MS. III, fol. 155.
34 Gardiner, *The History of England*, VII, 377–8; Ivan Roots, *The Great Rebellion, 1642–1660* (London, 1968) p. 40.
35 Clarendon, *The History of the Rebellion*, I, 85; Trevor-Roper, *Archbishop Laud*, rev. ed., p. 299; Hulme, 'Charles I and the Constitution', pp. 108–9.
36 For Laud's relationship with Harrison and Roe, see B.M., Stowe MS. 326, fols 59–61; Trevor-Roper, *Archbishop Laud*, rev. ed., pp. 113, 129.
37 *Clarendon State Papers*, I, 158.
38 *Ibid.*, pp. 158–9.
39 *Ibid.*, p. 159.
40 J. P. Cooper, 'The Fortune of Sir Thomas Wentworth, Earl of Strafford', in *Econ. Hist. Rev.*, 2nd series, XI, No. 2 (1958) p. 246. See also Aylmer, *The King's Servants*, p. 211.
41 Cooper, 'The Fortune of Sir Thomas Wentworth', pp. 246–7.
42 Gardiner, *The History of England*, VIII, 89–90; Trevor-Roper, *Archbishop Laud*, rev. ed., p. 225.
43 See above p. 195.
44 For evidence that there was less than £100 in ready money in Portland's house at the time he died, see *Strafford's Letters and Dispatches*, I, 388.

45 P.R.O., S.P. 63/254, fol. 187; S.P. 63/255, fol. 9; S.C.L., Strafford MS. III, fols 175–7, 180, 182; XIV d, fol. 285; *Cal. S.P. Ireland, 1633–1647*, pp. 83, 90; *Strafford's Letters and Dispatches*, I, 243, 262.

46 *The Works of Archbishop Laud*, VI, Part II, 397.

47 S.C.L., Strafford MS. III, fols 135, 199–202; Upton, *Sir Arthur Ingram*, pp. 221, 224–8, 230, 234; Cooper, 'The Fortune of Sir Thomas Wentworth', pp. 233–4; Wedgwood, *Thomas Wentworth*, p. 108.

48 S.C.L., Strafford MS. III, fol. 252.

49 *Ibid.*, VI, fols 182, 194.

50 *The Works of Archbishop Laud*, VII, 129–30.

CHAPTER 12

1 *Strafford's Letters and Dispatches*, I, 177, 242–3.

2 S.C.L., Strafford MS. III, fols 11, 116; XIV b, fols 147. See also P.R.O., S.P. 16/272, fol. 56.

3 P.R.O., S.P. 14/150, fol. 94; S.P. 14/155, fols 38–44; S.P. 14/164, fols 21, 98; S.P. 14/170, fol. 12; S.P. 14/171, fol. 42; Index 6809 (unfoliated); *V.C.H. Surrey*, II, 402–3; Gardiner, *The History of England*, VIII, 74; Dietz, *English Public Finance*, p. 265; F. J. Fisher, 'The Influence and Development of the Industrial Gilds in the Larger Provincial Towns under James I and Charles I' (unpublished M.A. thesis, University of London, 1931) pp. 197–8.

4 *The Works of Archbishop Laud*, VII, 141, 175; S.C.L., Strafford MS. VI, fol. 192. Clarendon, *The History of the Rebellion*, I, 92; Fisher, 'The Influence and Development of the Industrial Gilds', p. 222.

5 Dietz, *English Public Finance*, p. 265.

6 Scott, *English, Scottish and Irish Joint-Stock Companies*, I, 212–3.

7 P.R.O., S.P. 16/254, fol. 34; *V.C.H. Surrey*, II, 402–4, 412; Gardiner, *The History of England*, VIII, 73–6, 284; Scott, *English, Scottish and Irish Joint-Stock Companies*, I, 215–18.

8 P.R.O., S.P. 16/221, fol. 1; S.P. 16/231, fol. 15; Fisher, 'The Influence and Development of the Industrial Gilds', pp. 149–51, 157–8. See also Nicholas, *Mr. Secretary Nicholas*, p. 95.

9 P.R.O., S.P. 16/229, fol. 79.

10 *Ibid.*, S.P. 16/231, fol. 15.

11 P.R.O., S.P. 16/229, fol. 79; Smith, *The Herring-Busse Trade* (London, 1641) p. 1.

12 J. R. Elder, *The Royal Fishery Companies of the Seventeenth Century* (Glasgow, 1912) p. 67; Fisher, 'The Influence and Development of the Industrial Gilds', p. 151.

13 *Ibid.*; Scott, *English, Scottish and Irish Joint-Stock Companies*, I, 228.

14 Fisher, 'The Influence and Development of the Industrial Gilds', pp. 151–8.

15 On this point, see Trevor-Roper, *The Crisis of the Seventeenth Century*, pp. 85–9.

16 Martin J. Havran, *Caroline Courtier: The Life of Lord Cottington* (University of South Carolina Press, 1973) p. 130.

17 Joel Hurstfield, 'The Political Morality of Early Stuart Statesmen', in *Freedom, Corruption and Government in Elizabethan England* (Harvard U.P., 1973) p. 186.
18 Lloyd, *The States-men and Favourites of England*, p. 685.
19 P.R.O., S.P. 16/259, fol. 17; B.M., Add. MS. 30221, fol. 43.
20 *Epistolae Ho-elianae*, pp. 310, 320.
21 B.M., Add. MS. 32093, fol. 55; *V.C.H. Herefordshire*, I, 382.
22 B.M., Stowe MS. 326, fol. 60.
23 *Ship Money Papers and Richard Grenville's Note-Book*, ed. C. G. Bonsy and J. G. Jenkins (Buckinghamshire Record Society, 1965) p. x.
24 *Clarendon State Papers*, I, 94–5.
25 P.R.O., P.C. 2/44, fols 24–5; S.P. 16/269, fol. 51.
26 P.R.O., S.P. 16/285, fol. 7; M. D. Gordon, 'The Collection of Ship Money in the Reign of Charles I', in *T.R.H.S.*, 3rd series, IV (1910) 141.
27 Gardiner, *The History of England*, VII, 357–8.
28 *Ship Money Papers*, pp. x–xi.
29 *The Letters, Speeches, and Proclamations of King Charles I*, ed. Sir Charles Petrie (London, 1935) pp. 92–3; Gardiner, *The History of England*, VII, 376.
30 B.M., Egerton MS. 1820, fol. 419; *Strafford's Letters and Dispatches*, I, 357; Rushworth, *Historical Collections*, II, 265; Gardiner, *The History of England*, I, 375–7.
31 B.M., Add. MS. 29975, fol. 117; P.R.O., P.C. 2/44, fols 372–4.
32 Gardiner, *The History of England*, VIII, 84.
33 *Ibid.*, pp. 84–5, 102; *Ship Money Papers*, p. xiv.
34 B.M., Lansdowne MS. 232, fols 33–6. In 1636 the ship-money writs called for the raising of £199,700; in 1637, for £196,400; and during the three subsequent years for £196,400, £69,750, and £210,400, respectively.
35 On this point, see *V.C.H. Herefordshire*, I, 383. For other evidence about the opposition to ship-money, see *V.C.H. Somerset*, II, 203; *V.C.H. Middlesex*, II, 37; *V.C.H. Surrey*, I, 402; *V.C.H. Wiltshire*, V, 134; *V.C.H. Suffolk*, II, 189.
36 Gardiner, *The History of England*, VII, 378.
37 *Clarendon State Papers*, I, 77.
38 The negotiations with Necolalde can be followed in B.M., Egerton MS. 1820 (the letter-book of Sir Arthur Hopton, the English Agent in Madrid), and in the *Clarendon State Papers*, where many of the letters and documents of Secretary Windebank are printed.
39 *Clarendon State Papers*, I, 101.
40 *Ibid.*, pp. 216–17; B.M., Egerton MS. 1820, fols 279, 382.
41 Gardiner, *The History of England*, VII, 368–71, 378.
42 B.M., Egerton MS. 1820, fols. 435, 452; *Clarendon State Papers*, I, 247.
43 *Strafford's Letters and Dispatches*, I, 363; Stone, *The Crisis of the Aristocracy*, I, 480.
44 P.R.O., S.P. 16/295, fol. 19. See also S.P. 16/218, fol. 23.
45 P.R.O., E 403/2753, fol. 98; H.M.C., *Report on the Manuscripts of the Earl of Denbigh*, Part V, pp. 10–11, 14. For other materials pertain-

ing to the Feildings' journey to Venice, see P.R.O., S.P. 99/35, fols 13–14, 35, 40, 74.

46 S.C.L., Strafford MS. III, fol. 52; *Strafford's Letters and Dispatches*, I, 374, 387–9.

47 *Ibid.*, p. 389.

48 *Ibid.*; *V.C.H. Hampshire and the Isle of Wight*, V, 54; Chester Waters, *The Chesters of Chicheley*, I, 99; Whinney and Millar, *English Art 1625–1714*, p. 122.

49 S.C.L., Strafford MS. XXIV, fol. 58; *Strafford's Letters and Dispatches*, I, 389.

50 *Ibid.*; Chester Waters, *The Chesters of Chicheley*, I, 99.

51 *Strafford's Letters and Dispatches*, I, 389; H.M.C., *Report on the Manuscripts of the late Reginald Rawdon Hastings, Esq., of the Manor House, Ashby de la Zouch*, 4 vols (London, 1928–47) II, 79.

52 Clarendon, *The History of the Rebellion*, I, 67

53 *Ibid.* For materials pertaining to the sale of the Weston family properties after 1635, see P.R.O., Index 6810 (unfoliated); *Strafford's Letters and Dispatches*, I, 468; *Cal. S.P. Dom., 1637–1638*, pp. 424–5, 447; *Cal. S.P. Dom., 1639*, p. 354; *Cal. S.P. Dom., 1640*, p. 358; Morant, *The History and Antiquities of Essex*, II, 108–9, 215, 238; Wright, *The History and Topography of Essex*, I, 218, 427–8; *V.C.H. Bedfordshire*, III, 277; *V.C.H. Cambridgeshire and the Isle of Ely*, IV, 127–8; *V.C.H. Surrey*, IV, 79; Manning and Bray, *The History and Antiquities of the County of Surrey*, III, 198, 290; Brayley, *A Topographical History of Surrey*, III, 198; Chester Waters, *The Chesters of Chicheley*, I, 102, 106; Stone, *The Crisis of the Aristocracy*, p. 357.

Index